Myth Maker

Ellis Ashmead-Bartlett
The Englishman Who Sparked Australia's Gallipoli Legend

Fred & Elizabeth Brenchley

WILEY
John Wiley & Sons Australia, Ltd

First published in 2005 by
John Wiley & Sons Australia, Ltd
42 McDougall Street, Milton Qld 4064

Offices also in Sydney and Melbourne

Typeset in 11.5/15 pt Berkeley

© Fred and Elizabeth Brenchley 2005

National Library of Australia
Cataloguing-in-Publication data

Brenchley, Fred, 1942–
Myth maker: Ellis Ashmead-Bartlett: the Englishman who sparked Australia's Gallipoli legend.

Bibliography.
Includes index.

ISBN-13   978 1 74031 118 2.
ISBN-10   1 74031 118 3.

1. Ashmead-Bartlett, Ellis, 1881–1931. 2. War correspondents — Great Britain — Biography. 3. War photographers — Great Britain — Biography. 4. World War, 1914–1918 — Campaigns — Turkey — Gallipoli Peninsula — Journalists. I. Brenchley, Elizabeth. II. Title.

070.92

All rights reserved. Except as permitted under the *Australian Copyright Act 1968* (for example, a fair dealing for the purposes of study, research, criticism or review), no part of this book may be reproduced, stored in a retrieval system, communicated or transmitted in any form or by any means without prior written permission. All inquiries should be made to the publisher at the address above.

Photographs on cover and spine: Ashmead-Bartlett © National Portrait Gallery, London (negative no. 7709/4) Soldiers © Australian War Memorial (negative no. P02905.003)

Edited by Sharon Nevile

Printed in China by
Printplus Limited

10 9 8 7 6 5 4 3 2 1

Dedication

In memory of Nan Lundy

Born the year of the Gallipoli landing, and passed way in the year of its 90th anniversary — a wonderful Australian

Contents

Introduction vii

1 *An Explosive Start* 1
2 *All or Nothing* 14
3 *On the Road from Morocco* 26
4 *Three 'Gentlemen' of Gallipoli* 45
5 *A Race of Athletes* 61
6 *Igniting a Legend* 75
7 *'Enough Glory for All'* 93
8 *A Very Personal War* 113
9 *'This Should Draw All the Ladies of London'* 131
10 *'They Cannot Long Conceal the Truth From the Public'* 147
11 *'I'm Glad We're Dyin' Game'* 168
12 *In the Antipodes: 'Horrible–Horrible–Horrible'* 188
13 *War Office Blackball* 206
14 *Seven Marriages, One Legal* 214
15 *Journalism and the Making of the Gallipoli Myth* 240

Appendix 1: Report of the Gallipoli Landing 261

Appendix 2: Letter to the British Prime Minister 266

Bibliography 271

Index 279

Introduction

This is not a history of Gallipoli. There are plenty of good ones around.

Rather, it is the story of the journalist who scripted the Gallipoli legend, Ellis Ashmead-Bartlett; the reporter who proved the old adage that journalism is the first rough draft of history; and the Englishman who in so doing helped to construct Australia's national identity.

Ellis Ashmead-Bartlett was a journalist's journalist: self-confident, opinionated, witty, well connected, and a gifted war correspondent. He was a natural pack leader, always with a quip or the last word, and always surrounded by the best food and wines, not to mention, in his earlier days, women. Ellis was not only a gambler, but he appeared to have a gambler's luck with journalism, always being at the right spot for the big story. Yet there remained a strange tension within him. Although regarding himself socially as an insider, he had that naturally rebellious journalistic streak that led him to question authority. It was a combination that would prove explosive at Gallipoli, when Ellis began doubting the military competence of the expedition's leaders — doubts that grew to outright derision and resulted in his attempt to have a letter smuggled to England's Prime Minister Asquith. While others stayed quiet, Ellis Ashmead-Bartlett was prepared to risk his journalistic career to reveal the leadership blunders at Gallipoli. And he would do it yet again; risking his job to oppose communism in central Europe in the inter-war years.

Ellis Ashmead-Bartlett brings another dimension to what occurred at Gallipoli. While he witnessed and wrote about some of the major events, he also told of the power struggles behind the scenes, of the military's attempt to stifle press coverage, and the political in-fighting over the future of the expedition. But for Australians, of course, his superb documentation in both print and film remains a cornerstone of the nation's Gallipoli story.

As journalists, we came across Ellis Ashmead-Bartlett through an association with the C.E.W. Bean Foundation, which honours the works of Australian war correspondents. If Ashmead-Bartlett lit the Gallipoli flame, the famous Bean fanned and nurtured it to the point where it became the key symbol of Australian identity.

Acknowledgements

Our thanks to Francis Ashmead-Bartlett, Ellis's son, who generously gave of his time and personal family recollections. Francis lodged most of his father's papers, records and photographs with the Institute of Commonwealth Studies at the University of London. We would like to thank Ian Cooke, Yvette Bailey and the staff at the institute for their patience and help. At London's King's College Liddell Hart Centre for Military Archives, Kate O'Brien and Lottie Clarke were excellent; while at the Imperial War Museum in London Phillip Dutton was a godsend and a mine of information. Our thanks also to staff at the British Library, including their Colinton Newspaper Library, and the British National Archives (formerly the Public Records Office) at Kew.

In Australia we are grateful to the staff of the New South Wales State Library, the National Library in Canberra, the Australian War Memorial and the National Archives in Canberra and in Melbourne, where Loretta Tavellione and Leslie Wetherall were particularly helpful. Thanks also to the ACT Public Library Service and their online facilities.

Tracking down information about films and film-making in the early 1900s also meant seeking assistance from specialist libraries. Australia's ScreenSound (now the National Film and Sound Archive) was terrific, thanks to Kate McLoughlin and Cara Shipp. The War Memorial staff for film and photographs also supplied great assistance — thanks to Madeleine Chaleyer, Ian Affleck and Andrew Jack. In London, archivists at the British Film Archives were very helpful and painstaking, and we appreciated the expertise of the Imperial War Museum. Channel 9 backed the film search from the beginning with enthusiasm. Thanks to Max Uechtritz, Mary Davison, Ben Hawke and Peter Harvey.

Thanks also to Kate Fitzpatrick, Virginia Knox, Peter Lundy, Harry Gordon, His Excellency Lajos Fodor, Vicki Ashmead-Bartlett, Rebecca Lundy, Phillip Knightley, Jock Given, Daniel Reynaud, Penny Brenchley, Julian Brenchley, Wilma Norris, Dr T.E. Rogers of Marlborough College Archives, Wiltshire, Nye Hughes, Dr Lenore Colthart, Catherine Spedding and Sharon Nevile of John Wiley & Sons, Australia and an amazing group of good friends who offered constant support for the project.

The photographs in this book, except for those otherwise indicated, are from the Ashmead-Bartlett family collection, the majority of which is held at the University of London's Institute of Commonwealth Studies (ICS): the Ashmead-Bartlett Papers: photographs c1880–1930: ICS 84/D, folders 1–7. Others are from the Imperial War Museum (IWM); the Australian War Memorial (AWM); the National Library of Australia (NLA); and the National Film and Sound Archive (NFSA), a division of the Australian Film Commission (formerly ScreenSound).

Fred & Elizabeth Brenchley
Canberra, August 2005

1

An Explosive Start

IN the mid-1890s, as the teachers of the exclusive English school Marlborough were walking to church one Sunday morning, an explosion rocked the quiet Wiltshire hills. The geography master rushed to investigate. He returned triumphant. 'It's finally happened, just as I've always predicted,' he exclaimed. 'I've always told my boys over the years that this area of the country must be volcanic and that an eruption like this was only a matter of time. My theory is vindicated at last!'

His joy, however, was somewhat premature. It was quickly apparent that it was no act of God, but a devilish escapade by Master Ellis Ashmead-Bartlett and friends. Somehow or other they had secured detonators and explosives, letting them off in a local quarry as a joke on their geography master.

This, of course, is the raconteur Ellis's own version of events as told to colleagues later at the journalists' camp on Imbros Island off Gallipoli. But it was the sort of daredevil behaviour that never left him. For his colleagues, however, it was more an illustration of the curious mixture of the perpetrator's character — rebellious, although ambitious to be amongst the rich and powerful; disdainful of authority; and superbly confident, bordering on arrogant.

Ashmead-Bartlett was out to enjoy life, and those who accompanied him on his short 50-year journey found him an exciting and entertaining companion, if somewhat self-centred. Lord Birkenhead, Attorney-General and Viceroy to India, and himself a noted wit and orator, described Ashmead-Bartlett as the best conversationalist he had ever known. His shortcomings, said Valentine Williams, a journalist colleague, included an abruptness that could border on rudeness. But these were more than counterbalanced by a fine mind, pretty wit and 'a certain panache as though every succeeding day were big with adventure, whether this were a "scoop" for the paper or a run of luck at the gaming table'. For Williams, Ashmead-Bartlett was best summed up in Dryden's line:

> Has so much wit and mirth and spleen about thee
> There is no living with thee, nor without thee!

Charles Bean, the Australian journalist and historian at Gallipoli marvelled at his writing prowess and outrageous lifestyle, putting it all down to his upper class but 'careless' upbringing. For Bean, himself the son of a schoolteacher, Ashmead-Bartlett came from 'adventurous, reckless' stock, and was raised in the 'fast, flash' end of society. Ashmead-Bartlett, said Bean, had a life that 'was largely a progress from one excitement to the other'.

The adult influences on young Ellis that Bean alluded to were his father, Sir Ellis, and his uncle, William Ashmead-Bartlett. 'Uncle Willie' remained a confidant, sometime business partner and occasional financial saviour up to his death in 1921. 'Colourful' would be an understatement for these two Ashmead-Bartlett brothers. Born in America, with ancestors dating back to the Mayflower, and brought to England for an Oxford education, Ellis senior became heavily involved in Conservative politics and imperialist causes. He bested H. H. Asquith (later wartime prime minister) in a famous Oxford Union contest, going on to become a schools inspectors, barrister, MP, civil lord of the admiralty, and one of the most sought after speakers on the Conservative circuit. He was knighted in 1892. Sir Ellis married Frances Christina Walsh in 1874 (Ellis junior was the oldest of five sons and a daughter), but it was his affair with Blanche Hozier (mother of Clementine, later the wife of Winston Churchill) that caused a public sensation in 1889. Years later, young Ellis's rocky relationship with Winston over the Gallipoli expedition may have held an extra edge because of their families' history.

Just what this very public affair did for home life is not clear. Young Ellis later told friends that his parents were unsuited. He took his father's side, claiming that his mother, although very kind to the children, would have irritated anyone she lived with.

Apart from his public proselytising for Empire causes, such as keeping Ireland and making Swaziland a British rather than a Boer territory, Sir Ellis also put money into a new weekly newspaper, *England*, to promote imperialism. He was still fighting bankruptcy over that troubled publication a year before his death in 1902.

Sir Ellis died virtually penniless, and young Ellis went to live with Uncle Willie, who had gained a position helping the fabulously wealthy banking widow, Baroness Burdett-Coutts, dispense philanthropy, including to remote Australian Aborigines. The Baroness had refused many offers to remarry, reportedly including those from the Duke of Waterloo and Louis Napoleon. But in 1881, when she was 67, the announcement of her engagement to 30-year-old William Ashmead-Bartlett shocked British society. Prime Minister Gladstone even thought it could disturb foreign relations, sending an emissary, a Mr Knowles, to dissuade her.

'Mr Knowles,' the Baroness retorted to the prime ministerial emissary, 'have you ever read in the prayer book that a man may not marry his grandmother?'

'Yes.'

'Well then, it was perfectly well conceived that a man might very reasonably want to marry a woman old enough to be his grandmother!'

Such was the wealth and prestige involved with the great Victorian heiress and philanthropist that William had to gain Royal licence to assume her surname. Like his brother, William Burdett-Coutts also became an MP. It was said that the elderly Baroness never extracted 'undue morality' from her husband. As young Ellis said some years later, given the age difference this would have been absurd.

Ellis grew up, as the somewhat prudish Bean noted, amongst this 'fast, flashy, wealthy crowd which eddied around and at some points intermingled with the innermost currents of high society in England'. Fast and flashy it may have been, but it also provided Ellis with contacts beyond those of the normal journalist; contacts he would use throughout his career. Diplomats, officers, politicians and officials confided in him. His society contacts stretched to the top of politics. At Gallipoli his entrée back in London society created real resentment among the military leaders on the peninsula.

Ellis himself affected a moody self-assurance coupled with a superb conversation style and a certain panache when it came to pessimistic predictions. Friends said it was impossible to best him in retort. But he was inclined to be blunt which, added to his touch of prescience, often offended people. As war clouds gathered in 1914 Ashmead-Bartlett was in the Bachelors Club in London. A young friend already signed up as an officer asked him what he thought would happen.

'There will be war for a certainty in a few days,' replied Ellis.

'What will happen to us?'

'The British Expeditionary Force will be sent to France, and within two months most of you will be dead.'

'Well, you are cheerful,' responded his shocked friend. Within six weeks he had been killed in battle.

Ashmead-Bartlett was also blessed, if that is the word, with the cutting wit that journalists particularly relish. When he toured America with some British society friends, the head of a southern university greeted the visiting party with a speech, tearing off a pine branch to proclaim 'some of our greatest statesmen were educated by the light of these pine torches'.

'Oh, that's nothing,' interjected Ashmead-Bartlett, 'our present government was brought up in total darkness'.

On Imbros Island off Gallipoli, the journalists' camp was a couple of miles from the General Headquarters of Sir Ian Hamilton and his staff, but alongside a picket line of 100 Egyptian white donkeys.

'Did you hear those donkeys last night?' the New Zealand correspondent, Malcolm Ross, complained to Ashmead-Bartlett at breakfast one morning.

'Yes, and did you hear the answering bray from GHQ?'

Charles Bean said GHQ hated Ashmead-Bartlett's wit, which he obviously used against them. Bean related Ashmead-Bartlett's cutting comments about Hamilton's failed attempts to visit Suvla Bay on the morning of the new landings there in August 1915. Hamilton's boat could not start because of mechanical failure. By the time things were smoothed out it was about noon. 'Of course then it was too late — it was getting near time for lunch,' joked Ashmead-Bartlett.

After an initial private education at home, Ashmead-Bartlett was sent off to Marlborough for his final few years. Marlborough may have been one of England's great public schools, but it did not impress the young Ellis. He hated its regimentation. He hated organised games like football and cricket, preferring to get away by himself whenever possible. Blessed with an extraordinary memory, he was one of life's blotters who seemed to naturally soak up information. He could quote Gibbon by the page, and recite by rote the names and titles of all of Napoleon's generals. Give him a single line from Shakespeare and Ashmead-Bartlett could reel off the entire speech, and often the scene as well.

When in the mood, as he often was in the after-dinner glow of a fine repast at the journalists' camp on Imbros (Ashmead-Bartlett had imported a French chef) he was a gifted raconteur. The camp, with its good food and wine, epitomised the taste for the civilised life that Ashmead-Bartlett acquired during his childhood. Henry Nevinson, the distinguised journalist and German scholar who found himself on Gallipoli reporting for Britain's provincial press, said he was always astonished by Ashmead-Bartlett's 'air of magnificence'. He describes the campsite scene on Imbros:

'Among the rocks of that savage island, among the pigs and sheep that infested our camp searching for the last leaves and grapes of summer in a vineyard hard by, he would issue forth from his elaborately furnished tent dressed in a flowing robe of yellow silk shot with crimson, and call for breakfast as though the Carlton [Hotel] were still his corporeal home.'

Whether Marlborough nurtured young Ellis's gift for writing or not, it certainly did not foster a talent for spelling. His letters are sprinkled with primary school bloopers. And, oddly for a writer with a pen that one colleague described as dipped in 'volcanoes and fire', Ashmead-Bartlett hated writing with ink and paper. His forte was the portable typewriter. After his engagement in 1919 he even told his fiancée, Nina, that if she wished the marriage to go ahead she would have to tolerate typewritten letters from him.

Ellis's academic progress at Marlborough was patchy. He did quite well in his first few years, winning history and divinity prizes, but slumped to the bottom of the class in his final year as he lost interest. Although he was seen as having a quite reasonable academic standard, he was not regarded as a potential university scholar. Instead Marlborough channeled him into a wide diet of maths, divinity, German, French, Latin, English and geography.

The one thing young Ellis hated was boredom and middle-class life. Somehow he knew his life would be short, and he craved adventure and excitement. Indeed, he went straight to a warfront at 16 years of age. Sir Ellis Ashmead-Bartlett had been a great supporter of Turkey against an earlier Russian threat. In 1897, when the Sultan of Turkey invited him to Constantinople to see something of the Graeco-Turkish war, he decided to take young Ellis. Needless to say the teenager was delighted to get away from Marlborough for an entire term. The two assembled their travelling kit, including saddle bags, a Winchester Colt repeating rifle, one 'big revolver' and a smaller one. On arrival Sultan Abdul Hamid — 'the Shadow of God on Earth' — presented them with eight choice Arab horses from the imperial stables and an escort of 12 mounted troopers.

Young Ellis then found he was almost the first victim to fall in the war, which had arisen out of a dispute over Crete. His white Arab horse bolted in the darkness, with the youngster clinging on for his life. The horse eventually dumped him in a stony creek and ran off, leaving his rider bleeding profusely from a severe head wound. When the guards returned with the offending animal, Ellis said a strange ceremony ensued.

'They brought him before me, uttered some words in Turkish, and then each in turn doubled his fist and hit [the horse] a terrific whack on the point of the nose. My father then tried to explain that it would be wiser to leave the punishment of the horse to a later hour and to do something to stop the bleeding from my head. Their simple surgery was rough but effective. Each man carried a lump of tow which they used for lighting their pipes. This they stuffed in to the wound, and tied a handkerchief round my head to keep it in position.'

A surgeon at a Turkish field hospital later stitched the wound. Although at the time he believed that his youth saved him, the head wound would trouble Ellis for years. As the Turkish forces drove back the Greeks, however, he was more worried about not seeing any 'bloody battles' than he was about a mere head wound.

His military initiation came at the Battle of Valestino in early May 1897. As Turkish forces tried to turn the Greek flank, Ellis, displaying his usual self-confidence, gave his father the slip and went with them. In those days troops were armed with old-fashioned breech-loaded Martini rifles, which fire big lead bullets amongst much smoke. Young Ellis found himself in a wood with bullets buzzing about like 'angry bees disturbed'.

'The noise seemed awful to me. I was armed with a small Winchester Repeater and kept up an incessant fire, aiming at nothing except the trees in front, and scared to death,' he said.

'Suddenly I came upon a dead Turkish soldier with his forehead blown out by a bullet and lying in a pool of blood. This was the first dead man I had ever seen, and the sight filled me with an inexpressible horror. I stood and gazed on him in a kind of stupor for some minutes. The firing line had now passed out of sight and I was alone. No more fighting for me that day. I seized my rifle and ran from the battlefield, being chased in my disordered imagination by a thousand frightful specters.'

Ellis then fell in with a war correspondent from the *Standard*, a Mr Montgomery. Together they found their way to Larissa, where they gave Turkish commanders the first reports of the check their troops had suffered. 'We two Christians, it turned out, were Allah's first messengers. Montgomery was able to give a detailed account of the engagement. Reinforcements were dispatched, the position was saved, we were duly thanked and retired to bed exhausted.'

Not for the last time, Ashmead-Bartlett found himself the 'guest' of both sides in a war. Farewelled by their Turkish escort, father and son set sail. At Salonika they were betrayed by the Greek crew of their boat to a Greek naval vessel. But they were quite safe. The ship received a cable from Athens: 'Sir Ellis Ashmead-Bartlett is to be treated with every consideration and brought to Athens as quickly as possible'.

On arrival, the Greek prime minister came on board and, while preparations were being made to hand them over to the British ambassador, asked to see their luggage. 'When I came to showing him all the arms and trophies I had got up at the war, he did not seem particularly pleased … he rushed at me and seized me by the throat pretending to be angry,' Ellis wrote in his diary.

Despite his horror at the sight of the dead soldier, the war left the youngster with a taste for military life. On his return to England he joined the militia, participating in the big manoeuvres on Salisbury Plain, the greatest yet held in England. As the Boer War ground on his Bedford Regiment, under Viscount Cranbourne, was drafted in to supplement regulars.

'The majority of those who went to South Africa departed in much the same spirit as you would leave for a glorious holiday in some foreign land,' he wrote. Actually, he departed in a hail of oranges thrown at the departing British troops by Irish women who had been selling fruit on the quay. 'The air was full of oranges and the deck ran with orange juice,' he said. 'Truly the Irish are a strange race.'

Although he was only 19, the Boer War gave Ashmead-Bartlett the opportunity to demonstrate his ready grasp of military strategy. He had analysed the war before departure and, in what read like a remarkable prelude to Gallipoli, laid the initial failure of the British on four main factors — underestimating the enemy, poor advance scouting, the mobility of Boer forces, and the poor training of British generals, who were usually too old for the job.

The British had no accurate maps of the Transvaal, he said. 'Would a German cavalry regiment have behaved in the same manner? Certainly not. Every inch of the ground would have been surveyed and carefully mapped out.' And on the age of British field leadership he was scathing. 'Our generals are nearly all veterans of between 50 and 70 years of age, an age at which it is an impossibility for a man to be in a suitable state to take the field,' he said. 'This has been found time over an over again, the young active vigorous man will always win in the end. None of Napoleon's great line of famous marshals were above the age of 50, the greater part of them were 45 and under.'

The Boer War also saw the first signs of another of Ashmead-Bartlett's lifetime passions — gambling. He won £21 in a sweepstakes on the run to the equator and had to shout all the officers champagne. A second sweepstakes win was followed by a loss at shipboard poker.

There was also a glass of champagne as he celebrated his birthday on 11 February, as the liner *Canada* sailed down the African coast. 'I am 19 I think, but am uncertain,' he wrote, in a reference to the mystery surrounding the details of his birth. A birth certificate later cited by family members indicated he may have been born at Davos, Switzerland, in 1881.

South Africa was crawling with the Ashmead-Bartletts. Ellis ran into Uncle Willie at the Mount Nelson Hotel in Pretoria. And walking along the main street of Bloemfontein whom should he meet but his father, then trying to steer Swaziland into the British Empire. 'He did not at first recognise me, but I soon informed him who I was.'

As a junior officer, Ellis did a lot of marching about and camping, but appeared to see little action. He was fortunate in arriving during the second phase of the war as the British relieved the Boer sieges of Kimberley, Ladysmith and Mafeking, with the defeated Boer leader Paul Kruger fleeing. Ashmead-Bartlett believed the British generals at last were learning some lessons, eliminating frontal attacks and cutting off Boer retreats.

Good food and drink seemed to occupy an inordinate amount of the young officer's diary, as it did throughout his adult life. He wrote at length on the best cooking and eating for troops in the field, concluding that the best lunch drink for them was a whisky and water. Quite.

Despite such gastronomic treats, Ashmead-Bartlett fell ill, apparently a result of complications from the head wound suffered in his Turkish adventures. Doctors operated, and he was repatriated back to England. Details of this interlude in his life are sketchy, but in 1901 he turned up in Marseilles on junior consular duties while still recuperating.

Ellis was troubled that he could not return to the war, but consoled himself visiting all the cafes, 'consorting with all the finest coquettes in the place, and the little pleasure I had was derived from their society and bodies,' he confided to his diary. When a friend admonished him that he was an atheist and that he was destined for eternal fire, Ellis proclaimed that this left him cold as he had 'never cared two pence what happened after death'. If he found himself 'working in the lower strata' he believed he would 'certainly find a very large number of my oldest and dearest friends shovelling at the same level'.

Consular duties quickly bored him. Performing civil marriages and dealing with a ship's crew charged with mutiny brought on such ennui that he decided to visit the casino at Monte Carlo, taking £50 to gamble. 'I had but little money,' he said, but the 20-year-old dreamt of returning to London with immense wealth to enjoy the lifestyle he had come to enjoy during his upbringing, but found hard to maintain as an adult. This dream propelled his gambling habit for many years.

After taking a room at the Grand Hotel, Ellis hastened to the casino where he 'played furiously', unfortunately losing everything but 25 francs by noon. Somewhat revived by a bottle of wine over lunch, he took stock.

'I said to myself: "What is the good of 25 francs?" And with these words flung it on the table on red. Red turned up and I bet the 50. Red turned up again and I saw 100 before my eyes, but again I said: "What is the good of 100?" and left that on too. Again red turned up and I left it on until I made 800. Then I commenced to play more carefully. My luck was now in. I could do nothing wrong and by six o'clock on Easter Monday I had made 5000 francs, a large sum of money.'

While gambling, Ellis noticed a young girl standing in the casino room watching play but apparently taking little interest. Pretty, with a voluptuous figure, masses of fair hair and blue eyes, she had an expression of 'infinite sadness'. He felt that she looked like 'a little angel bemoaning the sins of the world'. Ellis followed her for a few days before introducing himself. When he asked her why she looked so sad, she burst into tears and the following story poured out. She was Elza Philipch from Budapest. Her parents were wealthy, but she had run away to France with a poor Austrian officer after her parents had opposed their marriage. For a month at the Monte Carlo tables his luck was good and they had enjoyed themselves. Then his luck ran out. He lost everything, and promptly shot himself.

'For some time I remained speechless after this tale, and finally kissed her as a mark of sympathy,' he wrote. They became friends, and then lovers. Young Ellis fell in love. 'Ah, that lovely night. The memory of it will never fade from my mind. The beautiful softness of her skin, the modesty of her demeanour, the evident reluctance with which she yielded the woman's supreme gift will ever remain as a divine oasis in the dreary desert of life.'

Between success on the tables and in bed, young Ellis's health improved. But he had to return to London. Elza begged him to take her with him as she had no friends in Monte Carlo. Initially he refused, but after a few tears, he consented.

In London he was due to take up residence with his mentor, Uncle Willie, and study for the bar. Elza would hardly fit into the Burdett-Coutts household. Ellis solved the problem by hiring a small furnished house for her in Montagu Street near the British Museum, staying with her at nights and sneaking home early in the morning. This was awkward because Uncle Willie, fearing burglars, refused to give him a latch key. One of the servants had to wait up for him and they soon complained about his extraordinarily late habits. Nevertheless, he kept up the love nest for months. It says a lot about Ellis's sheer confidence, even at 20 years of age. Living with an uncle and supposedly studying law, he was still able to keep a mistress in a rented home on gambling winnings. He kept up the double life through the summer months, taking Elza for excursions on the river and to dinner.

His gambling winnings soon ran out, however, and he began to resort to 'many shifts to keep my little illegitimate home together'. It was about this time he began borrowing from Jewish money lenders — 'the gentlemen of the Red Sea fiasco', as he called them. Eventually the strain became intolerable. Even Elza could see it. Ashmead-Bartlett told her she must return home to Hungary, and after some correspondence with her parents they agreed to take her back 'on certain [unspecified] conditions'.

Ashmead-Bartlett concentrated on his law studies, detesting the traditional practice of having to eat legal dinners for three years before being called to the bar. 'I found them an infernal nuisance, although the wine was good.'

The only relief was a trip to Ostend in Belgium with his mother. For some reason Ashmead-Bartlett took a revolver with him, and began practising shooting on the beach at Ostend. Belgian police arrested him and even charged him with intending to assassinate King Leopold, who was expected to visit that day. The British consul freed him, and Ashmead-Bartlett was hustled back to England that day, minus his revolver.

Spending two months swotting up before exams he even contemplated suicide he was so depressed. 'I never thought I would pass but

I managed it somehow,' he wrote later. The law, however, was as boring for Ashmead-Bartlett as the diplomatic service had been. He drifted around it for a while, dabbled with society, books and journalism, and even shot off to the West Indies where he took the first photographs of a major volcanic eruption at Mount Pelee.

Ellis had to face the painful fact that he was poor, yet wanted to live in high society. Handsome, 5 feet 10 inches in height, with a straight-jawed face and blond hair parted down the centre, he mixed easily, blessed with an easy conversational style plus the added pull of the Burdett-Coutts and his father's political life. He met the great financier Pierpont Morgan, and even the visiting Australian Prime Minister Edmund Barton, in London for the coronation of Edward VII after the death of Queen Victoria. 'Mr Barton is a fine looking man, whom if you dressed him up in the clothes of 100 years ago and put a suitable hat on his head would strongly resemble George Washington,' he wrote.

Money, or the lack of it, was a constant worry. He tried to speculate in property rentals for the coronation, but lost. Ashmead-Bartlett admonished himself when he thought he was falling in love with a young woman called Lena. 'If you have money it is all very well, but when you are under the painful necessity of having to earn a living it is a great mistake,' he said. 'Keep clear of all good women until you are in a position to marry one.'

Certainly he was in no such position. Another trip to Ostend's casino was a financial disaster, forcing a return in a second class cabin, and a declaration: 'I am now quite cured of all desire to gamble again as long as I live!'

That vow lasted only until he succumbed to the lure of a war correspondent's life.

2

'All or Nothing'

PHILLIP Knightley, in his classic work *The First Casualty*, called it the Golden Age of war correspondents. In the 70 years from the Crimean War to World War I a select band of men — there were no women — roamed the hotspots of the world. From the Crimean War to the American Civil War, Franco-Prussian War, Spanish-American War, Russo-Japanese War and South African Boer War, to Morocco and the numerous conflicts in the Balkans, they catalogued wars in a way that had never happened before.

They were reporters, spies, myth makers and national agitators in an era of empire and emergent nationalism, when newspaper barons were influential players. As William Randolph Hearst famously cabled his artist, whom he had sent to whip up emotions about a war with Spain over Cuba: 'You furnish pictures. I will furnish war'.

A new cabling language was created — one that omitted 'the, and, a, of' — as reporters utlisised expensive new telegraph lines that helped them get details of the latest battles to a seemingly insatiable public. Trains, ships, yachts, camels and later cars and aeroplanes were hired in what was also a golden age for reporters' expense accounts. They carried guns and expensive 'kit'. The lifestyle was either expensive hotels in exotic locations, with much drinking and womanising, or dodging bullets and living in hovels around battlefields.

Newspaper proprietors didn't much mind the expense, as long as it added to their prestige and, more importantly, sold newspapers. With newspapers the only means of mass communication, the press barons had to be first with reports, and hang the expense. A good war could double sales. Ashmead-Bartlett spent a small fortune hiring a ship to cover the Italian campaign in Tripoli in 1911, but he got a major scoop of an Italian massacre of Arabs that his Reuters agency sold widely. The Reuters boss later told him: 'My boy, it came as rather a shock when you spent all that money. It was a wicked thing for the Italians to massacre the Arabs, but it absolutely saved the situation.' He meant, of course, making a profit after Ellis's huge costs.

War correspondents hunted in packs, but were fiercely competitive. Camaraderie was fine behind the lines, but when it came to filing a report first it was every man for himself. Ashmead-Bartlett in World War I described the hardy, resourceful and unscrupulous character required:

> He must learn everything for himself [official information was almost unknown], he had to keep all his news to himself, he must grasp a situation at a glance, and very often when competition was excessively keen, he had to judge the finish of a battle without actually waiting to see the end. If you were a party of a dozen all working against one another on a campaign, life was, to say the least of it, hard. Only a few could withstand the mental and physical fatigue involved, and the constant excitement and unrest. You never, in fact, knew from hour to hour whether you were first with a despatch, or if an angry or respectful telegram would arrive from your Editor announcing that so and so had the story a day ahead.

War correspondents created a whole new genre of cliché-ridden newspaper reporting, as Knightley noted. Guns flashed, cannons thundered, struggles raged, generals were brave, soldiers gallant and bayonet charges made short work of enemies. Some romanticised war with colourful accounts, others exposed command incompetence and particularly medical supply scandals. They even brought

Myth Maker

down governments. Military officers in the field detested them as leeches. Some, like William Howard Russell, Richard Harding Davis and Luigi Barzini, wrote serious books as well as newspaper reports, becoming household names. Knightley recounted that newsboys in Milan sold *Corriere della Sera* not by shouting headlines but by yelling, 'Article by Barzini'.

William 'Billy' Russell's reporting of the Crimean War in 1854 set the pattern for this new breed of reporters. 'Am I to tell these things, or hold my tongue,' Russell wrote to the *Times* editor, John Delane. 'Go ahead,' replied the editor. But Russell's reports of army folly and blunders, particularly in medical treatment of the wounded, raised an outcry that he was unpatriotic. Lord Raglan, the army commander, attempted what would become the standard defence of trying to get rid of the troublesome reporter. Unsuccessful, he fell back on standard defence number two: the reports assisted the enemy. Russell's reports forced the government to upgrade medical services for the wounded. Florence Nightingale was also sent out to run a hospital for the wounded in Constantinople. But Russell's reports were so damaging that the government itself fell. 'It was you who turned out the government,' the Duke of Newcastle later told Russell, illustrating the new power of war correspondents.

Curiously, Russell's travails in the Crimea would find echoes with Ashmead-Bartlett almost 60 years later at Gallipoli. Ellis seemed straight from central casting for a war correspondent. He was a fast, colourful descriptive wordsmith, able to throw in historical allusions on cue. He stretched across all writing formats; a 'scoop' merchant with a gambler's streak that gave him the appearance of always being on the spot; an author of books; outspoken feature writer with just that touch of fame; and a sharp critic of military failures where necessary. Given his constant urgent demand to stave off bankruptcy, he even added new commercial touches like photography, lecture tours and cinema films.

Competitors revelled in his lively companionship and sharp conversation. They admired his journalistic style, but worried that they could not match it. Charles Bean both envied and admired Ashmead-Bartlett's remarkable account of the Anzac landing, but agonised that he could not write about bayonet charges like some correspondents did. 'Ashmead-Bartlett makes it a little difficult for one by his exaggerations, and yet he is a lover of the truth. He gives the spirit of things.'

Ashmead-Bartlett gave more than 'the spirit of things'. He was meticulous in detailing military movements, analysing battles and studying the topography of battlefields, even having expensive maps made to help him describe them. Interestingly, the Dardanelles Committee of Inquiry used his Gallipoli maps. And he was not just a battlefield reporter. Ashmead-Bartlett always sought to take a wider view of the overall military strategy — and that was to lead him into trouble with the military brass.

1904 was a turning point, not only for world history but also for Ashmead-Bartlett. The surprise Japanese attack on the Russian fleet at Port Arthur signalled the first war between a European and an Asian power. 'When the first shot was fired my blood boiled within me to be off,' wrote the 23-year-old. 'I sented [sic] the battle from afar, longed to take part in all the stirring events, and visions of great fights, cavalry charges, blood and slaughter arose within me.' He knocked on newspaper and wire service doors up and down Fleet Street, but there were no takers for the brash youngster, whether or not they had checked out his notoriously bad spelling. But Ellis was determined to go. He borrowed £200 from Uncle Willie, and another £100 from a money lender 'at an enormous rate of interest', bought his kit and booked a passage to Japan via America. His brother Seabury came to see him off, finding Ellis in high spirits that 'the world was really opening up before me'.

Closing up might have been more accurate. The Pacific crossing on board the liner *China* was lively enough. His travelling companions included Richard Harding Davis, the gun-toting Hearst journalist who had helped provoke the Spanish-American War, and John Fox of *Scribner's Magazine*. They amused themselves on the journey gambling, losing money to Chinese 'sharpers' on board playing fan-tan. On arrival in Yokohama the correspondents hired the famous No 9 Japanese Tea House with its beguiling geishas and, as Ellis admitted, indulged in the pleasures after an enforced celibacy on board ship. Ellis was into the high life of the new world of war correspondents on credit, and all this with no job.

In Tokyo, however, there was bad news. All the famous correspondents had hurried there, but the Japanese barred them from going to the front. After paying large hotel bills as the months ticked by, many editors began pulling out their correspondents. For Ashmead-Bartlett, the situation was grim. He was a freelancer, with no newspaper to pay his bills, and now not even a war to report in order to get some work. Fortunately, the Austrian owner of the Palace Hotel in Tokyo, Emil Flaig, gave him extended credit.

Running low on funds, Ellis was hit by another problem. Sir Claude Macdonald, the British ambassador in Tokyo, told him that serving British officers could not go to the front. Ashmead-Bartlett promptly wrote to the Secretary of State for War resigning his captaincy in the militia, which was accepted.

Meanwhile, the assembled war correspondents entertained themselves, congregating at a Tokyo house hired by Harding Davis's wife. They bragged to each about their rifles and kit, rode horses into the countryside, and plotted how they could join the Russian side. 'I do not think I ever saw a body of more touchy, irritable, nervous men than the correspondents presented during the enforced wait,' said Ashmead-Bartlett.

At one stage Ellis was so low on funds that he tried to sign up in the Japanese army, seeking a commission in the Guards. But the Japanese did not want any foreigners in their army.

Nor did they want any foreign press coverage. Richard Harding Davis even threatened the ultimate sanction — he would leave without even going to the front! The Japanese were unfazed. Phillip Knightley believed they regarded all foreign press as spies. Suddenly, however, the Japanese changed their minds, allowing correspondents to go to the front. Ashmead-Bartlett believed the change of heart was due to the Japanese need to curry favour in the Western press to raise loans in England and America. 'We were hurried off with almost indecent speed and loaded with favours,' he wrote.

Initially Ashmead-Bartlett was assigned to Japanese naval units, gaining a stringer's job with the *Standard* at £50 a month plus expenses. He also secured the job of special correspondent for *Collier's Weekly*, an American journal.

By November 1904 he was with General Nogi's troops in their attacks on the forts around Port Arthur, cabling reports to the *Times*. His description of Japanese forces scaling great bamboo ladders to breach the ramparts of the fort — urged on by officers yelling that victory would be a present for the Emperor on his birthday — displayed his ability to portray appalling war scenes:

> Then occurred one of the most extraordinary scenes I have ever witnessed in war. The Russians had huge forks on the end of long poles, and with these they pushed the ladders backwards, toppling the assaulters into the ditch beneath. Time and time again the Japanese rushed forward only to be hurled into the ditch which was choked with hundreds of dead, wounded and uninjured men. Those who were not hurt kept on making fresh attempts, and the Russians, to check the rush poured quantities of oil onto the mass below and then set the lot on fire with hand grenades. Great clouds of black smoke obscured the scene and from this inferno arose the terrible cries of hundreds of tormented men who were slowly burning to death. A horrible smell of burnt flesh wafted back on the breeze.

The Japanese broke off the attack, but General Nogi then ordered his engineers to dig under the fort to plant explosives. It was mid-winter in Manchuria, with the ground frozen solid and covered in snow. Ashmead-Bartlett lived in a 'wretched' hut in a 'miserable' village, sleeping on top of a brick stove with a fire of maize stalks burning underneath him. One night, as he was huddled beside the fire trying to keep warm, a Japanese messenger knocked on the door and handed him a note: 'General Baron Nogi presents his compliments and wishes to say that if it would interest you to see the Keikwansan Fort blown up, he will have the honour to blow it up at ten a.m. tomorrow morning and would advise you to be at your place at that time.'

Ashmead-Bartlett was certainly there, half sympathising with the Russians inside, blissfully ignorant of their 10 am fate. Right on the dot of ten the explosive trains were detonated, sending a huge column of smoke into the air. 'High above the smoke, you saw shapeless masses of masonry, great wooden beams, stones, rubbish and human forms blown in all directions.' The explosion was so large it also killed about 50 of the Japanese assault force assembled outside. Although temporarily checked, they charged through the breach, killing the Russian survivors.

Back in London, Ashmead-Bartlett wrote a fuller version in a book, *Port Arthur: The Siege and Capitulation*, to laudatory reviews. Winston Churchill told him he enjoyed it. One paragraph may have been self-analytical. Describing a furious Japanese assault, he wrote that they fought wildly, 'like gamblers who, having lost more than they could afford, determine to recover themselves by some desperate coup which must mean either success or still worse disaster'. Ashmead-Bartlett had already done that in Monte Carlo, and shortly would do it yet again.

The years following the Russo-Japanese War saw an introspective, moody Ashmead-Bartlett trying to come to grips with his gambling and high-life induced penury, while still uncertain about his career as a writer, although he had certainly given away the law. He clung, however, to high society almost as if it were his birthright. Still in his early 20s, he believed such contacts would both improve his mind and perhaps deliver the material fortunes he craved, even though his father had died virtually penniless in 1902. It was almost as if he saw himself in training for his expected upper-class life. 'While still young, it is wise to mix in society in order that a man may acquire those habits [of] free, easy, graceful and nonchalant [sic] which are the special perquisite of the upper classes in England and which make a man at home in every situation in which he may be placed,' he pontificated.

In 1906 he decided to attend the entire London season, that string of society functions that stretch through the English summer. And with single-mindedness he stuck to a punishing schedule of dinners, lunches, balls, weekends in the countryside, operas and morning calls, with all the accompanying flirting, gossiping, loves and match-making. 'It is far the best policy to enter into a thing thoroughly,' he wrote somewhat self-indulgently in his diary. 'If you intend to go through with the season, go through with it and do nothing else.'

At times he was ecstatic. 'It is delightful to whirl around a floor with your arm around the waist of a charming creature full of life and hope and enjoy the late hours of the early morning. To sup on indigestible quails and cutlets, to drink iced champagne, to swallow liquers [sic] and coffee, to be in fact a hero at closing time and a worm in the morning.'

At other times he flayed himself. 'Shameless idleness,' he privately admitted. 'It is with pain that I continue this record,' his diary records, 'this shameless record of over-eating and under-sleeping. However, I have set a time limit on this kind of life and I am determined to clear out of London and to retire to the country in the second week of July.'

The love affairs were tiring as well. He kept running into his old girlfriend Lena at country house parties. They had been lovers for several years. 'These post-mortem love affairs are most distressing to all,' Ellis lamented. 'They are easy to begin, yet hard to end.'

At one stage on a weekend outing he passed close to his old school of Marlborough. 'I contrasted my present position to my position of eight years ago and I wondered if I had used my time to the best advantage,' he said. 'A few minutes of reflection convinced me that I had not and therefore dropped the subject to think of something more congenial.'

A passing parade of women was certainly more congenial. Ellis enjoyed female company, and seemed captivated by elegant, older, titled women. 'Only England can produce women of quite that stamp,' he said. The Grecian-looking Lady Annesley, who complained to him about having to return to her old husband in Ireland, was one companion. Among the lunching ladies were Lady Jean Hamilton, wife of the general, and Lady Cunard, with whom he formed a liaison until her husband became jealous and barred him from the house. This was absurd, said Ashmead-Bartlett. 'Everyone except himself knows by this time that I love someone else.' He almost proposed to Lady Gwendoline Bertie until he recalled the 'cursed lines' of Alexander Pope: 'Chill penury ... quelled the genial current of the soul'. That brought him back to reality. But at the last ball of the 1906 season Ashmead-Bartlett told Lady Gwendoline that he loved her. 'What a terrible affliction to be really poor,' he confided in his diary. 'Nevertheless I feel that I shall surmount all obstacles and win her in the end, at least if I only set my mind to it. Everything comes to him who waits.' It didn't in this case, as we shall see.

Money was the constant worry, but Ashmead-Bartlett at this stage seemed to feel that a good living was his due and that someone would eventually provide it. Uncle Willie gave him some money, but refused a regular income. It seems he was already constantly juggling money lenders. He tinkered with a novel, *Cynthia*, and also a book about a prospective English Channel tunnel. However, this was scuttled when the government scrapped the idea. 'Verily life is a dreadful gamble,' he moaned.

Baroness Burdett-Coutts died in December 1906 at age 92, leaving Uncle Willie only property, although a lot of it, with the bulk of her money going back to her family. Ellis received nothing. Despite her reputation for philanthropy 'she never gave me even a present of any sort or description except a pair of mittens and a Japanese bible,' he wrote ruefully. Another uncle died, also leaving him out of the will.

On his 26th birthday in February 1907 he took stock of his life. What was the great lessons he had learnt from his strange mix of people, parties, work, stupidity and intellect, he asked himself. 'I have learned that in this life if anything is to be done one must rely absolutely on oneself,' he answered. 'I have learnt that work and application are after all the beginning and end of every accomplishment in life ... I have learnt that material troubles can be held in check and made to play only a secondary role in life if the mind is elevated on some higher goal, distant it may be, but ever coming closer, brought nearer by each succeeding day of toil and experience.'

As new book publishing ideas faded, however, and his need for money increased, Ellis was forced back to journalism. He joined up with the French army in its occupation of the Chaouia area of Morocco, taking the old township of Casablanca. Morocco was now a cockpit of colonialist tensions between the European powers, with France anxious to prevent Germany's predatory moves.

The campaign almost cost Ashmead-Bartlett his life. Moorish tribesmen had been besieging the French in Casablanca, but suddenly withdrew. Ashmead-Bartlett accompanied a small French force of some 200 sent out on reconnaissance under Colonel Prevost. Five miles out they were attacked by thousands of white-robed horsemen, some armed with modern rifles and others with old flintlocks. The French Foreign Legion formed into a fighting square, with the elderly Prevost in the middle barking orders, watched by a very apprehensive Ashmead-Bartlett. 'This was one of the most exciting moments I have ever known, because if they really charged home, it would be all up with us,' he wrote later.

The legionnaires redoubled their fire as the horde approached and, as Ashmead-Bartlett admitted, it began to look very black. But at a range of about 250 yards the Moors' courage failed, and they swerved, sweeping across the French line while firing wildly. The French suffered 50 casualties out of 200 men before a relief force arrived. In Casablanca two days later Prevost was shot dead by a Moorish sniper while talking to Ashmead-Bartlett.

The Morocco campaign paid Ashmead-Bartlett £125 a month, plus expenses, but back in London during 1908 he fell increasingly into the hands of money lenders. Worse, he had speculated disastrously in shares, and was gambling heavily at his club, Bachelors. It was almost as if he had a death wish, and he knew he was riding for a fall, with bills from money lenders gradually falling due, only to be dishonoured or renewed. Prospects of a future political life, which he now longed for, were fast fading. His diary at this time is full of self-pity at his omission from Baroness Burdett-Coutts's will and Uncle Willie's refusal to help him. 'Ten thousand pounds,' he said, would have allowed him to 'clear himself'. 'No, this was not to be, and in consequence through short-sightedness and lack of sympathy I have been dragged through the mire, suffered every form of humiliation and disgrace, and how long the blots will remain uneffaced it is impossible to say.'

In typically reckless fashion, Ashmead-Bartlett decided to raise money to clear creditors by a gambling burst on the card table at Bachelors with money he did not have. He lost £250 in one session, then urgently needed the money to settle this or he would be thrown out of the club. By tricking a Jewish money lender — calling at an hour of the day when it was impossible to make an instant check on his credit — he borrowed the £250. Then, in a do-or-die effort reminiscent of the Japanese soldiers at Port Arthur, he returned to the club's gaming room. This time he lost a further £100. Club friends chipped in to save him from expulsion when he could not settle the debt. With creditors now closing in he was forced to seek refuge in his old battalion's barracks, where summons servers were shown out at the point of a bayonet.

He was facing prison from various court orders and his army superiors petitioned Uncle Willie to save him. Uncle Willie finally relented, agreeing to settle his debts provided he agreed never to gamble again, nor to speculate on the stock market. As well, Uncle Willie required Ellis to 'turn over a new leaf', to which the young debtor commented ungraciously, 'or his cheque book might have been added'. The one consolation Ellis could take from the humiliation was that Uncle Willie wanted the money repaid. 'This last clause flattered me and proved that my uncle placed a higher value on me than I thought.'

But bankruptcy notices automatically meant he had to resign from his cherished club. Worse, his beloved Lady Gwendoline then announced her engagement to Jack Churchill, the younger brother of Winston. 'It was unbearable,' wrote Ashmead-Bartlett. 'I would have gone to a certain death with a light heart at that time and would have welcomed the end. The only person I ever cared about was engaged, my name was disgraced by the bankruptcy proceedings, I had been obliged to resign the Bachelors.'

It was time to flee England. The years of dandyism had ended in catastrophe. Ashmead-Bartlett had yet to find his own destiny.

3

On the Road from Morocco'

ASHMEAD-Bartlett's bolthole after the ignominy of financial collapse changed his life. It saw the emergence of the competing mixture of journalistic and entrepreneurial streaks that would drive the remaining 22 years of his life. He was usually a journalist, but often the craving to break out and make some real money, or to stand for parliament and become powerful, would obsess him. Even at Gallipoli he was dreaming of moneymaking schemes. This conflict was a reflection of his character and upbringing. A naturally rebellious child suspicious of authority usually makes a good journalist. But he also craved the trappings that went with an establishment upbringing — and which he could not live without.

As the financial disaster gathered around him an acquaintance from the Russo-Japanese War offered him a share in a deal to sell German rifles to Moulai el Hafid, then waging war against his half-brother Abdul Aziz, the Sultan of Morocco, in return for mining concessions. Ashmead-Bartlett even contemplated taking a 'small force' to Morocco to support Moulai el Hafid, but none of his friends had the ready money for such an investment.

Finally cleared of immediate debt by Uncle Willie, he raised a small amount and fled to the coast of Morocco, longing for 'some wild country where I could be lost to civilization and all my sorrows'.

Morocco fascinated him. His stint as a war correspondent with the French in the Chaouia district had convinced him that Moulai el Hafid would eventually capture the throne of the old Shereefian Empire. Abdul Aziz was corrupt, requiring the protection of France to survive. When Moulai el Hafid eventually won, Ashmead-Bartlett said Hafid believed he was inheriting an empire, but in reality it was only a pawn ticket.

The dynastic struggle had implications for European peace. In the first decade of the new century Morocco was the cockpit of Europe as France, England, Germany and Spain vied for colonial concessions. For Ashmead-Bartlett this was quite sad, and he laid out his feeling of the Moors' passing into the thrall of Europe in his later book, *The Passing of the Shereefian Empire*.

Arriving on the Moroccan coast, Ashmead-Bartlett in his usual flamboyant style bought a stallion and donned Moorish headdress for the journey to Fez. On the way he was confronted by what he thought was a terrorist, a wild man brandishing a poisonous snake wrapped around his body. A crowd gathered, and the man bit off the snake's head and ate it as the crowd gave him money. He was an entertainer, not a terrorist.

In Fez, an armed escort led him through narrow streets to the court of Hafid, who was just gaining the upper hand in the struggle with his brother. As the would-be Sultan's retinue sat around, Hafid told him the time was not right for business concessions. But he could do business once he was acknowledged as Sultan by the powers.

Believing his original business idea was off, Ashmead-Bartlett again turned to journalism. He wrote a long account of his meeting with the new Sultan, offering it to the *Morning Post*. No journalist had yet interviewed Moulai el Hafid, and Ashmead-Bartlett's article was published widely in Europe. 'I was the first to describe accurately the position of Hafid and tell the world he was bound to succeed, and that the cause of Abdul Aziz was lost forever,' he wrote in his diary. At this time France and England both backed Aziz, and the press was full of false reports that he was about to march from Rabat to Marrakech to be proclaimed Sultan of the south as well.

Such was the success of the article that the *Morning Post* appointed him their special correspondent. Ashmead-Bartlett was delighted. 'The work pleased me far more than struggling after concessions, and I really seemed on the threshold of a great success which would have

Myth Maker

helped me to forget the past and restore my name to favour — for everything was printed in the *Morning Post* under my signature — and make the unfortunate past speedily forgotten.'

Given Ashmead-Bartlett's eye for colour there was plenty to write about. Abdul Aziz's farcical attempt to westernise Morocco, or at least his court, was ripe pickings for any journalist. Aziz, the son of the previous Sultan and a favourite Circassian slave, imported western trappings and symbolism with what Ashmead-Bartlett regarded as a reckless disregard for its effect on the Moroccan people.

Motor cars were brought up in sections from Tangiers, and assembled in the palace grounds. These were followed by bicycles for the ladies of the harem, dolls, musical boxes, mechanical toys, then tennis courts, polo grounds and billiard tables. Even a bar was built, while reports that the Sultan's ministers had rolled him across a billiard table horrified locals. Pictures of the Supreme Calif dressed in ridiculous western clothes circulated, shocking the sensitivities of true Muslims.

Ashmead-Bartlett revelled in the story of an enterprising French businessman who brought a Parisian coquette to the Sultan's court, introducing her as his wife. The Sultan quickly 'fell prey to her experienced charms', as he wrote, with the businessman demanding instant reparation for such an insult to his honour. To hush up the scandal Aziz gave the businessman large tracts of land around Tangiers, which Ashmead-Bartlett claimed were worth more than £300 000.

The revived journalism career was short lived. Within a few weeks the *Daily Express* published an exclusive article headlined 'King Makers in Fez', detailing how Ashmead-Bartlett's consortium planned to sell Moulai el Hafid arms in return for mining concessions. An enterprising *Daily Express* reporter ('low class', Ashmead-Bartlett called him) had tracked down one of the consortium members, persuading him to hand over documents. It was nine-tenths falsehood, claimed Ashmead-Bartlett, 'but certainly contained an element of truth'.

'I knew it would do me frightful harm with the *Morning Post* and probably put an end to my appointment,' he forecast, and he was right. Asked to explain, Ashmead-Bartlett replied that he had been involved in a consortium, but had since ended his connections. The *Morning Post* dropped him. Ashmead-Bartlett acknowledged the paper's dilemma. It had backed his stance on Hafid despite opposition from the French and the British Foreign Office. Now these opponents could say, 'Look, you see why your correspondent is saying Hafid will win because he wants him to win ... for then the concessions which he wants will be of some value'.

Ashmead-Bartlett saw his renewed journalism career slipping away. It was a valuable lesson for him. Journalism and insider business deals never mix. It presents impossible dilemmas of journalistic ethics. Freed of his newspaper obligations, however, he returned to the concessions business, and after 'long and weary' negotiations secured from Hafid all new Moroccan mineral rights for 40 years in return for £300 000. Hafid also threw in a stretch of property along the Moroccan coast.

It was an extraordinary deal. Signed, as the document began, 'With the aid of God, who alone orders all things' it gave Ashmead-Bartlett exclusive rights to all minerals Morocco could produce for 40 years. The Sultan even agreed to supply labour for the mines. He would send criers to all parts of the country urging people to work on the mines 'for the benefit of Morocco'.

Ashmead-Bartlett rushed back to London with the piece of paper and one of the Sultan's courtiers. He also carried a letter from Hafid for King Edward. On the return journey, he saw an illustrated London newspaper with pictures of his beloved Gwendoline walking down the aisle with Jack Churchill. He swore to banish her from his mind, 'and never trust any woman again'.

Installing the Moor in his mother's house, Ashmead-Bartlett tried unsuccessfully to find backers for the mining deal. Unfortunately, his potentially lucrative concession was in the wrong country. Britain and France had signed an agreement that gave Britain business rights in Egypt and France those in Morocco. The Foreign Office thus opposed his deal, and that turned off investors.

Calling on King Edward to deliver Hafid's letter, Ashmead-Bartlett learnt of these changing fortunes of empire. 'Young man,' the King said, 'had you done what you have done 100 years ago you would have owned the country. As it is, in Morocco we have an agreement with the French, in return for similar concessions in Egypt.'

It was back to journalism, and back to Morocco. Following Hafid's victory over his brother, the Rifian tribesmen along the Mediterranean coast revolted against Spain, which was forced to send in 50 000 troops to suppress them. Ashmead-Bartlett secured a job as Reuters special correspondent for the war. In a mountain gorge he encountered a horrifying spectacle. The Rifs, renowned as fearsome fighters, had trapped a Spanish brigade, stoning to death those they had not shot. 'Hundreds of men lay there with their arms bound and their heads smashed to pulp,' he later recounted.

Two of his colleagues had a lucky escape, but Ashmead-Bartlett's horses did not. He had loaned them to Colonel Lewis, correspondent for the *Times*, and Captain Granville Fortescue, previously of the US army, who was working for American newspapers, so they could watch a major attack. Later, he saw them both on foot. The two had ridden forward too quickly, and became caught by a surprise Rifian attack. 'Both horses were shot dead, but neither Lewis nor Fortescue were hit,' he wrote. 'Fortescue lay down amongst some rocks but Lewis ran right through the Spanish line. Yet neither was touched by friend or foe. Such is luck.'

Ashmead-Bartlett had his own run of luck, and it was not on the gambling tables. He had suffered headaches before departure for Morocco, but ignored a doctor's warning not to go. The African heat, however, accentuated the problem, and he decided to return home. 'As I saw the rugged coast of Melilla pale away I congratulated myself on having come safely through yet another campaign and made my usual firm resolve that it should be really the last, and only the life of a politician should embrace me in its coils in the future,' his diary recorded.

Returning to London via Paris he relaxed with some of the society crowd but kept noticing that his vitality was down. Still, he delighted in affairs of the heart and love tangles. A rich American woman, a Mrs Leeds, who had an income of more than $1 million a year, was being chased by a pack of French lovers. One of them acidly commented, 'I thought I was at Court — but I find I am at a hunt!'

In London, doctors had some disturbing news. His lack of vitality and headaches were due to a return of the childhood head injury suffered when he was thrown from a horse in the Graeco-Turkish War in 1897. When his head was shaved the doctor was astonished by what he found. The hole in his head from the operation in South Africa had never properly healed. Only a thin layer of skin separated his brain from the outside air. And an abscess had grown steadily. The doctor declared it was extraordinary considering the life he had led that he had not died earlier. Ashmead-Bartlett could not have lived for another 10 days, the doctor declared, as the abscess had arrived at one-sixteenth of an inch from the brain. 'Had I stayed in Morocco, as I very nearly did, I would have just dropped dead from my horse one fine day. I shall probably regret many times in after life that I did not,' he wryly noted in his diary.

An operation was necessary, but Ashmead-Bartlett had also finally made the plunge into politics, securing Conservative Party nomination at the 1910 election for the safe Labour seat of Normanton in Yorkshire, a country constituency with many villages.

After a two and a half hour operation a doctor asked him if there was anything he would like. 'Champagne,' he replied, which the doctor allowed. Although the doctor forbade him from travelling, he had to campaign, arriving in a state of collapse in Durham, accompanied by a nurse and his brother Seabury.

The prospects of a winter campaign across the moors depressed him, and he began to wish he had never entered politics. Still, he fronted at numerous, well-attended meetings where the largely Labour audience was hostile to the Conservatives. 'The rowdyism was awful and the questions sent up to each meeting were enough to turn your hair grey,' he said. On election day he and Seabury were pelted with snowballs while driving around the polling booths.

Ashmead-Bartlett could read the writing on the wall, and when he encountered the worried Labour sitting member, a Mr Hall, at the Town Hall that night did his best to comfort him. 'Don't worry,' he assured Hall, who was perspiring with fear, 'you will get in by an even larger majority than before'.

Conservative supporters were crestfallen when Ashmead-Bartlett failed to cut into Hall's majority, but their candidate was not worried. 'An odd thousand or two votes mattered naught to me as I did not care a damn,' he said. Hall made a tactful speech and led Ashmead-Bartlett to a window, 'where a large mob awaiting the result hooted me for the last time'.

Not quite. He secured Conservative selection for Poplars, a safe Liberal seat, in another election that year, but suffered the same fate. It would be 14 years before he made another bid for a political career.

London was electrified in early January 1911 by what the press quickly dubbed 'The siege of Sidney Street'. Police had tracked down a group of Russian aliens wanted for the Houndsditch murders, to 100 Sidney Street, East London. They woke the landlady, a Mrs Fleishman, and told her that two of her upstairs boarders, known as Peter the Painter and Fritz, were armed and dangerous.

As Fritz and Peter the Painter held off police with gunfire, a huge crowd assembled. Home Secretary Winston Churchill was summoned to direct police operations. The Scots Guards were called in, bringing along 1200 troops and three field guns as Sidney Street took on all the overtones of a war zone. Ashmead-Bartlett was among the many journalists who raced to the scene, watching the final scenes as Peter the Painter and Fritz perished in the burning house. In the ensuing chaos he pulled off one of his most spectacular journalistic coups. Posing as a detective, he pushed through police lines and approached the disheveled Mrs Fleishman standing outside the wreckage of her house. In effect, he 'arrested' her, telling the landlady: 'If you will come with me I will take you home, find you clothes, give you a meal, and put you up for the night, and when you have sufficiently recovered you can tell me your whole story'.

Mrs Fleishman accepted. This was an era prior to chequebook journalism when she might have received a small fortune for her story. Right under the nose of hundreds of police, Ashmead-Bartlett whisked her away, found a taxi and took her home.

Watching from a nearby rooftop along with hundreds of onlookers was Harry Lawson, proprietor of the *Daily Telegraph*. He was obviously impressed with Ashmead-Bartlett's chutzpah. Refreshed at Ashmead-Bartlett's home, Mrs Fleishman poured out her story, with the 'exclusive' running in the *Daily Telegraph*. Meanwhile, Scotland Yard launched a major hunt for Mrs Fleishman, one of their chief witnesses. 'I rang them on the telephone and told them anonymously they could have her back on the following day,' said Ashmead-Bartlett cheekily.

Talks with the *Daily Telegraph* about a future career initially proved fruitless, although when this did eventuate some time later Lawson would prove the editor Ashmead-Bartlett needed, one who could offer him global assignments, tolerate large expenses, and flatter him to death to encourage his flair in breaking top stories.

Bored, Ashmead-Bartlett accepted an invitation to accompany society friends on a trip to America. It was a glorious indulgence, crammed with American high society, champagne that flowed, as he said, 'like tumbling cascades at Niagara', and women, lots of women. At one Bohemian party, the male guests were able to take different women upstairs. 'I have never been to a party like this,' said an obviously awed Ashmead-Bartlett.

There is an illuminating extract from his diary that gives an insight into his world of 1911, his views on American businessmen, and his ability to chat up American women:

> Most of these American businessmen are made of iron. They last for a short time and are thus able to lead this double life of business and pleasure. They have never studied and they seldom read. The dead world is totally unknown to them. They are not interested in any of the

great men, great epochs or great events of the past. Literature is banned by them. All you ever obtain from their society is at best a kind of genial bonhomie mixed with cocktails and endless dirty or semi dirty stories.

Only chorus girls can trap their springs of feeling and generosity. That is why Englishmen can have such a wonderful time in the United States. They know how to speak to women and to treat them with politeness and respect. Thus you are always on the mare something for nothing whereas these poor millionaires pay and pay and pay and all they get in return is deception, deception, deception.

Back in Europe, Ashmead-Bartlett moved between London and Paris, which was fast becoming his favourite city. Society and gambling occupied his time, but the latter was a disaster, as was all too often the case. He lost £400 in one week. 'I lost so much money gambling that I was obliged to economise,' he said, somewhat chastened but not sufficiently so to give it away. 'Really I cannot win at any game these days. But I won in the early part of the year so I suppose I cannot complain.'

Survival hinged on gambling winnings when they came, and borrowing. Uncle Willie may again have helped. At one stage in this period he complained of his 'acute' financial situation, 'but managed to raise some money'. To add to his troubles, bad health returned and he collapsed one day at the Badminton Club.

Once again, aspiring colonial power conflicts came to his rescue. In 1911 Italy began casting covetous eyes at the Turkish province of Tripolitania in North Africa, seeking greater Italian concessions. The Giolitti government in Rome, watching the French win in Morocco and renewed German interest along the North African coast, provoked a war and then landed Italian troops.

As the war threatened, Ashmead-Bartlett did the rounds of Reuters and the *Daily Telegraph*. 'This could be a godsend to me as my affairs are desperately involved,' he wrote in his diary. Hired by Reuters, he set out for Rome, where he promptly secured letters of approval from the Italian Foreign Office, helped by the fact that the Baron in charge was an old acquaintance from his society set. But at Messina in Sicily he could not find transport to the fighting across the Mediterranean, and also fell ill with a painful attack of kidney stones. He took large doses of opium as a pain-killer, but still rolled around the floor of his hotel in agony.

On the train to Naples, where he hoped to get a ferry to Tripoli, the pain was so severe he contemplated returning home. And in Naples there were no ferries. The *Daily Mirror*'s pictorial correspondent, Alfieri, also stranded in Naples, told him that he had found a small transport ship willing to take him to Tripoli but needed £600 to hire it. Would Ashmead-Bartlett pay half? 'We'll look absurd if left behind in Naples, and what a blow to our reputation,' Alfieri said. Ashmead-Bartlett agonised, and not just with the kidney stone pain — £300 was a huge figure to claim on any expense account, and he did not have the cash on him. He would need to draw a draft on Reuters.

Then, a little of his old spirit returned. 'There was something exciting and romantic in this strange expedition and I was fascinated with the prospect of being half lord and master of a steamer of my own.' The romance disappeared as soon as he saw the hired ship. It was an old 600-ton coal carrier in 'the most filthy possible condition' with a 'villainous looking' captain and crew. Its cabins were alive with lice and bugs. Still, it made the journey to Tripoli despite running out of food and requiring a stop in Messina.

A pack of war correspondents had turned up in Tripoli for the war: Lionel James from the *Times*, Jack Davis of the *Morning Post*, Maccullagh of the *New York World* and Reginald Kann of *Figaro*. Competition was intense, and the Italian authorities, feeling the heat of international opposition to their invasion, threatened severe censorship.

Ashmead-Bartlett and Davis hired another boat to sail along the coast to Benghazi, where fighting raged, but the Italians prevented

Myth Maker

them from landing. By the time they returned to Tripoli they had missed a major Italian attack, much to the delight of their colleagues. But going out into a nearby oasis they witnessed the aftermath of an Italian massacre on a village.

'They [the Italians] lost their heads and commenced an indiscriminate massacre of all the Arabs whether armed or unarmed within the oasis and even within the town itself,' Ashmead-Bartlett said. 'The troops, ill disciplined in their rage, killed off everyone they met in circumstances of the greatest barbarism. Even women and children were not spared. The Italian troops were seized with a blood lust which nothing could appease.' Outside the town they saw a heap of more than 100 corpses, including children. They had been dragged to the spot and shot, with no trial. 'We watched the Italians stalk one old man who was evidently endeavouring to make his way back to the town in order to surrender. He was shot in cold blood.'

Horrified 'beyond measure', Ashmead-Bartlett returned to Tripoli and wrote a long dispatch about the oasis massacre, carefully sending it to Malta for cabling there to escape censorship. Davis and some other correspondents also filed, but Ashmead-Bartlett believed their cables had been delayed by the Italians. 'I was satisfied that none of the other correspondents had been able to dispatch any cables ahead of mine, and that in regard to news I had not been forestalled in London,' he said. He was right. But before they knew anything was published most correspondents fled Tripoli, fearing they would be arrested by the Italians once their reports appeared in print. Ashmead-Bartlett and Davis even filed a protest with the Italians before leaving, and cabled a news report of this as well.

Returning to Rome, Ashmead-Bartlett learnt from the Italian press that the reports of the oasis massacre had caused 'a tremendous stir' throughout Europe. 'Mine had been reproduced in practically all the European and American papers.' He was advised to clear out of Italy before he was arrested.

Back in London, where he was commissioned to write more articles about the massacre, Ashmead-Bartlett defended himself and colleagues against a multitude of Italian charges that they had lied, created sensations, were enemies of Italy, had broken censorship and had even been drunk on whisky and gin while writing their articles. His criticism of Italy was savage, replete with historical and religious allusions:

> When a great nation sets forth on a crusade to substitute the Cross for the Crescent, the conduct of the Legions of Christ should at least compare favourably with the conduct of the Legions of the Prophet. The failure of civilization and of discipline to curb the primitive passions of man and the revival of the latent spirit of the Colosseum amongst the Italian troops have left an indelible stain on the soil of Northern Africa. They found an Oasis; they have left an Aceldama ['Field of Blood'].

Italy had secured its coveted toehold in northern Africa, but the fraying of the edges of the decaying Ottoman Empire was a constant source of work for Ashmead-Bartlett. In 1912–13 Harry Lawson of the *Daily Telegraph* employed him as a special correspondent for both the first and second Balkan wars. It was the start of an almost 20-year relationship with Lawson, later Lord Burnham, and the *Daily Telegraph*.

Following Italy's success in North Africa, the Balkan League of Greece, Serbia, Bulgaria and Montenegro challenged Turkey's control of Macedonia. In October 1912 Montenegro declared war, while the others demanded Turkey's exit from the Balkans.

Ashmead-Bartlett had been covering French army manoeuvres for the *Daily Telegraph* at £7 a column when an order came from Lawson: Go to Constantinople, join the Turkish army and get to the front. As he was rushing to pack he met his brother Seabury, who had lost his military career after an illness. 'Why don't you come?' he asked, telling Seabury he could also find him work as a war correspondent or assistant. The two must have looked like a small expedition when they gathered their bags at the station — typewriters, suitcases, hat bags, Gladstone bags, dispatch boxes, a saddle in a sack and a folded tent. There was so much baggage that on the train between Germany and Vienna it took up an entire first class cabin. One Teutonic inspector put his face into the cabin and, pointing to the saddle in a sack, declared that meat was not allowed in first class. 'Meat?' they responded. 'Yes. Have you not got a ham in that sack?'

In Constantinople, Ashmead-Bartlett eyed off the phalanx of rivals, including Lionel James of the *Times*, M.D. Donohoe of the *Daily Chronicle*, Ward Price of the *Daily Mail*, Allan Ostler of the *Daily Express*, and a cast of French, German, Austrian, Scandinavian and Russian journalists and photographers. He was not worried about the French and Germans. The French, he said in a burst of nationalistic rivalry, did little cabling and didn't spend much money on their work, while the Germans were 'hopelessly at sea' without the guidance of a censor. 'They are themselves the first to admit that they lack the spirit of enterprise, which renders the English press supreme during campaigns, when every opportunity must be seized like lightning, and not a minute lost if a rival is not going to beat you and obtain a "scoop".'

The jostling English were already at it. Ward Price had hired a motor car for the *Daily Mail* for a staggering £450 to travel to the front. Ashmead-Bartlett cabled home that he now contemplated hiring a motor plus two horses for £100 a month. This was 'very cheap' he assured the *Telegraph*, adding that following the *Mail*'s initiative 'I thought it was unwise to start without one'.

The cost of motor cars in Constantinople quickly shot up as the members of the press vied with each other. Soon Ashmead-Bartlett had to contemplate £500 to £1000 to buy one, urgently cabling London for more funds. 'Please keep my account at Ottoman Bank well supplied with money as they give no credit,' he told them.

The *Mail* scored with an exclusive interview with the Sultan. Ashmead-Bartlett fought back with some excellent dispatches.

Lawson replied after one in grammarless cablese: 'warmest congratulations on magnificent work follow it up'.

Establishing the truth, much less cabling it, was clearly a problem, with the Turks telling them the most outrageous fibs of victories while also flagging that field censorship would be tough. They wanted war correspondents to sign forms pledging to stay with the Turkish army until the end of the war, openly admitting this was a way to deter correspondents from going to the front. Ashmead-Bartlett surveyed the various routes to get his copy out, explaining his working rule: 'The first thing the war correspondent should say to himself is, "Where is the nearest point for sending off censored telegrams, and where is the nearest point for sending off uncensored dispatches should the need arise?"'

After several weeks of bureaucratic delays the great day arrived when all the correspondents were to leave for the front in a special train. The scene was utter confusion. Thirty-two correspondents assembled with baggage, servants and horses. Many ladies of the town were also on hand to bid them farewell. A French correspondent arrived on an emaciated cab horse, weighed down with extra saddle bags, revolvers, water bottles and filters. He was promptly christened Don Quixote by his colleagues, while an obese German who followed him earned the obvious nickname of Sancho Panza.

There was certainly a touch of eccentricity about the crowd. Lionel James entertained colleagues by sitting on his hands and chanting erotic Hindu songs in monotonous tones. Martin Donohoe, an Irish-Australian, reminded Ashmead-Bartlett of an old robber baron who had taken up the only legalised form of modern brigandage — the profession of war correspondent. A stout man with a bristling moustache, Donohoe appeared one day wearing a black fur cap and grey overcoat, looking so Bulgarian his colleagues feared the Turks would arrest him.

The war correspondents were corralled at Chorlou in Thrace as the Turkish and Bulgarian armies faced off not far away. The Turks fed them on daily doses of 'victories', but said telegrams could be sent only in Turkish, which of course none of them understood. The distant sound of guns heightened anticipation of a great battle to come.

Ashmead-Bartlett felt bound to wait for his brother Seabury to catch up. But after a few days he couldn't stand it any longer. He bought a cart for £14 and loaded it with enough equipment for a few days. 'I escaped from Chorlou and the Censor before dawn, and rode towards the sound of the guns,' he said, in words that were almost a motto for the free spirit of war correspondents in that era.

Over the next days he gained a unique insight into the great battle of Lule Burge, where the Bulgarians drove the Turks out of Europe, eventually sweeping the Turkish army back to the outskirts of Constantinople. He camped with the Turkish commander-in-chief, Abdullah Pasha, watched the major Bulgarian attack and retreated with the Turks and civilians.

'There is no more extraordinary or sadder sight in the world than to see the entire population of a panic-stricken city endeavouring to escape,' he wrote. 'I tried to make my way slowly to the rear but was dragged into a vortex of men, women, children, carts, stray soldiers, unarmed men and wounded, all hastening to escape from the enemy's shrapnel which had commenced to burst over the town from the hills behind. The confusion was awful. I lost my worldly possessions which I had left in the town hall, including my boots, and escaped in a pair of slippers.'

The Turks reportedly lost 20 000 men in 10 days as the army fell back to the lines at Cataldja on the European side of the Bosphoros, the death rate accelerated by an outbreak of cholera. Ashmead-Bartlett sympathised with Abdullah, the Turkish commander. For the entire day of the major battle he had stood on a mound with no wireless, field telephone or relay messenger system to connect him to his forces, outfoxed by the various Bulgarian armies.

'In all my experience I have never seen a more pathetic or instructive spectacle than that of this commander-in-chief in communicating with his divisional and brigade commanders,' he wrote. His description of the retreat of the cholera-ridden Turkish army revealed him at his historical best:

> The scenes on the road baffle description from my pen. They recalled to mind a picture I have seen from somewhere of the flight of the French army after Waterloo, or one of Napoleon's retreats from Russia. Not a vestige of order remained. Whole brigades and divisions had broken up. The men made no effort to preserve their places in the ranks. The strongest speedily got to the front, and the weak, sick and wounded struggled painfully behind. Thousands of wounded made pathetic attempts to keep up with their comrades, but each had to shift for himself, as not even the unwounded were in a condition to lend a helping hand. Many of the unwounded were so weak that they fell by the roadside and made no further effort to save themselves.

Ashmead-Bartlett knew he had witnessed a cracker news story, but what to do? It is all very fine for a war correspondent to witness a great battle, but he must get the news out. 'At that moment I would have paid any price for a couple of good horses, for a biscuit, or for a bottle of whisky. I thought how ironical it seemed that I should be sitting there with two hundred pounds in gold strapped around my waist, and yet be unable to buy even a cigarette.'

Despite days of 'sustained exertion, little sleep and semi-starvation' he resisted the temptation to sleep, knowing he must find out what his competitors had cabled. He hurried to Chorlou, where most of the journalists had set up tents or hired houses. 'I knew I must find out at once exactly what had become of all the other correspondents, but more especially of Lionel James and Donohoe, whose enterprise I feared.' Donohoe was trying to get some sleep when Ashmead-Bartlett barged in. He had seen some of the retreat, but had been forced to go down to Rodosto to buy petrol for his car. James, he said, had gone down to Rodosto to get a steamer over to Constantinople. For Ashmead-Bartlett this meant James had not witnessed the major retreat and therefore did not know the outcome of the battle.

Ashmead-Bartlett and Donohoe put their heads together. James would get to Constantinople first, allowing him to cable an early report of the battle of Lule Burge, but even this would be heavily censored by the Turks. If they could get to Constantinople and then across to Constanza in Romania, they could cable out the first uncensored report of this major Turkish defeat. They rushed to Rodosto, and after much frustration over chartering a boat, secured a steamer to Constantinople. Rumours filled the capital of a major battle and a Turkish reverse, but the pair said nothing, fearing the authorities would catch up with them. They found out that James had sent a censored report of the early fighting, and then returned to Rodosto to find details of the final stages of the battle. If they could get the steamer across to Constanza they would have a world scoop on their hands.

As they hid on the steamer to Constanza at its Constantinople wharf they heard the Turkish authorities searching for them. But they sailed safely, only to get hit by a savage storm. 'I never felt less inclined to sit down and write, and Donohoe was in an equally bad condition,' said Ashmead-Bartlett as the steamer arrived in Constanza. 'We were both worn out from the horrible baffling we had received from the waves, and my head swam.'

In Constanza both handed over some of the gold strapped to their waists to the local manager of the cable office, arranging with him a relay messenger from their hotel who would rush their copy by taxi to the cable office page by page. Then they sat in their room and worked.

'We each had a typewriter and kept at work the whole of the afternoon, until our minds were so weary we could no longer think and our fingers so sore we could hardly hit the keyboard,' he said. The messenger thought they were mad, but entered into the spirit of things. 'Whenever one of us managed to get a page ahead of the other, he would point this fact out, and beg each of us in turn to make an additional spurt.'

In London, Harry Lawson quickly recognised that Ashmead-Bartlett had pulled off yet another of his scoops. He splashed the report over seven columns. Lawson, who knew that all journalists in the field thrive on praise, sent Ashmead-Bartlett a cable that any journalist would be proud to have in their trophy cabinet: 'I offer you my heartiest congratulations on your magnificent feat of journalism, which well compares with the finest and bravest things that have been done in the past by English journalists'.

Ashmead-Bartlett went straight back to reporting the war. He was 'arrested' in the field by Turkish troops, but bribed his way out of what he feared could be an execution. He continued to run up large bills as he reported first the Turkish recapture of some positions, and then the Serbian side of the war.

'Send more money,' read one of his urgent but predictable cables to the *Daily Telegraph*, a demand that would echo down the years, as indeed did the stream of inquiries from the newspaper's accountants wanting him to explain expenses.

Valentine Williams, the *Daily Mail* journalist, shared a tent with Ashmead-Bartlett as they covered the Serbian operations. Williams said the way to get to know a man is to share with him for weeks on end the vicissitudes of heat, dirt, smells, bad food, flies and verminous trains and quarters, as the two did. Ashmead-Bartlett, he said, was self-centred, impatient, unreliable and frequently ill-tempered, not to say abominably rude in his relations with Serbian officers, of whom the two were guests. But these shortcomings were counterbalanced by a fine mind, wit, panache and an astonishing memory. Years later Williams wrote:

> He could quote Ceasar's *De Belle Gallico* by the page, and the same with Gibbon. I can hear him now, with enormous unction, reeling off the proper-minded Lecky's somewhat sanctimonious definition of a courtesan in *A History of European Morals*. Added to this, he was an absolutely first-class journalist. His style was trenchant and simple.

A third Ashmead-Bartlett war book followed, *With the Turks in Thrace*, written in collaboration with Seabury. In a letter from Constantinople, Ashmead-Bartlett later confided to a colleague that 'all the objectionable parts' about Turkey were written by Seabury without his knowledge.

He sorely missed the delights of Paris during his time reporting the Balkan wars. Constantinople he found 'a dreary hole' and he longed to be back in London or his 'beloved Paris', where he could live during the night and sleep by day. 'Here I am separated from all my beautiful ladies, and can only console myself by writing to them on this old Remington as no one has ever touched my meandering heart sufficiently to cause me to attempt a hand written epistle,' he wrote a friend.

4

Three 'Gentlemen' of Gallipoli

ELLIS Ashmead-Bartlett's 'beloved Paris' was much changed when he arrived just as World War I broke out in August 1914. More like a city of the dead, he thought. There were no porters at the railway station, no crowds in the streets, no night life, no cafes, no theatres or opera. 'I drove to my usual hotel — I found it a hospital,' he said. 'I drove to another — I found it closed. Paris seemed to be like a vast cemetery waiting to be filled.' He hoped that at least some of his lady friends were still around.

Ashmead-Bartlett had arrived after a remarkable 14-day journey that took him from London in a vast odyssey through Germany, Austria, Romania, Bulgaria, Serbia, Greece and Italy, as he tried vainly to report the early central European declarations of war without getting trapped behind lines.

The week before the outbreak of war he was staying in the English countryside with friends. The host, a rich financier, was sceptical about war, but Ashmead-Bartlett gave him his usual pessimistic, but well-informed outlook.

'Take my advice and close all your accounts without a day's delay,' he said. The financier scoffed. 'War is your livelihood,' he replied, 'you say there will be war because you wish it'.

'God knows I wish nothing of the sort,' Ellis replied. 'A European war will be the most dreadful calamity the world has ever known. I say there will be war because it has been my job to observe European events for fifteen years, and I am quite certain the great world calamity is at hand.' But the financier did not take his advice, and the subsequent market crash cost him a fortune.

As armies mobilised, the call quickly came from a panicking *Daily Telegraph*. He was ordered to join the Austrian army as it invaded Serbia in retaliation for the shooting of Archduke Ferdinand by a Bosnian member of a Serbian secret society — the so-called shot heard all around the world. Ashmead-Bartlett protested. If Austria had declared war on Serbia, Russia would be drawn in to support its Slav ally, and a general European war would follow. He would be better in another location. 'We want you to leave tonight in any case,' said Mr Lesage, one of the *Telegraph*'s executives. Ashmead-Bartlett also pointed out that, as he had been with the Serbian army only the year before, he was bound to be interrogated by the Austrians. With the *Telegraph* scrambling to cover the unfolding story, Lesage also brushed this aside, ordering him to take the nine o'clock train that night to Vienna. 'You must go somewhere at once.'

'Somewhere' involved a marathon train and ship journey, with Ashmead-Bartlett soon realising that his mission was impossible. The Austrians had made no provision for journalists, and he was warned he would be kept five days in the rear of its invading army. An Austrian friend told him he was also likely to be arrested as a spy. As the Austrian and other declarations of war unfolded, Ashmead-Bartlett's only escape was to travel south, returning to France and England via Italy. He constantly had to borrow money along the way as no cables arrived from the *Daily Telegraph*.

Britain had been working up a wartime press control regime for some 15 years before the outbreak of war. While editors proved difficult to convince, the clever Sir Reginald Brade, assistant to the Secretary of War, fixed that. 'Reggie' Brade, the ultimate bureaucratic machine man who had risen from being a humble clerk, negotiated directly with the press proprietors instead. They were not only better organised, he reasoned, but 'had more complete control of the press'. Students of the media who nurture ideas of editorial freedom should take note.

In prewar years Brade had slowly drawn the proprietors around to the idea of a wartime press bureau that would control the flow of information to the media as well as censor press copy, organise registration of war correspondents and handle voluntary censorship of sensitive information. Also envisaged was a scheme for an official 'eye witness', who would replace war correspondents in the field.

By 1913 the War Office's field service regulations stipulated that 'licensed' war correspondents with the army were to be allowed rations as well as a servant. They would be under the scrutiny of a chief field censor, who would define their area of work, issue 'official summaries of information', and be responsible for their discipline.

Correspondents were to pay a £300 surety to follow instructions not to refer to the strength, composition or location of forces, movement of troops, casualties, important orders and morale of troops, or to engage in 'criticism and eulogies of a personal nature'. As well, they were not to cause 'alarm, despondency, or unrest amongst the inhabitants of the British Empire or of any allied power'. This was the 1913 version of controlling war correspondents. It didn't leave the free spirits like Ashmead-Bartlett, who in Turkey 'escaped from the censor and rode towards the sounds of the guns', much room to roam battles and report exactly what they saw.

With Britain and Germany at war on 4 August 1914, a press bureau was hastily set up to provide, as Winston Churchill, First Lord of the Admiralty, said 'trustworthy information' to keep the country 'properly and truthfully informed' of 'what can be told from day to day, and what is fair and reasonable'. Journalists quickly dubbed it the 'Sup-press Bureau'.

The Press Bureau was established in a rat-infested two-storey Whitehall building, where journalists were kept waiting downstairs while officials worked on releases upstairs. A clerk would then come down the stairs, unlock a door, and hand out the information. The press was never allowed upstairs, and had to enter the building by a back door.

With the British Army shipped to France to meet the German invasion of Belgium and northern France, demand for news was insatiable. And not just printed words. The *Daily Mirror*, which featured photographs, saw its circulation explode upwards by some 650 000 copies in a few months. War posters and special editions also meant sales rocketed. London papers, with their wider coverage, pushed into regional areas for the first time to become national.

But how to get the news? While the 'Sup-press Bureau' dished out the official line, newspapers and the public demanded news from the front. Northcliffe's *Daily Mail* organised an elaborate system of couriers for reporters wandering France. But Lord Kitchener, Secretary of State for War, would not have a bar of reporters or photographers with troops. He got the French to agree, and even convinced press proprietors that the ban was at France's request.

At one stage the War Office agreed to send a group of 12 war correspondents to the front, including Ashmead-Bartlett, Henry Nevinson of the *Daily News*, Martin Donohoe of the *Daily Chronicle* and H. Prevost-Battersby of the *Morning Post*. They collected their kit, and even hired a French chef along with drivers and clerks. One hopeful sign was that they were told to sell their horses and purchase motor cars that would be necessary for the long advance into Germany.

Kitchener, however, was adamant, and none departed. To meet the news demand, papers continued sending individual journalists on assignment to France to report on whatever they could. This became quite dangerous in September 1914 when the War Office arranged with France that roaming reporters be arrested.

Nevertheless, journalists pulled off some big news scoops operating independently of the army. Hamilton Fyfe of the *Daily Mail* and Arthur Moore of the *Times* interviewed wounded British soldiers and wrote the first reports of the major retreat from Mons as the Germans pushed south. Using a car and courier they got their news reports back to London that same day. Moore attached a special message for the censor, pleading that his report be passed. 'I guarantee him that as regards the situation of troops I have nothing to say that is not known and noted already by the German General Staff,' he said.

Surprisingly, F. E. Smith, the Press Bureau chief (later Lord Birkenhead and a close friend of Ashmead-Bartlett) approved the British retreat for publication. Smith, who had been instructed by Lord Kitchener to do whatever he could for recruiting, scrawled the following appeal for enlistment on Fyfe's dispatch:

> England should realise + should realise at once that she must send reinforcements + still send them. Is an army of exhaustless valour to be borne down by the sheer weight of numbers while young Englishmen at home play golf + cricket? We want men + we want them now.

The effect of this news break was dramatic: newspaper circulations shot up, recruitment soared. Smith, however, was hauled over the coals and eventually resigned. After Prime Minister Asquith conceded to Chief Sea Lord Winston Churchill that Kitchener had an 'undisguised contempt' for the public, Churchill revived the idea to send an official war reporter, or 'eye witness', to the front who would supply news for all the papers.

Ernest Swinton seemed to fit the bill. A lieutenant colonel in the army, he was then deputy director of railways in the British Expeditionary Force in France and a writer of popular stories. But Swinton quickly fell foul of army jealousies — Sir John French, commander in the field, regarded him as a Kitchener spy, while the press mocked his 'eye witness' accounts as 'eye wash'.

Ashmead-Bartlett said the unfortunate Swinton's duty was to write 'charming stories of how our soldiers lived when they were not fighting, of their humanity towards women and children, and to relate those funny anecdotes about armies which have changed but little since the days of Julius Caesar'.

The *Daily Telegraph* decided to chance its hand, sending Ashmead-Bartlett and other correspondents on roving missions to France. Arriving in an 'empty and dull' Paris in September 1914, he linked up with three other correspondents, Richard Harding Davis, Granville Fortescue and Gerald Morgan. All four were veterans from the

Myth Maker

Russo-Japanese War. Ashmead-Bartlett was very fond of the American Dick Davis, a wonderful storyteller, whom he said had never really grown up; his mind always retaining its early freshness. Harding Davis had that unique journalistic ability to cut to the essentials of any situation, always maintaining an eye for the bizarre. Ashmead-Bartlett not only admired this, he used it effectively himself later at Gallipoli.

The four correspondents were trapped in Paris, each issued only with small round cardboard permits that allowed them to go to French General Staff Headquarters, where twice daily bulletins were issued. But Morgan decided to see how far the pass would take him. He hired a motor car and flashed his pass at sentries as he drove out of Paris toward the fighting front. They let him through, and he returned with this joyous news for his colleagues.

'Equipped', as Ashmead-Bartlett wrote, 'with a magnificent hired car', the four set forth. They successfully passed the barricaded gates of Paris with their 'magic pass' and motored towards Reims, the scene of bitter fighting. They found the magnificent old cathedral's priceless coloured glass windows had been badly damaged under intense German bombardment. The Cathedral of Notre Dame, where French kings had been crowned, had survived all other wars, but was under lethal threat in 1914.

The correspondents were horrified at the destruction. In the cathedral square someone had placed a tricolour flag in the outstretched arms of a statue of Jeanne d'Arc. 'The great shells had burst all round her, leaving the Maid of Orleans and her flag unscathed, but her horse's belly and legs were chipped and scarred with fragments of flying steel,' wrote Ashmead-Bartlett.

A priest let them in. 'Monsieur, they respect nothing,' he cried, showing them the gaping holes in ancient walls and glass that had been caused by the pounding of howitzer shells. 'We placed 123 of their wounded inside and hoisted the Red Cross on the spire in order to protect the cathedral, and yet they fire at it all the same and have even killed their own soldiers. Pray, monsieur, make these facts known all over Europe and America.' They did. Ashmead-Bartlett's story and photographs sent from Paris were the first accounts of the destruction of the Reims cathedral, which would not be fully restored until 1937. His story made riveting reading, with that touch of the bizarre he so admired in Harding Davis:

> Food was scarce in the town and meat almost unobtainable, but in the centre of the cathedral transept lay the raw quarter of a slaughtered ox, a horrid touch of materialism against a scene otherwise lacking all sense of reality. We moved around collecting fragments of the precious glass which the Kaiser had so unexpectedly thrown within our reach. We were brought back to reality by hearing the unmistakable whistle of an approaching shell, followed by a deafening explosion, and more fragments of glass came tumbling from aloft.
>
> The weary war-worn Teutons [prisoners] instinctively huddled closer to the Gothic arches. A dying officer, his eyes already fixed in a glassy stare on the sunlight above, gave an involuntary groan. We heard outside the crash of falling masonry. The shell was followed by another and more breaking glass. Our chauffeur came hastening in with the Virgin's broken arm in his hands. A fragment of shell had broken it off outside.

Apart from damaging the cathedral, the Germans also put a big hole in Reims's other great attraction — champagne. That night, as they stayed at a hotel out of town that had been occupied by Germans, their hostess could not offer them any of the famous local drop. It had all been drunk by the invaders, although they had bypassed the 30 million-odd bottles of champagne maturing in cellars around the area.

Flushed with the success of their 'magic passes', the four decided to try it again. Their luck ran out north of Reims, when they were arrested as suspected enemy agents. Just as the four were struggling to explain themselves, a French officer came up and said: 'Are you not Ashmead-Bartlett, and were you not attached to the French army in Morocco in 1907? I remember you very well there.' But they were still in a military zone without authority, and were ordered to be detained in a local walled farmyard which doubled as a temporary gaol. The Americans, Harding Davis and Fortescue, raised such an outcry that the field officers ordered them all to be sent under escort to the ancient military prison La Cherchi Midi in Paris.

While Fortescue was sent out with an escort to find the American ambassador, the other three correspondents persuaded their French gaolers to send out to the Ritz for champagne, wine and food. As they all sat down to an excellent meal — joined, naturally, by their gaolers — Ashmead-Bartlett played a trick on Harding Davis, who was still fuming to be freed.

The stone building with its iron-barred windows, gated courtyard and oil lamps had a revolutionary era atmosphere. Ashmead-Bartlett convinced Harding Davis that this was the prison from which Marie Antoinette departed to the guillotine. Wouldn't it be a great article for his paper to write about how he spent the night in Marie Antoinette's cell? 'Never had any idea appealed to him more,' laughed Ashmead-Bartlett. 'He became like a joyous schoolboy who had been promised an extra half holiday, and instead of regarding a night in the cells with horror and dismay, it became the obsession of his mind' — until the hoax was revealed.

The American ambassador duly arrived and vouched for the quartet, who were 'sentenced' to self-detention in the capital for eight days. 'Our dreadful sentence was worked out at Maxim's and the Café de Paris,' said Ashmead-Bartlett. It was several days, however, before Harding Davis would speak to him again, but eventually he recovered his sense of humour.

Some of Ashmead-Bartlett's other efforts to get near the fighting were not so farcical. In an attempt to join the Belgian Army with *Chronicle* correspondent Philip Gibbs, he signed up with an English 'flying ambulance'. He was somewhat perplexed about the name until he found out the reason for it. The ambulances would gather near a battle, then make a dangerous breakneck dash to the fighting, pick up wounded and dash out again.

Outside the little village of Dixmunde, where a battle raged, the ambulances assembled and then sped into the thick of the fighting, accompanied by French cries of 'les crazy Anglais'. Dodging shells and bullets, they managed to bring out wounded, although leaving behind a doctor who had wandered off to help others. As night fell, Ashmead-Bartlett signed on for another trip into Dixmunde to find the missing doctor.

> The scene was majestic in the extreme. Dixmunde was a red furnace. The flames shot upwards, showing clouds of white smoke above St Jacques further south. All along the line the shells were no longer bursting in clouds of white and black smoke. All had put on their blood-red mantles. Close at hand everything was bathed in inky darkness; farther off the burning towns and buildings showed up clearer than they had done during the day. We were at a loss what to do. [Dr] De Brocqueville had not turned up, and it seemed useless to hunt for him during the night. We therefore loaded up the car with what wounded we could carry, and made our way back to where we had left the remainder of the party.

In a sign that the tight restrictions on war correspondents accompanying troops might be relaxed, the War Office next organised visits for select groups. Ashmead-Bartlett went on two, but found them frustrating. 'We saw old battlefields, we heard highly technical accounts of mighty operations, we visited deserted trenches, ruined chateaux, and desecrated cathedrals, and sometimes went up to the front lines,' he wrote. 'From our experience of other wars we were thus able to reconstruct some stirring scenes, yet lacking in that decisive element of realism without which it is impossible to hold the reader for long.'

Realism gripped Ashmead-Bartlett in another direction, however. His creditors were circling again, and on 15 January 1915, the *Times* carried a report of 'A War Correspondent's Bankruptcy'. Ashmead-Bartlett's earnings were estimated at £800 a year, with annual expenditure at about £1500 to £2000.

Six weeks later the *Times* reported his cross-examination by the senior official receiver, Mr E. Leadam Hough. Ashmead-Bartlett said he was paid about £150 a month, although he was then without work, as war correspondents could not get to the front. His financial failure was due to his 'extravagance in living'.

> Mr Hough: 'Have you been in the hands of money lenders for some time?'
>
> Ashmead-Bartlett: 'Yes, for 12 years. That is one of the causes of my present situation.'

War saved him again. In January, Russia appealed for help against Turkish attacks on its southern front. Churchill rolled out his plan to capture Constantinople by sailing a fleet up the Narrows of the Dardanelles into the Sea of Marmara. Brilliant in concept, it would knock Turkey out of the war, help supply Russia, encourage wavering Balkan states and expose the soft underbelly of Austro-Germany. In retrospect, it might also have delayed the Russian revolution of 1917, changing the entire course of 20th-century history. But the flaws in execution showed up early. An Anglo-French naval force of mostly older ships invaded the Narrows on 18 March in a bid to knock out the shore batteries that prevented invaders reaching Constantinople. The fleet strayed into a minefield that the Turks had secretly laid; three battleships were sunk and another three crippled, with 700 men lost. The Royal Navy effectively retired, handing the attack over to the Army.

As a combined British, French, Australian and New Zealand force assembled in Egypt, the issue arose of whether war correspondents would be allowed to accompany it. Churchill told Kitchener there was not the same objection to 'press accounts' in this new theatre as there was in France. Unable to blame the French, and with the initial operations to be mostly naval, Kitchener simply turned the whole issue over to the Admiralty.

Churchill gave permission 'for the selection of three gentlemen, representing the whole of the press of this country, who are to be allowed to go out as war correspondents'. The Newspaper Proprietors Association would select one for the London papers, the Press Association another for the provincial press, while the Empire Press Union would select a third for dominion coverage.

The Press Association chose Lester Lawrence of Reuters news agency. Lawrence was an amiable, well-read former Berlin correspondent for Reuters. But Gallipoli was his first war, and he suffered from myopia, sometimes having to rely on others to tell him what was happening.

Initially, the newspaper proprietors could not agree. Several names were put forward and rejected. Then Harry Lawson said, 'Well, I am willing to let Ashmead-Bartlett go'. As Lawson had an exclusive lien on his services, the others were more than happy to gain the pen of the famous war correspondent.

The Empire Press Union could not reach agreement at all. The Admiralty then approved an application from Charles Bean, the authorised correspondent and later World War I historian then with the Australian Army training in Egypt. Bean was initially allowed to accompany the Australian troops from Egypt to Gallipoli, but not permitted by the British to write anything until his formal approval came through. Unfortunately for him, this did not happen until after the 25 April landing.

Instructions for Ashmead-Bartlett and Lawrence were hazy, in line with most of the planning about Gallipoli. Make your own way to Malta, and report to Admiral Limpus, there to gain a berth to the Dardanelles. General Sir Ian Hamilton, appointed by Kitchener to lead the expedition, fared only slightly better. After a cursory briefing from Kitchener he was hastily dispatched from London with out-of-date military maps to lead what was planned to be the world's largest amphibious invasion. Ashmead-Bartlett had maps made that were more up to date.

In Rome on the way to Malta Ashmead-Bartlett, through a society friend, met the Turkish military attaché who, as it turned out, he had known from the Balkan wars. The military attaché, who was out of favour with the ruling Young Turk regime in Constantinople, showed him the official Turkish report of the disastrous 18 March allied naval attack. The report, contrary to widespread belief, said damage to Turkish gun installations was almost nil. 'It served to confirm the opinion held by many that we had under-estimated our task, and that the attack on March 18 had never stood any chance of succeeding,' Ashmead-Bartlett commented.

Another bad omen greeted him in Malta. Admiral Limpus was sceptical, not only about the attack on the forts in the strait, but the whole invasion. 'We have given the Turks warning that we intend to strike, and they will be ready for us on the Peninsula itself,' he said. Limpus was more than a mere naval observer. He had headed the British naval mission in Turkey for some years, and was responsible for training the Turkish Navy. But when war broke out the Admiralty, acting under some curious fair play rule, deemed it unfair he should operate against his former pupils and relegated him to the Malta dockyard.

On 5 April, Ashmead-Bartlett and Lawrence arrived in Mudros Bay on Lemnos Island, off Gallipoli. They had travelled from Malta on the oil tank steamer *Sunik*, which was carrying bulk water for the invasion force. Both were overawed by the sight. Ashmead-Bartlett wrote:

> Our gaze fell on one of the most magnificent spectacles the world has even seen — the greatest Armada of warships and transports ever assembled together in history. Here for the first time I saw the mighty *Queen Elizabeth*, our latest and greatest battleship, carrying eight of the new 15-inch guns, shepherding a long line of pre-dreadnought

battleships, beginning with the *Lord Nelson, Agamemnon, Swiftsure* and *Triumph,* and followed down the tide by the *London, Prince of Wales, Canopus, Cornwallis, Majestic, Goliath* and many others. Cruisers, destroyers and countless transports packed this great sheet of land-locked water almost to overflowing.

Ashmead-Bartlett waxed historical about the invasion fleet. Several times he compared it to 'the last and greatest of the crusades against the Ottoman Turks', asserting that it increased his admiration for the knights of old who had attempted the same task with none of the modern advantages.

Its nearest parallels were the Spanish Armada, Napoleon's expedition to Egypt in 1798, and the Anglo-French expedition to the Crimea. But at Gallipoli the parallels ceased, he said. The Armada had not to force a strongly defended position. The feeble defences of Alexandria offered no opposition to Napoleon's guns. And while the Anglo-French army in the Crimea had to fight the battle of the Alma, they did not have to face an enemy in entrenched positions, protected by machine guns and artillery batteries.

As Ashmead-Bartlett did the rounds of the expedition commanders he became even more doubtful about its prospects. Navy commanders were not even expecting the two correspondents, but both the fleet commander, Vice-Admiral Sir John de Robeck, and his mercurial chief of staff, Commodore Roger Keyes, welcomed them all the same.

After spending a few days with the Navy on patrol in the mouth of the straits, Ashmead-Bartlett finally met Sir Ian Hamilton, hoping to find out details of the looming invasion, which were being kept 'a profound secret'. Like the Navy, Hamilton had no advance knowledge of the arrival of the correspondents. Could they land with the troops? Hamilton replied that he had no objection at all, and thoroughly disapproved of the manner in which the public had been kept in the dark.

'He himself was entirely in favour of having reputable war correspondents with the army,' Ashmead-Bartlett wrote. Later he would learn just what Hamilton meant by 'reputable'.

While this sounded promising, Hamilton's other news was disquieting. All their dispatches would naturally have to be censored, although nothing would be cut 'except that which came within the category of military secrets'. Then came the bombshell. William Maxwell, the former *Daily Mail* war correspondent, was on his staff and would act as censor. 'This news fairly staggered me,' said Ashmead-Bartlett, who had known Maxwell since the Russo-Japanese War. Maxwell had fallen out with the *Daily Mail* over his coverage from Belgium and France when war broke out, then accepting a military commission. 'I had a kind of feeling that Maxwell — having ceased to be a war correspondent — would take a fiendish joy in cutting up my dispatches,' thought Ellis. In fact, he did not, and actually became somewhat of an ally as relations between the press and military headquarters soured.

While Hamilton, a cultured man who wielded a formidable pen, at first seemed comfortable with press coverage, Ashmead-Bartlett worried about his chief of staff, Major General Braithwaite. Regarded by many as the string puller behind Hamilton, Braithwaite, said Ashmead-Bartlett, 'seemed to show a desire to utilise my services as an advertising agent rather than any independent eye witness'.

Also on Hamilton's staff was Jack Churchill, Winston's brother. Ellis resisted whatever temptation he might have had to ask about his former beloved, Gwendoline, who had married Jack in 1908 when Ashmead-Bartlett first fell into bankruptcy and fled to Morocco. Jack had certainly caught Hamilton's eye, however; Hamilton had written to Winston to assure him that his brother was doing fine at Gallipoli. Jack, he wrote, went about in very 'short' shorts, a shirt open at the neck and with his sleeves rolled up. 'We call him Lady Constance in consequence.'

Although the invasion plans were secret it quickly became known that the main British force, the 29th Division, would land on the southern tip of the Gallipoli peninsula, and the Australians and New

Zealanders (the 'colonials', as Ashmead-Bartlett called them) further north up the coast. A French force would land on the Asian side of the strait in a purely diversionary move. The plan was to split the Turkish defenders, allowing the British and 'colonials' to push across the peninsula to take out the Turkish guns along the strait. Hamilton told his commanders he wanted to take a good run at the peninsula 'and jump plumb on — both feet together'.

With the support of the Navy's big guns, there was a great deal of optimism about the plan. Just the presence of the awe-inspiring fleet pushed doubts aside. Given his experiences with the Turkish Army and its German commanders, Ashmead-Bartlett sounded a lonely negative note.

Although the military thought the first few hours of the invasion would be critical, he believed the critical period would come during the push inland when the Turks, out of the fire of the warships, massed their defences. From the outset he also doubted the multiple-landing strategy, believing that command would be extremely difficult to exercise, and much would depend on the initiative of brigade commanders.

With their poor intelligence and out-of-date maps, Ashmead-Bartlett already mistrusted the expedition's higher command. They just did not seem to realise the gravity of the enterprise they were undertaking. 'It seemed to me they rather regarded the expedition as being a kind of glorified picnic, and that the main consideration was the fact that they had an independent command to exercise which was extraordinarily pleasing to their "amour propre" [self-esteem],' he wrote in his diary.

Ashmead-Bartlett's diaries of this period need to be seen in the light that they were reconstructed after he lost the originals in a German submarine attack, and this might have enabled him to write with some hindsight. Nevertheless, two incidents confirm his early pessimism.

On 22 April, three days before the landings, he happened to bump into Hamilton on the quay ashore. He found him very confident, even relating a funny story about the Australians, although Ashmead-Bartlett did not say what it was. Nevertheless, he was appalled by the over-confidence of the British officers.

'Personally I was far from sharing his confidence, and ventured to remark on saying good-bye: "General, the task ahead is one of the most difficult that has ever been undertaken, and the Expedition can only succeed if you have sufficient troops to push right inland at the start, and if the Government keeps you well supplied with reinforcements".'

Ashmead-Bartlett says, in both his diary and later book, *The Uncensored Dardanelles*, that by this time he had become convinced that the expedition was almost certainly destined for disaster. The next evening he sat up late in the wardroom with the officers of *Queen Elizabeth*, contemplating 'the latest and greatest of the Crusades'. The officers and journalist even laid bets on what might happen. Every officer was absolutely confident of success, accusing Ashmead-Bartlett and his language of a 'leap in the dark' with being a pessimist — a charge he often attracted. 'I ventured to point out a few of the real difficulties that had to be encountered before we could call the Narrows our own.'

Shortly after the two correspondents arrived, the Navy decided to assign them to different ships. Lawrence was assigned to the *Triumph*, which was to support the main British landing, while Ashmead-Bartlett was sent to the *London*, which Commodore Keyes assured him would be at 'interesting and vital spots' during the landing.

Keyes was right. Fate had pushed Ellis Ashmead-Bartlett right into the path of Australia's short history, and it would be his pen that would now choreograph its most famous chapter.

5

A Race of Athletes

UNTIL 1915 Ellis Ashmead-Bartlett knew little about Australia's military. In the Boer War a couple of drunken Australian officers had kept him awake half the night playing the piano and singing in his hotel, but he didn't seem to mind this too much.

Apart from the Boer War, Australia — or, before 1901, its six colonies — had contributed only in minor ways to British Empire military expeditions in the Sudan, and the Boxer Rebellion in China. On the outbreak of war in 1914 there was enormous public support in Australia for Britain, still regarded as the 'mother country' despite federation of the colonies into a new nation in 1901. Australia, declared Labor Party leader Andrew Fisher in a famous phrase, would help defend Britain 'to our last man and last shilling'.

Just three months later the first Australian Imperial Force departed, supposedly on the way to the Western Front in France. After training in Egypt, however, events overtook it. The Australians, along with New Zealanders, instead found themselves off the coast of Gallipoli in April 1915, training for an amphibious landing on the Turkish coast — although most would have preferred to be in the main centre of action in Europe.

On board HMS *London*, Ashmead-Bartlett, wearing his war correspondent's rig of khaki, a verdigris green soft felt hat, and a camera slung over his shoulder, watched the Australians practise climbing up and down rope ladders on the side of the battleship. He was impressed by their physiques, but dubious about their discipline.

> This is the first time I had seen anything of the Australian troops and they certainly create an excellent impression with their fine physique and general bearing. But their ideas of discipline are very different from those of our old regular army. The men seem to discipline themselves, and the officers have very little authority over them even through the holding of military rank — personality plays a much more important role. This is easy to understand because many of the officers are little better trained than their men, and, therefore, lack the experience and authority which comes from years of service.
>
> Nevertheless, they appear a body of men who can be relied on in any emergency; whatever they lack in discipline and experience I feel will be compensated for by their native intelligence and initiative. A warm friendship has sprung up between our bluejackets from the North, and these men from under the Southern Cross.

Another reason Ashmead-Bartlett may have warmed to the Australians was that they provided such colourful copy. In a dispatch dated 21 April he told how the Australians were becoming weary of being cooped up on transports, where many had been for six weeks, with short stints ashore. As well, the transports had run out of alcohol.

'Now these Australians like their drink, and they are accustomed to it,' he wrote. 'Thus they are anxious to get ashore and stretch their limbs in a real fight, when these temporary discomforts will be forgotten. In a letter one of them wrote home the other day the following was found by the censor: "We are having an iron time; we live in an iron ship, sleep on an iron floor, have nothing to eat but our iron rations, and now, to crown it all, I hear we are commanded by a fellow called Iron Hamilton".' It was the first of many gags that Ashmead-Bartlett loved reporting about the irreverent humour of the Australians.

More seriously, Ashmead-Bartlett, with his long history of watching and analysing military campaigns, fretted about the prospects of the whole expedition. The assembled army was about to land on an unknown shore; no accurate maps were available; no general staff had patiently worked out every detail of the landing or measured its demands on demands; the commander-in-chief had exercised no previous fighting command (indeed, the army's best brains were in France); his staff were equally inexperienced; and the defending forces would have great advantage unless faced by an overwhelming force.

Ashmead-Bartlett may have been a natural pessimist, but on this occasion he was right. Commander Charles Dix, who was in charge of the tows that would take the troops to the beaches, wrote in 1932 that he recalled talking to Ashmead-Bartlett on the night before the landing:

> In conversation with me that evening he foretold the run of events with almost uncanny exactitude. He insisted that only in the event of having another division both at Anzac and Helles could speedy success be obtained, and that long-delayed success might, and probably would, mean eventual failure.

Despite censorship, Ashmead-Bartlett tried to get the truth — or at least his fears — known in England, by writing private letters. 'Thanks to the fact that my letters were being censored up to this time by the Navy and not the Army, I succeeded in a limited sense in doing so, but of course not in the manner in which I wished,' he wrote in his diary. It is a telling entry in the light of the political bombshell of a subsequent letter that helped end the entire campaign.

On 23 April Ashmead-Bartlett watched from the *London* as some of the big cruisers and transports left Mudros Bay with the British 29th Division that would land around Cape Helles on the southern

Myth Maker

end of the peninsula. Lawrence accompanied them. Meanwhile, the destination of the 'colonial troops' was still unknown.

Commodore Keyes promised he would get his dispatches away on time. 'There was an air of suppressed excitement about everyone,' Ellis said. 'All seemed to shake off the lethargy of too much waiting about, and to brace themselves for the coming struggle, the last and greatest of the Crusades which could decide whether the Turk could be driven out of Europe forever, or else leave the Crescent more triumphant than it had been since the capture of Constantinople by Mahommed the Second in 1482.' It was one of the many analogies Ashmead-Bartlett used to compare 1915 to the medieval crusades.

About 3 pm on Saturday, 24 April boats brought 500 men of the 11th Australian Infantry on board the *London*, distributing others around the fleet. The *London*'s crew handed over their entire accommodation to the troops, their last night of any comfort. At 5 pm this second division of the fleet, led by the imposing dreadnought *Queen Elizabeth*, and with a host of accompanying battleship and transports, steamed out of Mudros.

'As we passed along the lines of transports bands played various tunes and the national anthems of all the allies, deafening cheers greeted our departure,' Ellis noted in his diary. 'It was the most majestic and inspiring spectacle I have ever seen, but withal there was an atmosphere of tragedy because we knew that there were many on this battleship who would never see another sun sink in the west.'

Instead of steaming straight towards Gallipoli, which would have caused them to arrive too soon, the convoy headed due west to a rendezvous point. Although the actual landing point was still secret, the best hope was only for some local surprise, as even Hamilton realised that spies on the islands would already have reported on preparations for departure.

Ashmead-Bartlett was such a prolific writer, always looking for new commercial opportunities, that there are at least three versions of the historic events of the next 24 hours: his personal diary, reconstructed after being lost in a German torpedo attack; his news account of the day, which became part of an instant book, *Despatches from the Dardanelles*; and his 1928 book, *The Uncensored Dardanelles*.

About six o'clock the Australian troops fell in on the quarter deck, with the ship's crew on the other side. The *London*'s Captain Armstrong read Vice-Admiral de Robeck's proclamation wishing them well, while the ship's chaplain led prayers for victory. The Australians filed to the mess deck, where the crew served them a hot meal before they turned in to get as much rest as possible before dawn.

'It was the last sleep for many a brave warrior from "down under",' said Ashmead-Bartlett.

The *London*'s officers then shouted the Australian officers a farewell in their wardroom. 'Many a man who had not tasted any drink for a long time past was invigorated by cocktails, champagne, and whiskies and sodas,' he said. 'We all gave up our cabins to the officers in order that they might obtain as much rest as possible, and when I turned in about half past ten I snatched a few hours sleep on the floor.'

The fleet stopped at 1 am after cruising east from the rendezvous point. All troops on board were roused. Ashmead-Bartlett did a tour of the mess deck where the Australians were having their final hot meal. At two o'clock they fell in by companies on numbered squares on the deck.

In his famous report of the landing, Ashmead-Bartlett put raw emotion into the pre-dawn assembly of these untested troops. 'The Australians, who were about to go into action for the first time under trying circumstances, were cheerful, quiet, and confident, showing no sign of nerves or excitement,' he wrote. 'As the moon waned the boats were swung out, and the Australians received their last instructions. Men who six months ago were living peaceful civilian lives began to disembark on a strange, unknown shore, in a strange land to attack an enemy of different race.'

An unusual convoy now sailed directly towards the Gallipoli coast, the battleships towing pinnaces which in turn towed boats of troops.

Myth Maker

At 4.30 am the *Queen*, *London*, *Prince of Wales* and *Majestic* stopped about 3000 yards off the shore and cast away. 'It was still very dark and each pinnace, towing four boats, looked like a great snake as it slowly forged ahead,' Ellis reported. 'We, who assembled on the bridge of the *London*, were now to pass some nerve-racking minutes of suspense, which seemed like hours. Very slowly, the twelve snakes of boats steamed past the battleships, the gunwales almost flush with the water, so crowded were they with khaki figures. To our anxious eyes it appeared as if the loads were too heavy for the pinnaces, that some mysterious power was holding them back, that they would never reach the shore before daybreak, and thus lose the chance of surprise.'

As the water shallowed the battleships slowed, allowing the 'snakes' to move on ahead toward the beaches. All on the bridge strained their eyes and ears to catch any Turkish alert. Even the stars above the hills were mistaken for lights. Ashmead-Bartlett and others startled as a signalman shouted: 'There's a light on the starboard bow'. It was only a star on the horizon.

Dawn was breaking, and the fear on the bridge was that the boats would not make it to shore while it was still dark. Precisely at 4.50 am, said Ashmead-Bartlett, the Turks spotted the boats. A light flashed for 10 minutes before fading. Anxiety on the bridge rose, as the boats appeared to be almost on the shore. Destroyers moved past the battleships to offer close fire support.

'At 4.53 am there came a very sharp burst of rifle fire from the beach, and we knew that our men were at last at grips with the enemy,' he wrote. 'The sound came as a relief, for the suspense of the prolonged waiting had become intolerable. The fire lasted only a few minutes, and then a faint British cheer was wafted across the waters. How comforting and inspiring was the sound at such a moment! It came as a message of hope, for its meaning was clear: a foothold had been obtained on the beach.'

The return of boats brought the first news. They contained three wounded sailors, all hit in the first round of fire. Ashmead-Bartlett said a 16-year-old midshipman shot in the stomach regarded his wound 'more as a fitting consummation to a glorious holiday ashore than a serious wound'.

The war correspondent's report of what happened next, variously reported in his diary, press account and later book is worth quoting at length as it laid a foundation stone of the Anzac legend. Here is what Australians read in the press, and later in a specially published booklet for schools:

> The boats had almost reached the beach when a party of Turks entrenched ashore opened a terrible fusillade with rifles and a Maxim. Fortunately most of the bullets went high. The Australians rose to the occasion. They did not wait for orders or for the boats to reach the beach, but sprang into the sea and formed a rough line. They rushed the enemy's trenches, although their magazines were uncharged. They just went in with cold steel.
>
> [Some versions of Ashmead-Bartlett's various reports contained an extra sentence here that did not appear in Australian papers, reading: 'I believe I am right in saying that the first Ottoman Turk since the last crusade received an Anglo-Saxon bayonet in him at five minutes after five a.m. on April 25'.]
>
> It was over in a minute. The Turks in the first trench either were bayoneted or ran away, and the Maxim was captured.
>
> Then the Australians found themselves facing an almost perpendicular cliff of loose sandstones, covered with thick shrubbery. Somewhere about half way up the enemy had a second trench, strongly held, from which a terrible fire poured both on the troops below and the boats pulling back to the destroyers for a second landing-party.
>
> Here was a tough proposition to tackle in the darkness, but those colonials were practical above all else, and went

> about it in a practical way. They stopped a few minutes to pull themselves together, get rid of their packs, and charge their rifle magazines. Then this race of athletes proceeded to scale the cliff without responding to the enemy's fire. They lost some men, but did not worry, and in less than a quarter of an hour the Turks had been pushed out of their second position, and were either bayoneted or fleeing.

Ashmead-Bartlett's celebrated dispatch (the full text is in Appendix 1) went on to relate how the troops had been landed in the wrong place. The Australians had been aiming further south, where the country was more open, but Ellis put the best spin on the mistake, saying it deprived the Turks of a clear line of fire on their attackers.

With the sun fully up, Ashmead-Bartlett reported that from the bridge of the *London* he could see the Australians had actually established themselves on the ridge amidst confused fighting. New troops were disembarking from boats. His press dispatch continued, describing the fighting for the high points as the Australians launched out from the beach into craggy terrain they had not expected, and began to meet the stiff resistance of Kemal Atatürk's forces:

> But then the Australians, whose blood was up, instead of entrenching, rushed northwards and eastwards, searching for fresh enemies to bayonet. It was difficult country in which to entrench. They therefore preferred to advance.
>
> The Turks had only had a weak force actually holding the beach, and relied on the difficult ground and their snipers to delay the advance until reinforcements came. Some of the Australasians who pushed inland were counter-attacked and almost outflanked by oncoming Turkish reserves. They had to fall back after suffering heavy losses.

The Turks continued to counter-attack throughout the whole afternoon: but the Australasians did not yield a foot of the main ridge. Reinforcements poured up from the beach, but the Turks enfiladed the beach with two field guns from Gaba Tepe. The shrapnel fire was incessant and deadly.

In these early days censorship by the Navy was remarkably light, and Ashmead-Bartlett could openly state that the Australians suffered 'heavy losses' and had to 'fall back', and that later in the day, as the pressure of the Turkish counter-attack intensified 'their line had to be contracted'. Despite later criticism of exaggerations, Ashmead-Bartlett did not attempt to hide the disastrous day's fighting.

His reporting of the wounded, however, almost certainly fell into the over-colourful category. Poor planning to handle wounded — and the refusal to arrange cease-fires to retrieve wounded — later became a central point of his criticism of the expedition's leaders, but on the 25th his press report of the difficulties of getting wounded down from the hills and off the beach onto ships read:

> The courage displayed by these wounded Australians will never be forgotten. Hastily placed in trawlers, lighters, or boats, they were towed to the ships. In spite of their suffering they cheered the ship from which they had set out in the morning. In fact, I have never seen anything like these wounded Australians in war before.
>
> Though many were shot almost to bits, without hope of recovery, their cheers resounded. Throughout the night, you could see in the midst of the mass of suffering humanity, arms waving in greeting of the crews of the warships. They were happy because they had been tried for the first time, and had not been found wanting.

It is difficult to imagine severely wounded soldiers — Australian or any nationality — cheering in such fashion. Still, as Charles Bean said, although Ashmead-Bartlett may have made it difficult for other correspondents because of his exaggerations, he was also a 'lover of the truth', and he was aboard the *London* as wounded returned.

Interestingly, Ashmead-Bartlett in his later *Uncensored Dardanelles* makes no mention of cheering wounded. Rather, he said they arrived in a 'never-ending stream' and accommodation on the single allotted hospital ship quickly gave out. 'As usual, with the start of all British expeditions, the medical arrangements were totally inadequate to meet the requirements of the hour. Optimism had minimised our casualties to the finest possible margin, but the Turks multiplied them at an alarming rate.'

Rather than cheering and waving wounded, his later account said the boats returning from the beach 'all brought the same tale of things going badly: heavy casualties, the beaches choked with wounded, who could not be moved, while the enemy's attack showed no diminution in strength or persistency'.

Ashmead-Bartlett saved perhaps his best prose for the concluding paragraphs of his press copy about the Australasians on 25 April 1915:

> For fifteen mortal hours they occupied the heights under incessant shell fire, without the moral or material support of a single gun ashore, and subjected the whole time to a violent counter-attack, by a brave enemy, skilfully led, with snipers deliberately picking off every officer who endeavoured to give a command or lead his men.
>
> There has been no finer feat in this war than this sudden landing in the dark and the storming of the heights, and above all, the holding on whilst reinforcements were landed. These raw colonial troops in these desperate hours proved worthy to fight side by side with the heroes of Mons, the Aisne, Ypres, and Neuve Chapelle.

This initial report ended with some details of the 26th, the repeated Turkish attempts to drive the attackers back into the sea and the plastering of Turkish positions by close inshore British warships.

> The scene at the height of the engagement was sombre and magnificent. It was a unique day, perfectly clear, and one could see down the coast as far away as Seddul Bahr. Three warships were blazing away, and on shore the rifle and machine gun rattle was incessant. The hills were ablaze with shells, while masses of troops stood on the beaches waiting to take their place in the trenches.
>
> The great attack lasted two hours. We received messages that the ships' fire was inflicting awful losses on the enemy.
>
> Then amidst the flash of bayonet and a sudden charge by the Colonials, before which the Turks broke and fled amidst a perfect tornado of shells from the ships, they fell back, sullen and checked.
>
> They kept up an incessant fire throughout the day, but the Colonials had now dug themselves in.

The main criticism of Ashmead-Bartlett's press report that historic day should be not of exaggerations, but omissions. There are hints of 'holding on' and 'desperate hours', but Ashmead-Bartlett concluded his dispatch with the heartening news that the 'colonials' had now 'dug themselves in'. In reality, as he knew, it was extremely close run, with the Australians contemplating evacuation within a few hours of landing.

Although he had observed the day's action from the bridge of the *London*, Ashmead-Bartlett then hitched a ride to the beach about 9.30 pm on the night of the 25th, dodging a 'hailstorm' of bullets as the boat approached the shore. Here is his later description from *Uncensored Dardanelles*, but absent from his press story:

> I climbed ashore over some barges and found myself in the semi-darkness amidst a scene of indescribable confusion. The beach was piled with ammunition and stores, hastily dumped from the lighters, among which lay the

dead and wounded, and men so absolutely exhausted that they had fallen asleep in spite of the deafening noise of the battle.

In fact, it was impossible to distinguish between the living and the dead in the darkness. Through the gloom I saw the ghost-like silhouettes of groups of men wandering around in a continuous stream apparently going to, or returning from, the firing line. On the hills above there raged an unceasing struggle lit up by the bursting of shells, and the night air was humming with bullets like the droning of countless bees on a hot summer's day. Nevertheless, this little stretch of beach was so angled that it provided a haven of refuge — if a precarious one.

Ashmead-Bartlett stumbled toward what he saw was a group of officers, hoping to get news of the Australians' position on the ridges. He saw the shortish figure of General Birdwood, the English officer in charge of the Australians and New Zealanders, obviously giving instructions. Although dressed in a khaki uniform, Ashmead-Bartlett was wearing a green floppy hat. Suddenly a voice rang out: 'Who are you and what are you doing here?' Before Ashmead-Bartlett could answer the same officer shouted: 'Seize that man, he is a spy'.

Soldiers rushed up and imprisoned him. For the second time in only a few months, Ashmead-Bartlett found himself arrested as a spy in a war zone, and lacking any papers to prove otherwise. 'I am Ashmead-Bartlett, the official war correspondent', he protested, producing a rough pass he had obtained from Captain Armstrong of the *London*. But this satisfied nobody, and the excited officer who had arrested him began shouting: 'Does anyone here know this man?'

Out of the darkness a gruff voice said, 'Yes, I do', and Ashmead-Bartlett was freed. His saviour, he later discovered, was the boatswain on one of the pinnaces, who recognised him by his green hat. The boatswain, who joked he had saved him from 'hexecution on the spot', was 'suitably rewarded'.

Ashmead-Bartlett now became a bit player in the late-night drama of whether the Australians should be withdrawn. The naval beach officer commandeered his pinnace, saying it might be needed to go around all the transports asking them to send in their boats to pick up the troops. 'It is impossible for the Australians to hold out during the night, they are being too hard pressed,' the beach officer told him.

A similar view was being pressed on Birdwood. Ashmead-Bartlett felt otherwise, believing withdrawal could lead to a massacre on the beach. He watched the small group of officers struggle with whether or not to recommend to Hamilton an immediate evacuation of the stretched Australians. 'It was a dramatic scene while General Godley was writing this momentous dispatch in semi-darkness to General Birdwood's dictation, surrounded by a small group of Staff Officers, by the dead and wounded, and a miscellaneous collection of stores and ammunition. On these few words, penned on the battlefield, in the darkness of the night, relieved only by bursting shells, the fate of the whole expedition depended.'

The naval landing officer and Ashmead-Bartlett delivered the withdrawal recommendation to the *Queen Elizabeth*, Hamilton's flagship, and then toured around transports warning them to get their boats ready in case an evacuation was ordered.

It was not. On board the *Queen*, aides woke up Hamilton, who had just retired to bed, telling him he had to urgently decide 'a matter of life and death'. Hamilton quickly sized up the situation, and issued his famous order that the Australians, having 'got through the serious business', now had to 'dig, dig, dig'. Just at the moment he was deciding, wireless news arrived that an Australian submarine, the *AE2*, had penetrated the treacherous Narrows of the Dardanelles and made it into the Sea of Marmara, where it could now attack Turkish sea supply lines. Hamilton added this encouraging news to his 'dig, dig' message to the troops.

Ashmead-Bartlett, having toured the transports, now returned to the beach, where he was again immediately arrested by the same officer, whose nerves 'seemed to have completely deserted him'. Quickly released, he found the situation much improved. The Turkish guns were almost silent.

In his diary he doubted that Hamilton's 'dig, dig, dig' message ever reached the firing line. 'What really saved the situation was the sudden cessation of the Turkish attacks at midnight, which gave the Australians the chance of temporarily entrenching themselves and to prepare against the attacks which they knew must come in the morning,' he said.

Ashmead-Bartlett's competitive war correspondent's nerves began to jangle as he sat down aboard the *London* to write his dispatch. He had a first-hand account, and he desperately wanted to be first into print. But he knew Lawrence, who was down covering the British landings on Cape Helles, would be trying to do the same — and Lawrence was now closer to the cabling point, as the *Queen Elizabeth* had sailed south to Helles.

'I had an uncomfortable feeling that being nearer the *Queen Elizabeth* he might be getting off a lot of stuff ahead of me,' he confided in his diary.

Lawrence, however, was covering his first war, and knew none of Ashmead-Bartlett's tricks of the trade.

6

Igniting a Legend

AUSTRALIAN newspaper editors, never a quiet bunch, must have been unusually agitated in late April 1915. They knew Australian forces were participating in a major attack in the Middle East. But they did not know exactly where, and they had no coverage. This was the first military action by the new nation, and newspapers were reduced to running skimpy official communiqués and scuttlebutt from the bars of Athens, Constantinople and Alexandria.

Charles Bean, the official Australian press representative, who already had an understanding that he would later write the history of the force, had last filed from Cairo. Bean, a *Sydney Morning Herald* leader writer, had won the official press position in a union ballot, beating the younger Keith Murdoch. The position paid £600 a year and Bean was also supplied with a horse and batman. Bean — a gangling, bespectacled 35-year-old redhead — had a reputation as a stickler for facts, a true reporter who, as Ashmead-Bartlett so aptly commented, 'counted the bullets'.

Bean's reporting from Cairo had included the sensational story of the sending home of some soldiers for drunken, larrikin behaviour. In the typical circumlocutory reporting style of the day, Bean, who had been briefed by the army to 'prepare' Australians for the return in disgrace of these men, began his December 1914 report: 'It would be a deceit upon the people of Australia if it were reported to them that Christmas and the approaching New Year have found the Australian Imperial Force without a cloud in the sky.'

Bean went on to report caustically that some of the men were not just uncontrolled and slovenly but also dirty. 'A percentage of these will probably find their way back from here, the reason for whose return has been that they have damaged their country's reputation, and a few of them have been got rid of as the best means of preserving it.' The report caused a sensation in Australia and resentment among the troops remaining in Cairo; resentment only forgotten in Bean's later self-sacrifice living in the trenches with the troops through Gallipoli, as well as his dedication to factual reporting.

The eventual destination of the newly trained Australian force was a popular guessing game among the Cairo troops. An unidentified military correspondent writing in the *Sydney Morning Herald* in early April 1915 reported that while Syria, the Suez Canal and the Dardanelles were rumoured, there was no doubt where the men wanted to go — France. 'Their dearest hope is that they may help to drive the Huns out of Belgium,' he reported.

With the failure of the naval attack on the Narrows of the Dardanelles on 18 March, the Australian and New Zealand Army Corps training in Egypt was inevitably caught up in the subsequent land invasion. Bean jockeyed to accompany them, and eventually General Birdwood approved him going along as a military officer — but only if he undertook to write nothing until authorised by London. Bean, who would have preferred an official 'eye witness' role, seems to have accepted this without qualm. 'There's no question of my attempting to evade censorship,' he wrote in his diary. 'I'm the representative of my country and not of a newspaper.'

Australian newspapers were having a good war. Circulation boomed among readers avid for war news in pre-radio days, although newsprint prices also soared. The *Sydney Mail* converted into a pictorial magazine almost entirely devoted to war scenes. Both it and the *Bulletin* used regular patriotic covers against the 'Hun', with the *Bulletin* maintaining its 'Australia for the White Man' logo, and using the war to argue for even higher tariff walls. The *Mail*'s circulation boomed.

Cabling costs were a real problem for newspapers in meeting war news demand, however. The major Australian metropolitan papers relied on cabling agencies in London, which sent through important stories from the London papers and official communiqués. With cabling costs rising some 600 per cent and newsprint supply scarce, newspapers resorted to smaller issues and shorter stories. Some major war developments were covered in only a few sentences. Not for them a typical Ashmead-Bartlett dispatch, which could run to 2000 to 4000 words, covering several days of action and written in a news-feature style.

With Bean temporarily 'silenced', the papers became desperate for news of what was happening with the Australian force. Nobody doubted Britain's strategy in opening a front against Turkey, although it was rarely reported in terms of the modern 'crusade' analogy sometimes used in British newspapers, including by Ashmead-Bartlett. In early March, as the fleet assembled off the Dardanelles, the *Sydney Morning Herald* opined somewhat obviously that 'Constantinople now takes its place as a supremely important centre in the strategy now unfolding'.

As the allied navy pounded the forts along the Dardanelles Strait, Australia's press carried reports of foreigners fleeing the capital, with refugees claiming the Turks were dismantling guns in Constantinople in the hope that the allies would regard the city as an open town. Later, Athens correspondents were reported from London as saying the 'check' that the allied fleet had suffered in the straits on 18 March was 'sufficiently grave to make a radical change in the operations necessary'. This, the *London Daily News* was quoted as saying, was 'but the prelude to an attack by an overwhelming force'.

The *Daily News* was right about that, although 'overwhelming' would prove an optimistic forecast. But an attack — where, when, how — all those questions for which newspapers crave answers. From Cairo in early April Bean cabled back a report of his conversation with Sir Ian Hamilton, the newly arrived commander-in-chief of the expedition. Under the headline 'Tribute by Sir Ian Hamilton', the report showed no evidence that Bean had quizzed the putative commander on where the Anzacs were going, although some had

Myth Maker

already departed and Bean himself was urgently pressing for permission to accompany them.

'Having had the privilege of a conversation with Sir Ian Hamilton after the inspection of the Australasian troops, I asked whether he noticed any change since his previous inspection a year ago at the other end of the world (in Australia),' Bean reported.

'It was a most gratifying sight,' Hamilton said. 'Of course, they are now trained troops, steady and disciplined. The officers understand now how to make a suggestion. As for the men, I am sure they have grown since their arrival in Egypt. I have seen many of these men in Australia actually and they never appeared as big as they are today. I believe hard work of the right sort in the open air in this splendid climate has made bigger and stronger men of them.'

Nothing more, at least in print, of where the troops might be going. In private conversation, Bean secured Hamilton's assurance that an accompanying pressman could do a better job than any official 'eye witness', as Britain was then using in France. Hamilton also gave Bean the War Office lie about French opposition to accompanying press, saying that as the coming 'eastern show' was in British hands the government would be freer with information.

The 'show', however, unfolded with Bean still gagged, and the Australian press scrabbling for information about the nation's troops. On 10 April, the Turkish Sultan was briefly reported as 'confident', saying he regarded the Dardanelles as 'impregnable'. On 23 April, the *Sydney Morning Herald* carried an imposing photo of Hamilton, replete with military sashes and medals, with the caption reading: 'To lead the attack on the Dardanelles'. The accompanying two paragraph story from London quoted the *Daily Telegraph*'s Cairo correspondent saying 'colonials', who had developed 'faster and better than their best friends hoped', would constitute the 'backbone' of the attack. At least the destination was becoming somewhat clearer.

But a 24 April report claimed British troops had landed at Enos, on Turkey's European shore near the current border with Greece. This was 'confirmed' by fugitives in Bulgaria. The rumour mill was in overdrive for the next few days, with 'unofficial reports' from Athens claiming that 'decisive action' had commenced in the Dardanelles, with landings at Enos, Suvla on the Gallipoli peninsula, and Bulair at the neck of the peninsula.

Two days after the 25 April landing the Australian press was still only reporting naval barrages. Then, on 28 April, newspapers printed Admiralty and War Office statements that a 'general attack' of the fleet and army had 'resumed'. 'In spite of serious opposition from the enemy, who were behind strong entrenchments and entanglements, it was completely successful, and before nightfall a large force was established ashore,' the report said. Amazingly, this report, which obviously involved the Australians being landed somewhere, did not lead the *Sydney Morning Herald*'s war coverage. That was devoted to major accounts of battles at Flanders on the Western Front.

On 29 April, four days after the landing, the *Herald* was still scratching, with only a two-sentence report of War Office and Admiralty statements that 'after a hard day's fighting the troops on the Gallipoli Peninsula have succeeded in thoroughly making a good footing with the navy's effective help'. The *Herald* carried a map of the Dardanelles. Other short reports said the French on the southern shore of the Dardanelles had taken 500 prisoners, while a 'report from Athens' spoke of 'much excitement' in Greece at the allied landing.

The following day the fighting was given added prominence by reports of 'steady advances' and claims by Turkey that it had inflicted losses on the allies, 'and to have captured a number of Australians'. Even so, the *Herald* carried only four short reports, the longest of four paragraphs. The same map was again featured. Athens bar gossip reached a new level: the allies had captured an entire Turkish battalion.

By now the politicians were getting in on the act. The British Secretary of the Colonies sent the Australian Governor-General, Sir Ronald Munro-Ferguson, his 'warmest congratulations on the splendid gallantry and magnificent achievement' of the Australians, with Sir Ronald replying he was confident they would 'carry the King's colours to further victory'.

The ever-helpful Athens rumour mongers were at it again, this time reporting that 'portions' of the Australians landing on Tuesday (two days behind the actual event) had 'immediately installed batteries on the coast'. If only, their commanders would have groaned. Shore artillery would have meant the Australians had conquered a sizeable area, and would have been far more effective than naval guns. Indian mountain artillery had struggled to support the Australasians.

Surprisingly, the Australian government itself was having trouble cutting behind this fog of official palaver and Athens rumour. On 30 April the *Herald* reported Prime Minister Andrew Fisher telling Federal Parliament that his government had no information of what Australian troops were where. 'They had twice within the last 48 hours asked to be provided with that information, in order to make the whole of it public, but they had not yet received it,' the *Herald* reported Fisher admitting.

By now, six days into the landing, the lack of information from the front was starting to cause disquiet, and not just in Australia. On 1 May, in a column of news with four decks of headlines — For King and Empire, Australia's Braves, The Dardanelles, and King's Congratulations — the *Herald* reported 'The Times of London' in condescending tones saying that nothing had moved the 'mother country' more than the devotion of her daughters, citing the 'gallantry' of Australians. The *Times*, however, complained that 'news' available in Melbourne and Wellington was not announced in London. The *London Daily Mail* also complained that Britons had 'not been allowed' to hear anything of the 'magnificent services' of the Australasians in the Dardanelles.

Meanwhile, in Australia the complaint was on the other foot. Defence Minister Senator George Pearce said news of the actual landing was allowed to be published in Britain but not in Australia.

The cautious Pearce said the government would not make any protest about this 'until it was known that troops had actually landed'. This must be one of the most extraordinary admissions of Gallipoli — six days after the landing and the Australian defence minister could not even confirm that it had occurred.

With all the official talk of 'gallantry' and 'congratulations' from the King it was obvious that casualties had been heavy. Sure enough, on 2 May, the Australian government released an initial list of 18 dead and 37 wounded. In a report starting across two columns (indicating it was very important) the Herald reported: 'The Allies now hold the end of the Gallipoli Peninsula, and the colonial troops have maintained their positions, Turkish reports to the contrary being untrue.'

Time, of course, would show that the Turkish reports were more accurate than those Australians were receiving from British cable services. The allies were barely holding on. In reports thick with further congratulations from the King, this time to Hamilton, and from Winston Churchill to Australia, the *Herald* gave limited London details of the actual landing. 'The allies have since rested and consolidated their positions' the report said, which would have come as welcome news to the battle-weary troops.

Agitation for real news was growing, and by 4 May the *Herald* was editorialising on 'Our need of news'. Many people, it said, believed a case could be made out against the censorship. The *Herald* itself should have been one. Its own editorial of 5 May said cable reports 'proved' the allies had crossed the peninsula and captured the important position of Maidos, overlooking the Narrows. Unfortunately totally incorrect; Maidos was a headquarters of Kemal Atatürk's defenders.

The Maidos capture myth persisted for a couple of days, aided by more Athens reports that 'heavy naval guns co-operating with the army, isolated a number of Turkish columns at various points of the peninsula, and forced them to surrender'. These cheerful reports said the Turks were burning every village from which they had been driven. In reality, of course, they had been driven from none.

On 6 May the *Age* ran a London report from the Athens correspondent of the *Evening News* claiming that the allies had 'repulsed' Turkish attacks, and were now 'advancing into the interior'.

The London papers became so desperate for real news that the *Daily Chronicle*'s correspondent hired a launch to visit the Gallipoli coast, and filed a report based on what he had seen. The valley across which both sides were fighting 'seemed a river of flame,' he reported from his offshore launch.

Such was the mixture of official camouflage, Athens gossip and seaside snippets that the Ashmead-Bartlett eyewitness report dropped into on the afternoon of 7 May. To Australian newspapers desperate for some reality — relief from the 'gallantry', 'furious onslaughts' and 'Turks repulsed' nonsense they had been fed so far — his ripping account of the first days must have been a godsend. Little did they appreciate, however, the drama of how it came into their hands. Bean, their official correspondent, still had no approval to file. He later admitted to a 'pang of jealousy' on hearing that, three days after he had accompanied the troops ashore, another correspondent was moving about what was now designated the ANZAC area.

He was right to be jealous. By 28 April Ashmead-Bartlett had completed a sweeping word picture covering the eve of the invasion, the landing and the battles of the first two days. But he couldn't file, a frustrating experience for any journalist with a major story. Captain Armstrong of the *London* had forwarded his lengthy report to the *Queen Elizabeth*, now down at Cape Helles with the British forces, but Ashmead-Bartlett, always conscious of not just getting the story out but also being first, was still 'greatly exercised' that Lawrence of Reuters was closer to the flagship.

Ashmead-Bartlett sent an urgent message to Commodore Keyes seeking a transfer to Cape Helles. Apart from ensuring copy dispatch he also needed to cover the British operations, which, after all, were the major punch of the invasion. Hamilton's headquarters, said the historian Robert Rhodes James, regarded the Australians as 'indisciplined amateurs' who had been entrusted with the simple part of the landing.

Keyes willingly sent a destroyer to bring Ashmead-Bartlett down to Cape Helles. The commodore had his reasons for this grand escort: he wanted Ashmead-Bartlett to write an account of the British landings around the cape beaches. Ashmead-Bartlett, however, was dismayed, not by this prospect but by the fact that his cables had not yet been sent. By this time he had written two. They had been censored, but remained unsent. The reason, said Keyes, was that Hamilton objected to any stories going through until he had got off his own official dispatches.

From London to Sydney, governments, newspapers and citizens were bemoaning the lack of information, and here was the reason. The literary minded general, who could certainly craft a colourful line, wanted to be first. Perhaps, also, the events of the first few days were so disastrous that Hamilton wanted to ensure the initial feedback was couched in his own terms.

Surprisingly, Ashmead-Bartlett, who always regarded himself as an 'insider' did not object, at least in his diary. 'This was of course reasonable, and I could raise no objection although a little disappointed,' he wrote at the time. Years later, in *Uncensored Dardanelles*, he appeared to change his mind, saying he had never heard of such a thing before. Official dispatches, he said, were never published until years later. Even though Hamilton did write some dispatches for release to the media, the excuse given by Keyes to delay newspaper cables was phoney. Hamilton had been sending cables back to the War Office for three days before Keyes told Ashmead-Bartlett his had not gone through.

Still, there was some good news. Handing Ashmead-Bartlett an envelope containing the unsent cables Keyes told him that Lawrence had not got off any either. Lawrence had not even sent in any to be censored. 'So whatever happened, I was certain to be ahead of him,' Ashmead-Bartlett wrote confidently in his diary.

Telling Ashmead-Bartlett that all the cable capacity on naval ships off Cape Helles was fully occupied by the military, Keyes directed him to HMS *Euryalus*, the ship directing transports to and from Malta and Alexandria. A transport could take his cables for dispatch from one of these ports. But on the *Euryalus*, Ashmead-Bartlett found little encouragement. No boat was leaving that day or the next. Officers sent him to the cable ship to find out if the necessary approval had been given to Malta or Alexandria to pass on the cables. An officer told him this approval had been given, but Ashmead-Bartlett was beginning to despair about ever getting his cables through this bureaucratic eye of the needle.

'Finally I decided to leave the whole matter in the hands of Allah,' he despaired, retiring to his new digs aboard HMS *Implacable*, where the captain kept him up half the night drinking port. But Ashmead-Bartlett did one final thing to give himself an edge: he marked his cables to be sent from either Malta or Alexandria 'Urgent'.

Bean later revealed how this twist made Ashmead-Bartlett first. It was not meant as a direction to telegraph it through at 'urgent' rates, but only his desire that Greek post office officials in Alexandria deal with it promptly, Bean said Ashmead-Bartlett had told his colleagues. But the Greeks took it as a direction, and sent the cable through at urgent rates.

'Lawrence afterwards felt that this was a breach of an understanding with him, but he accepted Bartlett's explanation,' Bean wrote in an obituary for Ashmead-Bartlett in 1931, describing Ashmead-Bartlett as the writer of 'swift, brilliant messages', while Lawrence was 'one of the most unselfish and sweet-natured colleagues that any man could wish to be associated with'.

Ashmead-Bartlett's 'urgent' directive cost the London newspaper proprietors an 'enormous bill' said Bean, but they soon made it up selling the copy to news-hungry dominion newspapers.

The tortuous path of the cable — from HMS *London* off Gallipoli to ships at Cape Helles, to an Alexandria post office and then London — finally ended on the desks of Australian newspaper editors on Friday, 7 May 1915, fully 12 days after the landing. The effect was electric. Here was the first eye witness account, written in direct and compelling terms. It talked not in official gobbledegook but used stirring phrases such as 'a race of athletes' and how the Australians 'had proved worthy to fight side by side with the heroes' of the Western Front.

'Splash' is the modern term for what happened to Ashmead-Bartlett's report — front page lead treatment. But in 1915 most papers still carried classifieds on their front pages, a practice which the *Sydney Morning Herald* did not give up until World War II. The afternoon Melbourne *Herald*, however, carried news front and back. When the report arrived late on 7 May in time for its late edition it ran a cut down version on its back page, leading with the 'no finer feat' angle, and carrying three headlines (all in italics):

No Finer Feat

Australian proves her valour in furious Turkish conflict

Onslaught proves irresistable

Next morning Ashmead-Bartlett's report was the lead story across the nation's newspapers. The *Sydney Morning Herald* carried it across the double drop of dual column copy spread under four decks of headlines (all in italics):

Australasians

Glorious Entry into War

Historic Charge

Brilliant Feat at Gaba Tepe

Historian K.S. Inglis said the *Herald's* issue carrying the Ashmead-Bartlett story bore more evidence of handling than any other in the paper's history. The two drops of dual column copy contained teaser subheadings such as 'Australasians in trouble' and 'Pressure by enemy', while an editorial that day was headed, 'The Glory of it'.

In Melbourne, the *Age* decorated the Ashmead-Bartlett story with no less than eight decks of headlines:

> Gallant Australians
> Full story of their Fight
> A Thrilling Narrative
> Troops landed in Darkness
> Attacked on Seashore
> British Correspondent's Tribute
> No Finer Feat in this War
> Heroes of Mons Equalled

The *Age* assured readers that Ashmead-Bartlett wrote after 'witnessing the operations, being aboard a war ship with the 600 Australians who formed the covering party for the troops who landed at Gaba Tepe'. The Melbourne *Argus* headlined across an entire broadsheet page: 'Australians at Dardanelles: Thrilling Deeds of Heroism'. It assured readers of Ashmead-Bartlett's credentials, saying he had represented the London *Daily Telegraph* in the Balkan wars, 'when his stirring and reliable messages brought him to the very forefront of war correspondents'.

In Brisbane, the *Courier* outdid its interstate rivals with 12 decks of headlines on the Gallipoli landing, starting with 'Our Noble Boys', and 'How They Fought and Died'. But the *Courier* ran the latest casualty list before Ashmead-Bartlett's account. By 8 May the total number of Australian dead had reached 160.

Ashmead-Bartlett's report had an instant effect on recruiting. By Monday the *Sydney Morning Herald* reported record numbers signing up. 'Australia has been thrilled by the story from Gallipoli,' the paper reported, with the Ashmead-Bartlett story acting like a 'bugle call'. Men had begun queuing outside recruitment stations early Saturday morning, 'many of them with copies of the morning papers in their hands, reading the story of Australia's baptism of fire in Europe, and only anxious to get their chance of following in their footsteps'.

Growing up in high society: the boy Ellis Ashmead-Bartlett, standing, and his father, Sir Ellis, seated on his right

At Marlborough College, Wiltshire, in 1897: Ellis is 3rd from right, 2nd row from top (Marlborough College archives)

Ellis aged 16 in Constantinople, Turkey, with his parliamentarian father, Sir Ellis, and a Turkish official

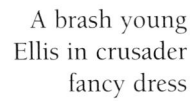

A brash young Ellis in crusader fancy dress

The cocky fledgling soldier

His first short-lived career as a young army officer in the Boer War

Outside his war correspondent's tent, probably in North Africa.

Back in London as the elegantly dressed sophisticate

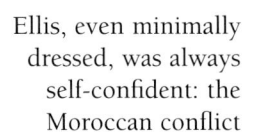

Ellis, even minimally dressed, was always self-confident: the Moroccan conflict

Marriage in Paris to Nina, the beautiful Argentinian heiress

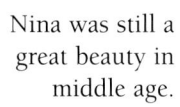

Nina was still a great beauty in middle age.

A mature Ellis Ashmead-Bartlett

(ABOVE) The quintessential war correspondent in action: Ellis Ashmead-Bartlett typing on an ammunition box, his movie camera on his left
(IWM, Ephem 00275)

(RIGHT) Always looking for a commercial angle: Ashmead-Bartlett's photo was later turned into a successful advertisement for Empire typewriters.
(IWM, Ephem 00275)

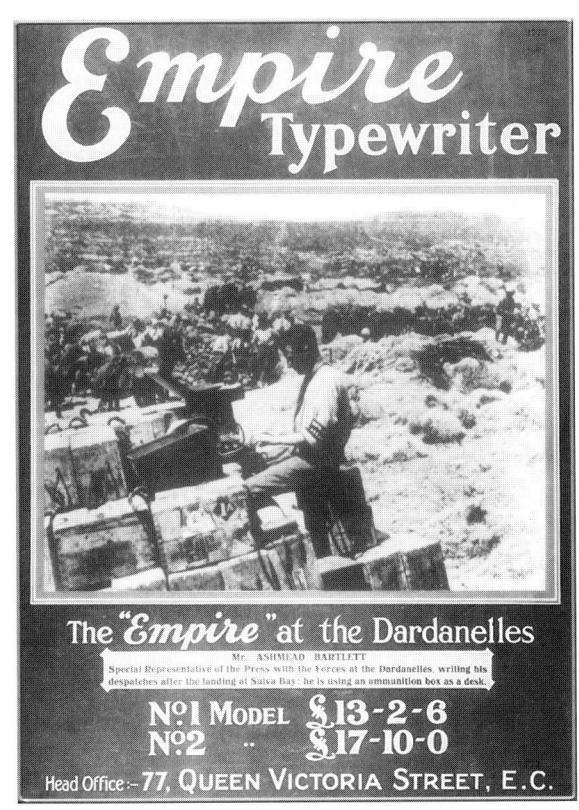

That same Monday Australian newspapers carried Ashmead-Bartlett's follow-up dispatch, covering the action of the 26th and 27th, by which time the 'colonials', he said, had created a little 'colony', cutting into the cliff with roads, dugouts and bomb-proof shelters. 'An improvised township is springing up as the troops dig themselves in and make themselves comfortable,' he reported. The 'colonials', he said, were extremely good under fire, often exposing themselves rather than keeping under the shelter of the cliff. 'One of the strangest sights was to see numbers bathing in the sea, with shrapnel bursting all round them.'

The Turks on the 26th had tried to drive the Australasians into the sea, with infantry attacks and a constant 'rain of shrapnel', he reported. 'They were soon disillusioned. These Australians were determined to die to a man rather than surrender the ground so dearly won,' he wrote, concluding that 'they now occupy such a position and are so thoroughly entrenched that all the Turks in Thrace and Gallipoli will never drive them out'.

Given the saturation newspaper coverage of Ashmead-Bartlett's landing report, Gallipoli soon began to be framed by the wider Australian press, as well as in popular lectures, verse, booklets and film, not to mention the public's heart.

Ballarat schoolteacher Jeanie Dobson put down her copy of Ashmead-Bartlett's account in the Saturday paper and penned a letter which was delivered to wounded Australian soldiers. The letter, widely distributed in the Empire, said:

> DEAR AUSTRALIAN BOYS — Every Australian woman's heart this week is thrilling with pride, with exultation, and while her eyes fill with tears she springs up as I did when I read the story in Saturday's *Argus* and says, 'Thank God, I am an Australian'.

Within a few days of the initial report the *Herald*'s 'War Notes' column was declaring that no Australian or New Zealander could read Ashmead-Bartlett without a 'thrill of pride'. Their 'little' army had secured a firm foothold on shore, and beaten off attacks by well-led, well-equipped, and determined troops.

The *Bulletin*, the soul of Australian nationalism, quickly adopted Ashmead-Bartlett. Its 13 May issue said 'Young Australia' had gone through the fiery crucible of baptism in war with a fine, honest courage and determination, continuing: 'Ashmead-Bartlett's account of their landing at Gabe Tepe — the silent boat journey by dark; the disembarkation under a withering fire; the ascent of the cliffs; and, later the grim work with bayonet and rifle on the shrapnel-swept plateau — makes a stirring story. It thrilled Australians with admiration for their soldier sons, and with pride that they had so nobly justified the confidence of their home.'

The following week the *Bulletin* published a poem by C. J. Dennis, the so-called 'laureate of the larrikin', whose *Songs of the Sentimental Bloke* was a runaway publishing success. A year later his *Moods of Ginger Mick* told how the larrikin was transfigured by Gallipoli, and it became another best seller. The seeds of Ginger Mick's swing from street warfare to national defence — spurred by Gallipoli — can be seen in the following stanzas of this poem that appeared in the *Bulletin* on 20 May:

> *Through the smoke I saw him strivin',*
> *Craig of Queensland, strong and tall,*
> *Like a harvester at hay-time, shouting 'set*
> *'em! On the ball!'*
> *And little Smith, of Collingwood, he*
> *howled a fightin' tune*
> *On the day we chased Mahomet over Sari's*
> *Sandy dune.*
>
> *For Green is gone, and Craig is gone, and*
> *God! How many more,*
> *Who sleep the sleep at Sari Bair beside the*
> *sun-kissed shore?*

*An' little Smith, of Collingwood, a bandage
'round his head,
He hums a savage song and vows swift,
vengeance for the dead.*

*But Sari Bair. O Sari Bair, the secrets
That you hold
Will move the hearts of Southern men when
All the tale is told.
The sun that lit your smiling bay bore witness
to the deed,
The day our father's fighting blood woke in
the Southern breed.*

Ashmead-Bartlett's account of the landing instantly reached deep into Australian schools. On 18 May Arthur Griffith, the New South Wales Minister for Education issued a special booklet to all schoolchildren containing Ashmead-Bartlett's account, and the first report of Bean, which was published on 14 May and in the *Commonwealth Gazette* of 17 May. Bean, who landed at Anzac Cove earlier than Ashmead-Bartlett on 25 April, had to wait for permission to send newspaper cables back to Australia. By the time it came through, his report of the landing was a week behind Ashmead-Bartlett's, receiving far less prominence. It was a more nuts-and-bolts report, with Bean concluding Australian soldiers that day had made a name 'which will never die'.

Although Bean did not have his English colleague's flair, his prose did not lack colour. For instance, he told of the Australian officer who questioned the order to retire, only to be then told to advance. While Bean later criticised Ashmead-Bartlett's exaggerations, his own account of 25 April had English sailors with 'tears of enthusiasm' over the 'whirlwind' charge of the Australians up the cliffs, with 'bayonets flashing'. Sailors with tears in their eyes seems about as hard to believe as Ashmead-Bartlett's cheering wounded.

Bean, who later did more than any other single person to nurture the Gallipoli flame that Ashmead-Bartlett ignited, generously acknowledged the historic importance to Australia of his colleague's 'magnificent' dispatch. 'Probably the finest of its kind ever penned by a war correspondent,' he said.

With Australian schoolchildren already reading *Australians in Action: The Story of Gallipoli* booklets, the Rev. W. H. Fitchett, a leading exponent of the British Empire and president of the Methodist Ladies College in Melbourne, wrote in the *Argus* on 24 May that Gallipoli 'is a tale of heroism which has thrilled the world'. The same day — Empire Day — he drew rousing applause from an audience when he invoked a comparison between Waterloo and Gallipoli, saying the daring of climbing the cliffs was an 'Australian touch' that even surpassed Waterloo. And Fitchett was right; the world was thrilled. Ashmead-Bartlett's account also received headline treatment in the British papers, anxious for some positive news in the gloom of fighting in France and the news the same weekend of the German sinking of the *Lusitania*. The *Daily Telegraph* editorialised about the 'prowess of the Australians and New Zealanders in scaling precipitous heights'.

Being the first report of Gallipoli, Ashmead-Bartlett's account of the Anzac landing overshadowed the British landing at Cape Helles on the same day. This had the effect of permanently locking the Anzacs into the lead imagery of Gallipoli.

For Australians, the first coverage of Gallipoli ignited a patriotic fervour. Ashmead-Bartlett's report was not only distributed to schools. It was also published with war fund-raisings and as part of theatre playbills. Filmmakers were quick to meet the public rapture about the new nationalist symbol of Gallipoli. Film versions soon followed, trumpeting their closeness to Ashmead-Bartlett's report. A feature film, *The Hero of the Dardanelles*, screened in July 1915 with a dramatic 'landing' of the Australians shot at Tamarama beach in Sydney. Posters for the films tapped the popularity of Ashmead-Bartlett's cable. 'The "Imperishable Glory" won by the Gallant Australians at Gallipoli most graphically and faithfully portrayed in accordance with Ashmead-Bartlett's historic despatch', the poster for the film proclaimed.

Australian newspapers knew they were onto a 'star' attraction with Ashmead-Bartlett. By the time of his next major dispatches covering the failed attacks on Krithia, his name had made it into headlines, with the introduction for the coverage saying: 'Another thrilling story of the fighting on the Gallipoli Peninsula is told by Mr Ashmead-Bartlett'.

Why did Ashmead-Bartlett's cable and his subsequent reporting strike such an immediate and deep chord in Australia? Ashmead-Bartlett removed a deep anxiety. Would the new army perform in its first test? Some soldiers had already been sent home for drunken larrikinism in Cairo. Was the Australian army an undisciplined rabble, as British military leaders obviously feared? Canadians had already shown their mettle in checking a German advance near Ypres on the Western Front. Could Australians do as well? As the *Herald* commented on the Dardanelles landing: 'Even while we mourn the loss of our men who have gone, we cannot but rejoice that they showed the same brave spirit, the same devotion to duty, as the Canadians'.

The new nation was but 14 years old, welded loosely from six colonies and as yet with no national capital. The story of stirring deeds at Gallipoli not only showed what the nation's manhood was capable of, it demonstrated a new national awareness. Bean was the first to spot this, with his memorable phrase that on 25 April 1915 'the consciousness of Australian nationhood was born'.

The stirring story of how the Australians had scaled cliffs and then held on in the face of a daunting Turkish counter-attack reflected the emerging character of the new nation. It blended the independent spirit of the bush with the larrikin 'have a go' of the cities. Ginger Mick's exploits at Gallipoli would show in verse how it had helped mould a new national Australian character in popular culture.

Such were the wellsprings Ashmead-Bartlett tapped on 8 May 1915. There was another important factor, however, in the public embrace of the stirring tale: the author was English. An Australian journalist might have been expected to praise his nation's troops. But here was an English reporter — and a well-credentialled war correspondent to boot — lavishing honours on them, likening their performance to some of the great battles on the Western Front. The young nation craved such praise from the 'mother country'. The historian Ken Inglis noted that the fact that Australians heard the Gallipoli story from an Englishman first, rather than from Bean, may actually have helped the country to make a national legend of the landing.

The full blown Gallipoli legend, replete with Anzac Day as the most symbolic Australian national holiday, would take some time to mature. But there is no doubt who had ignited the flame.

7

'Enough Glory for All'

NEWSPAPERS carrying the initial Ashmead-Bartlett stories trickled back to the peninsula by late May. A 'very good show', Ellis thought of the coverage.

Typical of his professionalism, even after the frustration of sending the initial Anzac report, he had quickly sized up the Cape Helles landings of the British 29th Division, the 'Old Contemptibles', on 25 April and filed a lengthy report within a day. The British landed in the face of stiff Turkish opposition at four of the six beaches. Losses were heavy and the advance slight. Hamilton had landed not with 'both feet', as promised, but a few toes.

In his report of the British landing, Ashmead-Bartlett wrote bluntly that 'the results justify the sacrifices'. The allies — a French force landed on the Asiatic side of the Dardanelles as a feint — had established a jagged line across the southern tip of the peninsula below the heights of Achi Baba, with its flanks secured by the gunfire of warships.

'It has cost us dearly to get astride the Gallipoli Peninsula, but there is no finer tale in our history than that of the deeds which were performed on Sunday, April 25, by Australian, New Zealand, British troops, supported with equal gallantry by the officers and men of the warships,' he wrote in a cable that was splashed across British newspapers.

A pattern was already being set. British newspapers, along with some Australian, began heading stories 'another thrilling dispatch from Ellis Ashmead-Bartlett'. He was becoming a media identity. *Bystander* magazine of 19 May ran a picture page on the 'Eyewitnesses' to the war, commenting: 'Particularly meritorious are the vivid dispatches of Mr Ashmead-Bartlett from Gallipoli'. *Ladies' Field* magazine ran a flattering portrait, saying that while many war correspondents could not reach the front because of restrictions, Ashmead-Bartlett was doing 'brilliant work'. *Newspaper World* described his 'descriptive matter' sent back from Gallipoli as 'amongst the finest stuff that has come through during the war'.

Ashmead-Bartlett's colourful historical allusions didn't please everyone, however. A letter writer to the *Irish News* disputed his claim of the Anzac landing that 'the first Ottoman Turk since the last crusade received an Anglo-Saxon bayonet in him at five minutes after five a.m. on April 25', a sentence omitted from Australian papers. The bayonet, said the pedantic letter writer, was unknown in warfare until 1693 — 300 years after the last crusade — when it was used by the French, and not adopted by the British for another 10 years!

More serious critics began to note the difference between Ashmead-Bartlett's reports and the now published accounts of Hamilton. The *Pall Mall Gazette* said Hamilton's reports cast a 'more hopeful light' than Ashmead-Bartlett's 'vivid word pictures'. Hamilton had reported that 'every day sees improvement in the Anglo-French position'. The *Pall Mall Gazette* commented that while that was good, they had learned (from Ashmead-Bartlett) that the Dardanelles could only be reduced by a long campaign. There was no longer any question of a coup de main.

After his initial guts-and-glory reporting style of the landings, Ashmead-Bartlett gradually became more pessimistic about the prospects of the expedition. Amazingly, within a month of his glowing 'fine feat of arms' style reporting of the 25 April landing, he was virtually at war with Hamilton and his staff. He was the first correspondent to throw doubts on the leadership of the campaign — and it cost him dearly.

Hamilton's character was a crucial part of the Gallipoli failure. Courteous, cultured and a stylish writer, Hamilton was also courageous, twice recommended for the Victoria Cross. But he had never commanded an army in battle, he was 62 years old — approaching retirement — and had been overlooked for the Western Front when Kitchener appointed him to head the Gallipoli expedition. Hamilton idealised Kitchener, accepting only a scant briefing from him before hurrying off to the Mediterranean.

At Gallipoli, however, his vacillation became painful. The commander, for instance, failed to enforce suggestions to his divisional commander on Cape Helles, Major General Hunter-Weston, to land more forces at an unopposed beach, or to conduct some of the frontal attacks at night. He acquiesced to French demands to evacuate the Kum Kale invasion on the Asian side of the straits, despite its success. Later, in the Suvla Bay landings, he tolerated inaction in attack for far too long. But the catalyst for Ashmead-Bartlett's disillusionment with the commanders was the disastrous battles for Krithia in late April and early May 1915, as the allies tried to take the small village standing before Achi Baba and its command of the mouth of the Dardanelles Strait. Hamilton stayed aboard his command ship, the *Arcadian*, while Major General Hunter-Weston ashore directed wave after wave of open-ground daylight attacks against entrenched Turkish positions. Only a small area of land was gained, with heavy losses, including those of an Australian and New Zealand force brought down from Anzac Cove.

Ashmead-Bartlett's reporting began to inject a note of warning about the expedition. But his personal diary was scathing. And his later book, *Uncensored Dardanelles*, became damning. But by then his relationship with Hamilton was poisonous, and his contempt for Hunter-Weston (he called him Hunter-Bunter) ran deep.

Cabled stories by Ellis contain a heartbreaking description of wasted Australian lives in the Krithia frontal attacks. After two and a half days of unsuccessful attacks Hamilton had come ashore to discover that an Australian force was still in reserve. He ordered a late afternoon attack, again over open ground. To encourage the hesitant French on the left of the line, Hamilton wanted the Australians to surge forward with maximum display. An aide called on Brigadier General W. McKay of the Australian Brigade, asking if they had any bands or flags to accompany their attack. McKay said no — such displays would have only drawn the attention of Turkish fire.

Oblivious to this ludicrous request, Ashmead-Bartlett described the vain charge:

> They were met by a tornado of bullets, and were enfiladed by machine guns from the right, and the artillery in vain endeavoured to keep down this fire.
>
> The manner in which these dominion troops went forward will never be forgotten by those who witnessed it. The lines of infantry were enveloped in dust from the patter of countless bullets in the sandy soil, and from the hail of shrapnel poured on them, for now the enemy's artillery concentrated furiously on the whole line.
>
> The line advanced steadily as if on parade, sometimes doubling, sometimes walking, and you saw them melt away under this dreadful fusillade, only to be renewed again as reserves and supports moved forward to replace those who had fallen.
>
> In spite of all obstacles, a considerable advance towards Krithia was made, but at length a point was reached from which it was impossible to proceed further. Not a man attempted to return to the trenches. They simply lay down where they were and attempted to reply to their concealed enemy, not one of whom disclosed his position. Only a few hundred yards had been won, it is true, but these Australians and New Zealanders were determined not to budge, and proceeded to entrench themselves where they were. But it became obvious at the end of an hour that the attack had spent its force, and that the hope of taking Krithia by direct assault must be abandoned.

Doubts were creeping into his reporting. Ashmead-Bartlett concluded his 16 May cable of the Krithia battle with the first public suggestion that the plan to win Constantinople was being met by an 'indomitable foe' and that 'extreme patience' would be necessary. 'Our men have done everything mortal man could do,' he said, sounding a clear warning to the reading public that Gallipoli was a looming disaster. Krithia was never occupied.

Privately, he was beginning to wonder whether the force would have to be withdrawn. Hamilton had already told him confidentially that the Turks were in far stronger numbers than he had anticipated. In the wake of the disastrous landing at the Cape Helles beaches and the first abortive attempts to take Krithia in early May, Ashmead-Bartlett wrote in his diary that the expedition had failed as a minor operation. Success would now depend on 'very large' reinforcements, which could be ill-spared from the Western Front.

After the second battle ended on 8 May with its useless slaughter he noted that 'the first stage of the campaign had definitely failed'. He began to question whether Hamilton was facing the facts, and whether he was telling the government the real state of affairs. At the same time Hamilton in fact had secretly cabled Kitchener that the expedition so far had been a failure, 'as my objective remains unachieved'. But in following this two days later with a request for two more divisions, Hamilton told Kitchener 'everyone is in good spirits and full of confidence'. The solution, he had decided, was to hammer away until the Turks became demoralised. This was Hamilton's breezy 'all continues to go well' optimism that marked the commander's private and public dispatches.

Turks aside, Hamilton was certainly demoralising his own side. He told Ashmead-Bartlett after the Krithia battles that he was still confident of taking Achi Baba, and that Kitchener had promised him two extra divisions. Turning to his chief of staff, Braithwaite, in the journalist's presence he said, 'We must not worry the old man too much. He is very pleased with us now, and in time we shall get what we want out of him.' The remark stunned Ashmead-Bartlett. It was

Myth Maker

strange to regard your duty to your country as secondary to worrying Kitchener for reinforcements, he thought.

The bloody battles for Krithia began to change Ashmead-Bartlett's view of the Gallipoli campaign. Not only would large reinforcements be required, but Britain now had an eastern campaign of 'huge dimensions' as well as its great campaign in France. 'We have voluntarily brought this upon ourselves by attacking the Turks, when we should have done far better to let them stew in their own juice until the grand settlement which must follow the termination of the war,' he wrote in his diary. He was far more constrained in his censored dispatches, saying that after Krithia those who thought the Gallipoli campaign would be speedily won would be disappointed.

As he watched the carnage at Krithia, and worried that with the military censorship the real facts of Gallipoli were not getting out, Ashmead-Bartlett made a fateful decision. He would write a memorandum on the situation at Gallipoli and present it in the form of a letter to be published in the press. This would test whether 'the military authorities out here were concealing the truth from the authorities at home'.

The military leaders at Gallipoli, he noted in his diary, were afraid that if the truth were known they would be recalled, 'and then goodbye to KCBs, KCMGs [knighthoods] and all the other damned honours they have in mind. But this is only playing with a great question when the whole safety of our country is at stake. But our leaders in the field are very little men. That is their trouble.'

Although the memo was subsequently lost, his other writings reveal what was going through Ashmead-Bartlett's mind at this stage. The invasion had been too dispersed over no less than eight landing points. The 'fatal error' had been sending the five brigades of Anzac troops off on a separate landing rather than using them to push in right behind the 29th Division at Cape Helles. This, he believed, would have 'stood a very fair chance' of taking Krithia and Achi Baba, rather than leaving the dominion troops 'clinging like ants to the hills around Anzac [Cove]'.

'It would be dangerous to prophesy that it would have succeeded in any circumstances, but the chances of success which it did possess were thrown to the winds by the fatal abandonment of the most elementary rule of war, namely, to concentrate your army and strike at the enemy's most vulnerable points and not to deliver half a dozen widely separate attacks, without retaining any reserves with which to follow up an initial success,' he later wrote. 'Too late Sir Ian Hamilton realised his mistake.'

Ashmead-Bartlett was also developing his other theory about the campaign: that the main attack should have been up at Bulair at the neck of the Gallipoli peninsula. This would have cut the Turkish forces in half. In fact, the Navy had mounted a feint at Bulair on 25 April, but its force was quickly withdrawn to support the besieged Australians at Anzac Cove.

The senior naval officer in charge of the Bulair landing told Ashmead-Bartlett that his men had penetrated inland without finding any resistance before they were ordered to withdraw. It sowed a belief that Bulair was the lost key to Gallipoli success. 'Had we occupied the Bulair lines that night the campaign would probably now be over,' he wrote in late May.

The letter to the press became the mainspring of all his subsequent troubles with Hamilton and his senior staff. Submitted to the censors it was rejected in its entirety by Hamilton and Braithwaite. Maxwell gave him the bad news, telling him that Hamilton had added, 'under no circumstances must it be allowed through'.

'They [Hamilton and Braithwaite] realised three things which they never forgave,' Ashmead-Bartlett noted in his diary. 'Firstly, that I had a perfect conception of the extent of our so-called success up to date; secondly, that I knew too much and disapproved of the strategy of the campaign; and thirdly, they saw for the first time that I was not prepared to be an official eye-witness, but was determined to remain an independent one who could not be got at in anyone's interests.'

It was a declaration of journalistic independence. Little more than a month after joining the expedition he was not prepared to toe the official line. Indeed, he was determined to get out what he saw as the truth. Ashmead-Bartlett may have been the well-connected insider, but his rebellious journalistic instincts overrode any class loyalty. Gallipoli was badly led, he had decided. The whole expedition was shaping up as a disaster. He wanted the story out. From this point Ashmead-Bartlett became a gadfly to Hamilton's conduct of the campaign. The problem for Hamilton was that Ashmead-Bartlett was not just a troublesome journalist: his social and political connections in London were just as strong as the cultured general's.

The May memorandum must be seen against the generally optimistic tone of reporting at the time. On 17 May, for instance, the *Sydney Morning Herald* carried two headlines about Gallipoli fighting: 'Pushing Forward' and 'Slowly, Surely'. Days later, another read: 'Steady Progress'.

Such reassuring news was backed up by patriotic messages from Hamilton. Under the headline of 'Glowing Tribute', Hamilton told Australians on 13 May that their troops had 'upheld the finest traditions of our race during this struggle still in progress'. They had, he said, created an 'imperishable record of military virtue'; small wonder that Hamilton barred Ashmead-Bartlett's memo from publication. The English journalist was the only one prepared to blow the whistle on this optimistic camouflage.

Lester Lawrence, the myopic Reuters correspondent, was having his own problems, not only with the censors but with the Reuters chiefs back in London. Lawrence, billeted on HMS *Cornwallis*, poured out his troubles to Ashmead-Bartlett when Ellis visited the battleship. Half of it was due to Lawrence's inexperience, thought Ashmead-Bartlett. Reuters was not satisfied with their correspondent's work. Ashmead-Bartlett generously gave Lawrence some of his own cables to read through, saying these might help him to get the knack.

Visiting Anzac Cove in late May, Ellis reported on the big Turkish push to drive the Australasians into the sea. In attacks from the top of Monash Gully, and against close Australian positions at Quinn's

Post and Courtenay's Post, the Turks suffered enormous casualties, estimated at between 7000 and 8000 killed.

'The ground presents an extraordinary sight when viewed through the trench periscope,' he cabled. 'Two hundred yards away, and even closer in places, are the Turkish trenches, and between them and our lines the dead lie in hundreds. There are groups of twenty to thirty massed together, as if for mutual protection, some lying on their faces, some killed in the act of firing; others hung up on the barbed wire.'

A tour around the Australian front line with Birdwood — 'Birdie' as the troops knew him — provided Ashmead-Bartlett with more good copy on the irreverent Australian rank-and-file attitude to British officers. Birdwood asked one Australian how many Turks he had killed in the furious onslaught. 'That I can't say, General; but, look out here, there are eight acres of them lying around.'

By now German submarines were menacing the British fleet supporting the troops. Some of the big battleships such as *Queen Elizabeth* withdrew to the safety of Mudros. Ashmead-Bartlett was lunching aboard the *Swiftsure* on 25 May when a young midshipman interrupted Rear-Admiral Stewart Nicholson. 'Beg pardon, sir, the *Triumph* is listing.' The lunch party rushed to the deck to see *Triumph* listing after a fatal hit by a torpedo. A sister ship to *Swiftsure*, the *Triumph* hung at an angle for some minutes before turning belly up and sinking. Chastened, the Admiral, officers and Ashmead-Bartlett returned to the wardroom and fortified themselves with a port or two.

The Admiral then transferred his headquarters to HMS *Majestic*, the oldest of the battleships off Cape Helles, and obviously deemed expendable as she was the last battleship left to protect the onshore army despite the threat of submarines. Ashmead-Bartlett accompanied him, but on the evening of 27 May he had a queasy feeling that 'the end might come at any moment', and decided to sleep on deck. He was a poor swimmer and dreaded the thought of being sucked down with the ship if she was struck by a torpedo. A deck jump would enable him to get as far away as possible.

Many officers had the same uneasy feeling that night. Gathering in the wardroom with Ashmead-Bartlett they polished off the remaining champagne on board the 25-year-old battleship. Later, in his cabin, he packed some money in his wallet, placing valuable notes on the campaign in a leather bag. Unfortunately he left this bag behind as he settled down on a mattress above the aft turret, along with an uninflated lifebelt. It was a beautifully clear night, and he was soon sound asleep. Given his champagne intake Ellis slept well, only to wake and ask a sentry the time. 'Six fifteen, sir' was the reply, allowing Ashmead-Bartlett to turn over and sleep again.

Thirty minutes later he was disturbed by men running past him. One of them trod on his chest. 'What's the matter,' he cried. 'There's a torpedo coming' was the fleeting reply. Ashmead-Bartlett had only just scrambled to his feet when a dull explosion sounded from the port side. Although there was no shock on deck, the ship suddenly jerked and then began to list. 'Then there came a sound as if the contents of every pantry in the world had fallen at the same moment,' he recalled. 'I never before heard such a clattering, as everything loose tumbled about. You could tell at once she had been mortally wounded somewhere in her vitals, and you felt instinctively she would not stay long afloat.'

His plan had been to float safely away with his lifebelt, but he found to his disgust that he had forgotten to have it inflated. The crowd of men rushing by trying to escape swept him down to the quarter deck, where Ashmead-Bartlett contemplated leaping overboard to try to get to one of the rescue boats. An observer on another boat recounted to British newspapers how he watched Ashmead-Bartlett looking for an escape and glancing at his watch as the pell-mell of escaping men rushed past him. Ashmead-Bartlett by now was a minor war celebrity and this eyewitness account of his torpedoing made the newspapers.

'There he stood, reminding me of a 100 yards race in the role of a timekeeper watching the whole bunch of competitors speeding to the tape, looking at the men, and then his watch,' the observer said.

'There he stood gambling with death. He was there when seconds only divided him from the *Majestic*'s last plunge. Then at the last moment he took to the water, and was rescued. I never saw a cooler, calmer man.'

Dragged aboard a small overcrowded boat, a drenched Ashmead-Bartlett sat watching the *Majestic* turn turtle and contemplating what a splendid photograph it would make when someone called out: 'If you don't loose that rope we will be dragged under'. Men began jumping overboard when it was seen their boat was tied to the *Majestic*. At the last moment before the *Majestic*'s plunge someone finally found a knife and cut the rope.

He was taken aboard a French ship and given a suit of sailors' clothes as well as coffee and brandy. Some of the veteran reservists who crewed the *Majestic* were suffering from cold and shock, although Ashmead-Bartlett seemed unperturbed. 'I cannot say I felt any the worse,' he commented laconically

Back on a British ship the crew mocked his new French uniform. Commodore Keyes topped it with a hat. His sole worldly possessions now consisted of a wet pair of pyjamas, a silver cigarette case and £30 in notes, also dripping wet. With all his kit lost, including his glasses, portable typewriter and diary, Admiral de Robeck agreed Ashmead-Bartlett could go to Malta for a fresh outfit, but only if he did not write anything for the newspapers.

With a passage for Malta secured on the stores ship *Baron Ardossan*, Ashmead-Bartlett stole the biggest lifebelt he could find and carried it aboard. The captain chuckled: 'What are you carrying that belt for? I've got eleven hundred rounds of 12-inch ammunition on board as ballast, and if anything strikes us we shall all go so high that the only thing that could help you would be an aeroplane.' Ellis threw away the lifebelt.

On arrival in Malta, where he found it difficult to buy anything he liked, an idea began to form in his head. Why not now go all the way back to London? He was in a curious position, under naval command but army censorship, and he knew Hamilton's staff would be furious at his departure without their permission. But if he didn't write anything for the newspapers, what could be the problem?

Ashmead-Bartlett felt he could be 'useful' in advising the government on the realities of the Dardanelles; realities he did not believe were getting through in the official reporting or censored newspaper accounts, and were blocked when he tried to write an open letter to the press. Two incidents in Malta convinced him of that. First, Lord Methuen, Malta's governor, told him not to send any cables without his permission — an obvious indication that he had received instructions from General Headquarters (GHQ) on Gallipoli. Second, one of the Kings Messengers (official couriers) en route to England told Ashmead-Bartlett that Methuen had revealed to him that Hamilton himself had cabled to Malta, saying: 'Do not let Ashmead-Bartlett say a word about the Expedition, as he is a Jeremiah'.

Curious, Ashmead-Bartlett looked up the history of the prophet, only to find that Jeremiah was a pessimist. He was shocked. 'I have never been a pessimist, provided things are carried out in the right way,' he wrote, apparently oblivious to his long history of gloomy forecasts. He was fast becoming right about Gallipoli, however, and, as he noted when mulling over the pessimist charge: 'I am more than ever convinced we can never get through, working on our present lines'.

He decided to make a flying visit to London, sailing on the *Caledonian* two days after arriving in Malta. Admiral Limpus, the local naval commander, and other officers spurred him on, saying his information on Gallipoli would be useful if known in London. On board the *Caledonian* two Kings Messengers, one actually returning from Gallipoli, urged him to prepare a new version of his memorandum that had been rejected by Hamilton. He immediately set to work.

Ashmead-Bartlett's brief return to London in the middle of the Gallipoli campaign is a classic illustration of his style and contacts. Naval commanders and Kings Messengers en route took him into their confidence; he cabled ahead to his girlfriend, Gina, and to shops to order clothes as well as theatre tickets; and in London he saw politicians from Prime Minister Asquith down. Cabinet called him in for a briefing and Winston Churchill briefed him on sensitive war decisions made that very day in Cabinet.

Typically, Ashmead-Bartlett ordered from Malta a suite of rooms at London's Carlton Hotel, an old favourite. Events on arrival showed his cavalier attitude to such trifles as unpaid bills. The hotel management pointed out that he still owed them money from his last stay. While this was true, Ellis nevertheless took strong exception. 'I never heard such cheek in my life considering the money I have spent there, and I told them so to such good effect that they became most polite and affable.'

The suite was provided, and he set to work finishing his memorandum on Gallipoli, entertaining Gina, dining in the Carlton Grill with theatre friends and briefing politicians and his newspaper bosses. He was always discreet when referring to his lady friends. His diary, for instance, might note only that Gina called in the afternoon, and that 'I was kept occupied all the afternoon'.

The days were crammed with work and late nights. 'I am nearly dead,' he complained at one point, 'but I can always go for about ten days at a stretch with little or no sleep'. He determined to stay out of the limelight and refrain from public comment — probably because he would breach his censorship obligations — confining himself to seeing government leaders.

Catching up with family, he learned that his brother Seabury had been injured in the battle of Ypres, with two wounds in the head and one in the arm. But even family occasions were dominated by Gallipoli. At Uncle Willie's home, Holly Lodge, he briefed Sir Edward Carson, the attorney-general, who told him the matter was before the government at that very moment. Carson arranged for him to meet other cabinet ministers.

Asquith's Liberal government was in crisis, and not just over Gallipoli. The *Times* had exposed a shortage of shells on the Western Front, forcing Asquith to bring Conservatives into a coalition government. One casualty in the reshuffle was Churchill, who was dumped as First Sea Lord. This exposé came just after Hamilton pressed Kitchener for more shells for Gallipoli.

At a meeting with his very well-connected proprietor, Harry Lawson of the *Daily Telegraph*, Ashmead-Bartlett learned of the Cabinet intrigues between the French and Kitchener over the conduct of the war, which culminated in the leaked *Times* report and Asquith's need to form a coalition to continue. Lawson said he did not believe the government could survive any crisis over Gallipoli.

A dinner organised by Lady Randolph Churchill for him to meet Winston provided a private insight into the state of the man who masterminded Gallipoli, and where it had now left the British government and Empire. The air around the dinner table must have been heavy with the past affairs that entwined Ashmead-Bartlett and Churchill — Sir Ellis's brazen affair with Churchill's mother-in-law and the young Ellis's love for his sister-in-law, Gwendoline. All that was overlooked, however, as Churchill, seemingly addressing his mother, lectured the dinner guests on the failures of Gallipoli as he saw them. Ashmead-Bartlett was surprised at Churchill's change since their last meeting. He looked years older, his face was pale, and he was obviously depressed at being dropped from the Admiralty. The guests fell silent during Churchill's monologue.

Churchill harangued the dinner table about the failed naval battle of 18 March which then led to the land invasion. The battle should have been fought to the finish instead of the Navy withdrawing after the first day's losses. The fleet might have got through the Narrows. It was an obsession with him, thought Ashmead-Bartlett, who later noted in his diary:

> The facts are forgotten, or ignored — the forts still remain unsilenced, the three lines of anchored mines still untouched, the possibility of concealed torpedo tubes, the three battleships lying at the bottom of the Straits, a dreadnought sorely stricken, other ships limping wounded to cover, and the problem of what the fleet could have done had it entered the (Sea of) Marmora

only to find the Narrows closed once more against its return — all these factors, so patent to the admirals on the spot, seemed to carry no weight with him.

The loss of the ships leaves him undismayed. His only regret, like that of some ancient Anahuac god, is that the sacrifices were stopped, before the full number of victims, waiting to be laid on the altar of chance, had reached their destination.

As the ladies retired, Winston rounded on Ashmead-Bartlett, accusing him of coming home to run down the expedition and to crab about it to a lot of society gossips, to ridicule it for the sake of a newspaper story. Ellis pretended to be angry, pointing out the facts, and saying he supported the expedition — but he would only be silent if it was conducted in the right way.

Winston suddenly calmed down, confiding in Ashmead-Bartlett his determination that the expedition must succeed at all costs. 'Not only because he feels that strategically it must have a great effect on the war, but also because he knows it will mean his complete vindication, and restore something of his old prestige, because the mistakes will be speedily forgotten in the final success,' said Ellis.

The Cabinet was divided over Gallipoli, Winston told him, and would have to make a decision that week. He, Ashmead-Bartlett, must assist by convincing ministers to send out reinforcements and meeting the prime minister, Asquith. Churchill would arrange it for the next day. Ashmead-Bartlett acquiesced. 'I have always thought it would be fatal to give up at this stage and that also the task could be fairly easily accomplished if gone about in the right way,' he confided in his diary.

With Winston in a happier frame of mind, he asked Ashmead-Bartlett to accompany him home to his residence at the Admiralty, which he was just about to vacate. As they walked through the streets Winston told him how he had warned the Cabinet of what they were taking on after the naval defeat.

Myth Maker

'I told them that once an army was landed, it was quite another affair, and that they would be dragged into a great enterprise from which they could not withdraw,' Ashmead-Bartlett quoted him as saying. The 'great enterprise' warning seems at odds with the amateurish way the Gallipoli expedition was launched, hobbling it from the start.

At Admiralty House, Winston wandered through the empty rooms, his face flushed, his head bent and his hands behind his back, picking up an odd book or document, glancing at it, but his mind failing to concentrate on anything other than the Dardanelles. To Ashmead-Bartlett he looked the perfect picture of a fallen minister.

As he roamed the rooms, Winston picked up a bottle of brandy and took great gulps 'like some wretch who is strengthening his hand for suicide'. The deserted rooms, so recently full of sycophants and admirers, re-echoed his voice as once again he burst out on the naval disaster that led to the invasion. 'They never fought it out to a finish,' Winston moaned. 'They never gave my schemes a fair trial.'

'But they did and lost three ships and two others badly damaged before ever reaching the minefield,' replied Ashmead-Bartlett.

'That does not matter,' said Winston. 'They ought to have gone on. What did it matter if more ships were lost with their crews? The ships were old and useless and the crews mostly old reservists. They were sent out there to die, it was their duty. That is what they were mobilised for.'

Ashmead-Bartlett censored this Churchill outburst in his later book, omitting the callous references to the old naval reservists. Later, Winston calmed down, and the two worked through to 3 am poring over Gallipoli maps, trying to work out a plan to save the situation. Finally, Winston said he agreed with Ashmead-Bartlett's scheme for a landing up around Bulair, and told the journalist he wanted him to brief Asquith.

At 1 pm the next day Winston sent a message for him to come to 10 Downing Street. He was admitted into the Council Chamber and Asquith, looking, wrote Ashmead-Bartlett, as if he did not have a care in the world, went over the plan with both Churchill and the journalist. Asquith said he was in favour. 'It seems to me the only natural thing to do,' he said. Asquith ended the meeting by asking Ashmead-Bartlett to write him a memo, and also attend Cabinet the following day.

After meeting Asquith, Ashmead-Bartlett lunched, somewhat surprisingly, with Lady Jean Hamilton, who until Gallipoli had always been an admirer. His old friend Lady Cunard was also present as Ellis tried to cheer up Lady Hamilton, who was worried about the lack of success on Gallipoli and how that might reflect on her husband. Don't worry, he told her, the government had decided to see the expedition through at all costs, and would send out reinforcements. It was an insight into the manners of the era. Here was Ashmead-Bartlett comforting the wife of the man who had already labelled him a Jeremiah, and who would shortly become an implacable enemy. Little did Ashmead-Bartlett know that as he was sitting at Lady Hamilton's dining table her husband was actively conspiring to end his career at Gallipoli.

That night he completed the memo for Asquith. Anzac was a stalemate, he told the prime minister. An advance at Cape Helles might be possible, but would require 'a vast operation of war'. The solution was to get astride the peninsula near its neck at Bulair. The Turks would have to weaken their defences of Anzac and Helles to meet the new challenge.

'In conclusion,' he told Asquith, 'once you get astride the Peninsula the campaign is won. You have only then to clear the minefield and get your Fleet through to Constantinople. The real obstacle to success is the presence of submarines, and we must be prepared to lose some ships.'

At this point, Ashmead-Bartlett still believed the expedition could succeed, but was more critical of the point of landings rather than the military leadership. That would come later.

The following day, 12 June, he was summoned to 10 Downing Street, taking his memo for Asquith. He waited outside the cabinet room for an hour and a half as 'the choice and master spirits of the age', as he called them, deliberated. Kitchener emerged. Despite his fearsome reputation, Ashmead-Bartlett found him full of good-natured benevolence as he asked pointed questions about Turkish supply lines, the chances of success of new allied submarine penetration into the Sea of Marmara to attack Turkish shipping, and whether other new landing sites might be better.

Ashmead-Bartlett was stunned by one question, however. When he pointed out that the Anzacs would be pinned down as long as the Turks held Gaba Tepe on their right, Kitchener asked him why the Australians had given it up, and seemed surprised when Ashmead-Bartlett replied that they had never occupied it. Birdwood believed that Gaba Tepe was impregnable, with subterranean passages enabling Turkish supply from behind. Kitchener then was juggling huge strategic issues, and it might be understandable that he thought the Australians had once occupied Gaba Tepe, but it was a revealing insight into his poor knowledge of Gallipoli. After some discussion about the possibility of the Turks launching gas attacks on the close Anzac positions (they never did), Kitchener ended the conversation.

Later that day Ashmead-Bartlett called at the Admiralty for a farewell chat with Winston, and to find out what really happened at the cabinet meeting. Again he displayed a depth of sources that other journalists would kill for. Winston gave him a complete run-down of Cabinet's decisions. Asquith had read out Ashmead-Bartlett's memo, which was then discussed in detail. A majority of ministers supported a Bulair landing. But Winston thought that first they would try to starve out the Turks by sending more submarines into the Sea of Marmara. Cabinet was determined to see the expedition through, and would now send out the extra troops Hamilton called for. Cables were being drafted to send to Hamilton asking him questions about the campaign, but Ashmead-Bartlett's name would not be mentioned as it would make his position on return 'difficult'.

That was an understatement. Here was a journalist sending memos to the prime minister and influencing Cabinet on its Dardanelles strategy over the head of the commander-in-chief on the ground.

Hamilton, of course, suspected Ashmead-Bartlett's hand when he received the cables, and it only reinforced his disdain for his journalist critic.

This was Winston's last day at the Admiralty, and as he walked to his car he told Ashmead-Bartlett he would write to Hamilton on his behalf. Then he told the journalist: 'I consider you have greatly assisted us. We are all working for a common end. If Constantinople is taken there is enough glory for all.'

In almost three weeks in London Ashmead-Bartlett was at the heart of the British Empire power structure as the Cabinet wrestled with what to do about the looming Gallipoli disaster. He talked to and briefed cabinet ministers from the prime minister down, met the chiefs of the War Office and Admiralty, as well as discussing options with Lord Kitchener. Yet he wrote none of it. It was not until 1928 when *Uncensored Dardanelles* was published that these details emerged. Journalists and editors in those days might have regarded themselves as inside players, but to a modern editor he embodies the lament that the problem with journalists is that they know all the good stories, but don't write them.

The glory foreshadowed by Churchill was fine, but Ashmead-Bartlett urgently needed money to dig himself out of debt and sustain his lifestyle. When the wife of a friend ran into him in Jermyn Street, home of fashionable men's outfitters, she asked him why he was always falling into bankruptcy. 'The high cost of loving,' he quipped.

Even though he dabbled in high strategy during his brief London sojourn, Ashmead-Bartlett still found time to make some new commercial deals. The Newspaper Proprietors Association formally thanked him for his much praised dispatches, and he responded by indicating that a pay rise would be an acceptable reward. More importantly, his literary agent Hughes Massie arranged a deal for him to write a book on the Gallipoli expedition, to be published by Hutchinson. He received a £500 advance as well as a 'big royalty', plus reserving the American rights. This was a good deal, he said, considering the state of the wartime book trade. Showing his eye for commerce, Ashmead-Bartlett was keen to get the book out quickly, as he feared that immediately the Dardanelles campaign ended interest in it might collapse. Later, he changed his mind on this point.

Hughes Massie made another suggestion. Why not take back a newfangled 'cinematograph' camera and record some moving film of the Gallipoli expedition? Why not, thought Ashmead-Bartlett, conscious of the possible film revenues but also worried about the difficulties of operating this new technology.

It was a decision that would provide Australia with a priceless piece of national heritage — the only cinema footage of Gallipoli.

8

A Very Personal War

ASHMEAD-Bartlett had a champagne return to the Gallipoli peninsula, rounding up all the British and French on the boat to Malta to toast the 100th anniversary of peace between the two countries after the Battle of Waterloo. But the bubbles quickly turned flat back at Gallipoli.

Dining with both Admiral de Robeck and Commodore Keyes the next night he sat up late telling them 'almost everything' that had passed in London. It was a slightly different story the following day when he met General Hamilton, to whom he related 'most' of his London interviews.

When he arrived on 23 June, Ashmead-Bartlett found that the reporting ground rules had changed. The first change was that Hamilton had moved his GHQ from the ship *Arcadian* to a series of tents on a sandy slope at Imbros Island. A trawler service shuttled people between the Anzac and Helles battlegrounds on the mainland, and to Lemnos Island, where the fleet was harboured at Mudros Bay. To Ashmead-Bartlett, the Imbros site was execrable.

'If GHQ invariably select the strongest points of the enemy's line against which to deliver their attacks, they have shown just as little skill in selecting the site of their own camp,' he wrote. 'After the comforts of the *Arcadian*, this sandy wilderness at Kephalos is a Via Dolorosa for the whole of GHQ. Burnt up by the sun, blown about by the siroccos, tormented by millions of flies, they pass a miserable time, and their meals are largely composed of a fine sprinkling of sand.' Sand aside, the fine-mouthed Ashmead-Bartlett, who had closely studied nutrition for armies in South Africa, was appalled by the food. 'It never does any good for a commander-in-chief and his staff to be badly housed and badly fed during a campaign.'

Hamilton's chief of staff, Braithwaite, curtly told him of the next change: Ashmead-Bartlett was to set up a press camp. More correspondents were coming out, and he was to make a camp for them at K Beach, about two miles from GHQ. Braithwaite told him that from now on the war correspondents were to be under the control of the Army, and would have nothing further to do with the Navy.

'I found at once a rather hostile attitude towards me,' said Ashmead-Bartlett. 'I knew this would be so on account of my visit home. They [GHQ] are a lot of sensitive children and fear any form of criticism. As a matter of fact I have criticised no-one by word or in print. But they know I have seen the heads of government, and that is what they dislike.'

Maxwell, the former war correspondent now the censor at GHQ, filled him in. There had been a series of intrigues against him to prevent his return, Maxwell told him. Ashmead-Bartlett believed these had failed because of the 'safeguards' he had taken, presumably a reference to his determination not to write a word for newspapers while in London, and not speak to other journalists. 'I played my cards very carefully and had calculated on all this beforehand,' he believed.

But Maxwell knew about only a smidgen of the conspiracy by Hamilton to rid himself of the one war correspondent who posed any problem for him. On 3 June Hamilton had cabled Kitchener:

> (Secret and personal) After being wrecked in the "Majestic", Ashmead-Bartlett obtained leave to go to Malta in order to buy an outfit. Just before he started we had refused to pass for publication a telegram and a letter. It was a regular Jeremiad, with demands for more men, more munitions etc, and in a tone not unlike Repington's letter from France. [Perhaps Harry Lawson was right when he told Ashmead-Bartlett in London that public disclosure over the lack of troops and munitions

on Gallipoli might have really sunk the Asquith government. It was Repington's letter on the shells scandal in France that had forced Asquith into a coalition, dumping Churchill from his Cabinet.]

... I now hear that he has left Malta and gone to England, so I am sending you this warning, for, although he is a good writer, he is a pessimist of the first water. Now that he has gone home he had better stay there, and some more cheerful correspondent should be sent in his place.

Hamilton went a step further, trying to make Ashmead-Bartlett's departure a fait accompli. Compton Mackenzie, the well-known writer, was working in the intelligence section at Gallipoli, and Hamilton now pushed him into a new role of reporting for the Newspaper Proprietors Association — Ashmead-Bartlett's job. The snobbish Mackenzie, however, at first demurred, preferring to keep his officer's commission rather than be a war correspondent.

Hamilton convinced him otherwise, telling him that Ashmead-Bartlett was getting £2000 a year for his job, and that he had cabled Kitchener suggesting the Newspaper Proprietors Association be approached on Mackenzie's appointment. Maxwell was outraged when he heard about it, saying the proprietors would strongly resent having an 'amateur' foisted upon them.

Mackenzie was no amateur, but he was no war correspondent either. In one of his first dispatches he drew an extended analogy between Lancashire landing, the Helles Point landing beach, and a British seaside beach. The *World* newspaper unfavourably compared his work to Ashmead-Bartlett's. Mackenzie wrote too well, said the *World*, never seeming to get to speak 'beyond the brain'. Readers paused to admire, but with Ashmead-Bartlett 'the interest was too intense for any other emotion', with his descriptions leaping to the eye.

With Ashmead-Bartlett keeping a low profile while in London, at least in the media, Kitchener was forced to cable Hamilton that stopping his return would not be easy.

'Steps have been taken to prevent Ashmead-Bartlett from communicating anything through the press to the public, and Ashmead-Bartlett has promised verbally to speak to no one but his editor who can be trusted,' Kitchener said. 'He is, however, the servant not of one paper but of the whole London press, and unless you authorize us to lodge a definite objection with them, which we shall have to look to you to help us to substantiate, we shall have difficulty in denying his services to them'.

Hamilton was not prepared to lodge a formal objection to Ashmead-Bartlett. His method was more the back door approach. Changing his tune somewhat he claimed his real aim in stopping 'a particularly despondent telegram' was to prevent neutral countries becoming pessimistic about the success of the expedition. England then was hoping to bring Bulgaria in on its side against Turkey.

When Kitchener cabled him with questions about the Anzacs' tenuous position that had arisen from the 12 June cabinet meeting, Hamilton guessed the source — Ashmead-Bartlett — and changed his mind, now wanting him back. 'I fear the Jeremiah referred to in my [earlier cable] has been busy and believe he will do less harm here than at home,' he told Kitchener.

Surprisingly, on 17 June, as Ashmead-Bartlett was on his way back, the War Office offered Hamilton a new way to diminish the troublesome journalist's authority — competition. Would Hamilton be prepared to accept two or three more war correspondents, the War Office asked. Provincial newspapers had complained that, although they had the services of Lester Lawrence of Reuters, the London dailies had both Reuters and Ashmead-Bartlett.

Arthur Balfour, the new First Lord of the Admiralty who had just taken over from Churchill, not only agreed but, as Gallipoli was now mainly an army show, transferred the control of war correspondents on the peninsula over to the War Office. Hamilton jumped at the chance, pushing for an older war correspondent, Henry Nevinson, whom he had known in South Africa.

Hamilton immediately envisaged that new correspondents would cut Ashmead-Bartlett down to size. As the single correspondent for the entire London press, Ashmead-Bartlett had become 'an unduly important personage', he told Kitchener. Newcomers would 'counterbalance' his baleful influence. But Hamilton did not just want competition. For a general who publicly professed support for freedom of the press he showed his real colours in a frank note to Winston Churchill on the new arrivals: 'It is much easier to deal with a dozen, who can be set one against the other, than with a single individual'.

So much for press freedom. Having suffered defeat in banishing Ashmead-Bartlett, Hamilton, says Nicholas Hiley (who devoted his PhD thesis to media controls in the first two years of the war), was now aiming to divide and rule as a control mechanism. Not only that, now he had operational control of war correspondents Hamilton also wanted them rounded up into one position at K Beach — and away from GHQ.

Charles Bean, angered by the order that both he and the New Zealand correspondent, Malcolm Ross, must also relocate from Anzac Cove to the new correspondents' camp at K Beach, quickly divined the reason. Protesting to Maxwell about Hamilton's 'thunderbolt' on relocating, he was told: 'The reason for rounding up the rest of us was in order to round up Ashmead-Bartlett. They weren't at all satisfied with his proceedings, and wanted to have him thoroughly under control — and so made the rule to apply to the lot of us.'

Bean's plea to stay with the Anzacs showed the key difference between him and Ashmead-Bartlett. Bean was there not so much to report the wider war but to focus just on the Australians, and later to write a history. 'I have not attempted to sum up the general trend of the campaign, except in one, or possibly two small references to events already long since published in England,' he said in his letter to GHQ seeking to remain at Anzac Cove. 'I do not know, I do not want to know, and, needless to say, have not attempted even remotely to touch on any future plans.'

Bean also made it clear he was not in the business of criticising military practices, even when they affected the Australians. A case in point was the problem of keeping the Australian division up to strength, because diarrhoea cases were repatriated all the way to Alexandria — where they were usually well on arrival, but still given the choice of going to England or elsewhere. The result, said Bean, was that men who could be back in six days were often away six weeks.

The issue was much discussed within the military, and Bean was asked why he did not report it. He refused. It would have meant criticising the military's so-called Lines of Communication.

'It is strictly against the regulations for me to criticise and I have not been asked by the Authorities to do so,' he wrote in his diary. 'My job is to tell the people of Australia all I can about their troops here and I should be sent back if I tried to do anything else — that I know only too well. Besides, even if I were free to criticise L [Lines] of C [Communication], I'm not on the spot — I'm at the front and not the base. The unofficial correspondents in Cairo and Alex[andria] will take it up and it will be righted through a Press agitation and not the official channels — I have no doubt.'

With Bean's obvious disinclination to rock the boat, Hamilton agreed to an exception. The order that all correspondents must locate to the new camp on K Beach, Imbros, would remain in force, but Captain Bean and Ross could visit Anzac for three or four days at a time on a trial basis, and if this did not work it would be reconsidered. This, said Hamilton, recognised the desire of Dominion correspondents to 'practise their profession'. Bean thought otherwise, noting how he had been prevented from covering the landing while Ashmead-Bartlett and Lawrence reported. Hamilton was even more generous in private, telling Bean and Ross he did not mind how long they stayed on Anzac on their 'visits'.

'We caught his meaning,' Bean said, 'and thenceforth lived happily at Anzac, but with the inestimable privilege of being able to visit Imbros for a day or two holiday whenever we wished'.

Holiday it may well have seemed for anyone living in shell-blitzed dugouts, for Ashmead-Bartlett, given the job of setting up the new correspondents' camp, typically created a minor paradise in the hell that was Gallipoli. He showed no sign at all of resenting Hamilton's crude attempt to corral him. Instead, he created a haven of good food, wine and intellectual conversation that became a magnet for dissident officers as Hamilton's campaign failed and his leadership came increasingly under question. Hamilton, in effect, gave Ashmead-Bartlett the platform to be a serious gadfly to the ineptness of the expedition's leadership. Ashmead-Bartlett's lifestyle mocked Hamilton's attempts to constrain him, creating new tensions with GHQ.

Visiting K Beach to examine the proposed camp site, Ashmead-Bartlett likened it to being 'stranded on an inhospitable shore like Robinson Crusoe'. He quickly determined that the site was unsuitable. On flat, sandy soil adjacent to an army rest camp it was all heat, dirt and flies, 'unsuitable for anyone who has to concentrate their mind and endeavour to write an intelligible account of what was passing at the Dardanelles'. Instead, half a mile away, he found the perfect spot, nestling inside a grove of large trees. He pegged out a central area amongst grape vines. Told by GHQ that more correspondents were arriving, he borrowed some soldiers and had tents pitched with little paths in between. Later he obtained a large double-flyed hospital marquee to use as a mess tent. But there was no cook, although the military provided servants.

On a mission to get supplies in Malta Lawrence picked up a chef who, as Ashmead-Bartlett said, 'turned out a fair success'. The journalists bought local wine, and Ashmead-Bartlett somehow tapped some champagne supplies as well. 'Ashmead-Bartlett's camp' became famous. Bean later claimed that such was Ashmead-Bartlett's marvellous standard of living that he had not only a chef but also an international restaurant manager from Paris. Lawrence, said Bean, complained about the costs of sharing the mess at the camp 'but as always he just let Bartlett do as he wished'.

Ashmead-Bartlett also struggled to meet camp costs. Early in July he wrote to the *Daily Telegraph* that he needed 'more money', urging the paper's manager to send cash immediately as he had already borrowed £50 from Lawrence. 'Expenses will be greater than hitherto as I have to establish a camp on shore, get servants, stores and camp equipment,' he said. The newspaper was always chasing Ashmead-Bartlett to account for expenses, a common occurrence on every newspaper.

There is an interesting sidelight to Ashmead-Bartlett's camp. While he was moving from ship to ship and covering both the Anzac and Cape Helles stories he asked Lawson at the *Daily Telegraph* to equip him with a yacht. A yacht would enable him to 'get about' and be 'independent', he told Lawson. In typical style, he suggested a large and 'well provisioned' yacht, suggesting it could be hired in England and sail out to the Dardanelles. The idea, not surprisingly, was knocked on the head.

The three new correspondents were Henry Nevinson of the *Manchester Guardian*, representing the provincial press; Herbert Russell for Reuters, and Sydney Moseley of the Central News and Exchange Telegraph agencies. Phillip Schuler of the Melbourne *Age* and Charles Smith of the Melbourne *Argus* arrived later, while Keith Murdoch of the Sydney *Sun* would make a stunning, if brief, appearance in September.

Nevinson, who was 59 when he arrived at the Dardanelles, was a scholar of German literature and a confirmed pacifist despite having taken up war corresponding. Nicknamed 'The Grand Duke' because of his noble air, silver moustache and row of ribbons, he was often saluted by the troops. His description of Ashmead-Bartlett emerging from his tent in a yellow silk robe shot with crimson, and calling for breakfast as though he was still at the Carlton remains one of the best word pictures of the high-living journalist.

For Bean, nights at the camp were great fun. Apart from card games, Ashmead-Bartlett held court on his colourful experiences in school, the law courts, society and family. 'We could not have had better entertainment in London,' Bean said. 'He was the cleverest conversationalist I have ever known, and for two hours after dinner he would scintillate, urged on now and then by well-directed thrusts from Nevinson or Ross, who seemed to know exactly how to apply the necessary leverage to keep that wheel turning.'

The raconteur Ashmead-Bartlett entertained them with stories ranging from his experiences in Morocco to his disastrous investments in South American mines. Bean liked the story of how to beat bankruptcy in England. According to Ashmead-Bartlett the trick was to get the court case called exactly on time. By the time solicitors for creditors could get into court the case could be over.

Nevinson had a slightly different view. Ashmead-Bartlett liked everything 'fine and civilised', Nevinson said, so that he could entertain his 'notable guests'. But Ellis's association with the rich and great from boyhood had given him a proud self-confidence and a self-centred view of the world. As well, his scornful and often antagonising wit made him a difficult, although attractive, companion in camp.

It was Ashmead-Bartlett's camp in name and fact, said Bean. 'Things always go his way when he's about,' he said. But he recalled that in their campsite soirees Ashmead-Bartlett always deferred to the elder Nevinson, who teased him that, although he would stand for the Conservatives in Parliament, by conviction he should be on the other side. Ashmead-Bartlett admitted the truth of this. Bean always felt that Ashmead-Bartlett was a radical by intelligence but a conservative by tradition and temperament.

The new arrivals quickly picked up on the tension between Ashmead-Bartlett and Hamilton. In keeping with his divide-and-rule scheme, Hamilton called in the new correspondents, telling them they were free to go anywhere, see anything, speak to anyone and write anything. If truthful, he told them, their articles would be passed.

It seemed to work. Nevinson, an old friend, said Hamilton's 'generous amiability' was accompanied by 'deep indignation' about 'a quasi-civilian who has lately been home on leave and by his hostile criticism of the campaign has spread despondency', indicating that the general quickly tried to undermine Ashmead-Bartlett to his colleagues.

Moseley, who seemed out of his depth, said the new correspondents found a 'state of war' between Ashmead-Bartlett and Hamilton. 'All of us I think were inclined to work in with the Commander-in-Chief in the extremely trying situation,' he said. Moseley spent only a short time at Gallipoli, and was sent home ill after the other correspondents complained to Hamilton. At Gallipoli, Hamilton said Moseley just did not fit in. But later, in England, Moseley ingratiated himself into Hamilton's friendship and became a pawn in the general's battle with Ashmead-Bartlett.

Ashmead-Bartlett did not help his own cause. He was too free with details of his London visit. Other journalists took this as bragging, and it rubbed them up the wrong way. Bean, for instance, noted in his diary how Ashmead-Bartlett, over breakfast at the camp in early July, told them he had briefed leaders in London how things were going wrong. 'It seemed to me typically and exactly the thing that a War Correspondent ought not to do, but I am bound to say I think he's a competent man, though certainly inaccurate,' he said. This was obviously an early Bean view of the interchange between war correspondents and politicians. Later he would brief Prime Minister Billy Hughes on the leadership of the Australian forces on the Western Front, opposing the appointment of John Monash as Australian Corps Commander.

Compton Mackenzie took a similar view on the 'zipped lip' role of war correspondents. Whether he was right or wrong, said Mackenzie, Ashmead-Bartlett must have known he could not persuade Hamilton to change his mind. 'If he wished to remain as the only war correspondent with the Expedition, it was his duty to sacrifice his opinions with as much self-abnegation as others were sacrificing their lives.'

Questioning that sacrifice of life was obviously not a thought for Compton Mackenzie. In his *Gallipoli Memories*, the novelist recounted in somewhat condescending terms a conversation with Ashmead-Bartlett as they walked to Hunter-Weston's command on Cape Helles one day after arriving on a launch. Ashmead-Bartlett hated walking, and had failed to persuade Mackenzie to use some horses. 'So he walked alongside me, grumbling at the heat,' wrote Mackenzie.

> He had been much gratified by his reception in London, where the newspaper proprietors had received him in conclave presided over by Lord Burnham [Harry Lawson's new title] and solemnly thanked him for his Dardanelles services to Fleet Street.
> 'I was rather taken aback at first when I walked into a room at the *Daily Telegraph* editorial offices and found a large number of grave gentlemen sitting round a table. But they were very kind to me.'
> 'Were they really?'
> 'Yes, it was rather a change from the way I'm treated out here by the staff.'
> He went on to say that he hoped his visit to London would have convinced the authorities what a set of incompetent jealous self-seekers were in control at Gallipoli.
> 'I'm sure you did your best to convince them.'
> 'Well, I think I managed to open their eyes a bit to what's going on.'

Mackenzie said he began to wilt as Ashmead-Bartlett 'rasped on' about his plan for a Bulair landing. Ashmead-Bartlett told him not to be upset by his returning to Gallipoli. In fact, said Ashmead-Bartlett, Mackenzie was welcome to his job reporting for the London newspapers. 'Here I broke in hastily to insist that only on Sir Ian's orders would I have ventured to take his place, since I was too well aware of how little I knew about strategy or tactics,' Mackenzie said. 'I added I had done my best to avoid being appointed Official Eye-Witness.'

Myth Maker

'I wouldn't have minded,' Bartlett interposed contemptuously.

'I'm afraid I wasn't bothering about you, Bartlett, I was only thinking about myself.'

'In any case,' he continued, with a suggestion he was putting me on to a good thing should I care to avail myself of the tip, 'I don't think I shall stay out here much longer. It's pretty clear that the whole show is a wash out. I saw Hughes Massie, my agent, when I was in town, and he's sure he can get me an offer from America for a book about the Dardanelles. A thousand pounds advance on a straight twenty-five per cent. Not bad, eh? Hamilton and Braithwaite can stop my book in England of course, but they won't be able to stop it in America, and I'll go over there to write it if necessary.'

Mackenzie went on to tell an amusing story about how some officers didn't like Ashmead-Bartlett's style. Ashmead-Bartlett had turned back to the beach, but as Mackenzie approached the headquarters command the shrapnel started. On arrival the big guns were booming, and not a soul was in sight. As the novelist was about to dive into a dugout, the head of an officer appeared from a hole at his feet.

'Oh, it's you, Mackenzie!' he exclaimed. 'We thought it was Ashmead-Bartlett, and we didn't want to ask him to lunch,' Mackenzie reported him saying. 'He shouted jovially, and from other dugouts all round emerged the relieved faces of the Army Corps Staff.'

Whether Compton Mackenzie reported his conversation with the correspondent or not, Ashmead-Bartlett was soon summoned before Hamilton's chief of staff, Braithwaite, and 'abused' for openly criticising the conduct of the campaign. Braithwaite was imposed on Hamilton, and at Gallipoli he was seen as the power behind the vacillating general. Braithwaite's view, said John Laffin in his book, *Damn the Dardanelles*, was that the Staff always knew best.

'He [Braithwaite] declared that as a private individual I might hold what views I liked, but as a War Correspondent I had no right to any except those which were given to me officially,' said Ashmead-Bartlett. 'This really made me laugh. It is quite a new aspect of the case. I must no longer think and see for myself.'

Braithwaite's 'official drip feed only' view of the role of war reporting seemed to cut right across Hamilton's more generous views to the new arrivals. Hamilton obviously knew of the meeting, later telling Ashmead-Bartlett's editor that the correspondent acknowledged his fault and had given his word of honour not to infringe regulations again.

For his part, Ashmead-Bartlett told a different version. Braithwaite, he said, threatened to send home anyone who spoke against the conduct of the campaign. 'This was an empty threat, quite lost on me, because it would mean withdrawing the entire army from the peninsula!' Braithwaite refused Ashmead-Bartlett's request to supply the name of the informant. Ashmead-Bartlett denied he had ever criticised the Army publicly, but reserved the right to do so in private conversation. The two parted on friendly terms.

There is no doubt Hamilton was behind the threat. He wrote to Churchill on the day of the meeting that 'your old friend' Ashmead-Bartlett was going to be hauled over the coals for 'letting himself go freely' to officers. 'As such conversations tended to spread despondency and alarm, they were reported to my headquarters, and I am going to give him just one warning, and, if he disobeys it, Press or no Press, he goes right home.'

Hamilton then tried another tack — heightened censorship. On 18 July Ashmead-Bartlett was again summoned to GHQ, this time by Hamilton's chief of intelligence, Colonel Ward, who told him that an entire dispatch he had written on Lancashire landing at Cape Helles had been returned without a single line being passed by the censors. The reason given was that the story made British soldiers look afraid. Ashmead-Bartlett was astounded. He said he had only written the article to get the men on the beach landing parties some recognition.

He had shown it to some of them, he said, and they were delighted to think their service would be recognised in the press,

The real reason, Ashmead-Bartlett said, was that GHQ did not want the true position known back home. Maxwell told him there were now at least four censors on Gallipoli — himself, who takes out little or nothing; then Ward; then Braithwaite; and finally Hamilton.

'How they find time is what beats me,' said Ashmead-Bartlett. 'They all hold different views on what should be written, and each successive censor feels it his duty to take out something his predecessor has left in. Thus only a few dry bones are left for the public. The articles and cables resemble a chicken, out of which a thick nutritious broth has been extracted. One private letter was not allowed to pass because it was supposed to criticise the authorities at Malta.'

This is a revealing example of Hamilton's real views on press freedom, certainly as it applied to Ashmead-Bartlett. Hamilton even wrote privately to Lawson in a back door attempt to have the troublesome correspondent recalled. He noted, first of all, that Ashmead-Bartlett had done some 'brilliant work out here'. Then, he canvassed his own views on censorship, saying there were few soldiers in the army keener to give 'these gentlemen a free hand'. However, he had to draw the line at 'any sort or writing which could raise the morale of the Turks, lower that of our own men, or make the neutral States think less well of us than we deserve'. Ashmead-Bartlett's cancelled dispatch, he said, was pervaded by 'a spirit of depression and fear'. This is quite a stark contrast to Ashmead-Bartlett's view that the soldiers he had written about had liked the article.

Lawson replied that the Newspaper Proprietors Association was quite happy with the work of Ashmead-Bartlett.

Hamilton's hypocrisy on censorship was evident in other ways. He permitted the naming of individuals and units and he specifically told censors not to delete criticisms of his own action from reporters' dispatches. Ashmead-Bartlett found that censorship of cabled description of fights was 'excellent', and welcomed the opportunity to name regiments, brigades and divisions.

But censorship of long and descriptive letters back to papers was another matter. Whole letters were stopped, often those with no value to an enemy — the standard being applied on the Western Front. Ashmead-Bartlett warned Lawson in mid-July that the newspaper proprietors should be aware of the new difficulties of reporting from Gallipoli. 'I am afraid you will find a great falling off in the quality of my work, but this is entirely due to the censorship on letters which is the severest I have ever known, ten times more so than when I was with our Army in France,' he told Lawson.

In England after the war Hamilton made great play of claims that Ashmead-Bartlett's dispatches encouraged the Turks. He produced a debriefing report of two 'Arab Officers'. 'Mr Ashmead-Bartlett's articles in the *Daily Telegraph* used to be translated and read to the [Turkish] troops,' it quoted as information from the two. 'They had a great effect in giving them hope and courage.'

In that case one wonders what the Turkish troops thought of Ashmead-Bartlett's dispatches in the two months after his return to Gallipoli. At the very time that Hamilton was playing divide-and-rule games, and using censorship and appeals direct to his editor to have him withdrawn, Ashmead-Bartlett was perhaps at his most positive in terms of publicly reporting the campaign.

During June and July Hamilton and his Cape Helles commander Hunter-Weston mounted another series of murderous frontal attacks on Achi Baba. The official casualties on the allied side were 7700 British and 4600 French. Ashmead-Bartlett wrote of an attack on 28 June that the British Army had won 'a great local tactical victory, gaining a mile of territory, and capturing many prisoners and weapons'. The success, he said, had 'had a most inspiring effect on the whole army, and seems to open up the brightest prospects for the future if only our gunners are kept supplied with an unlimited quantity of ammunition'. Hardly a doomsayer. In the same dispatch he said that having been absent from the front for a few weeks, it

Myth Maker

appeared to him that the enemy's powers of resistance had appreciably weakened. 'It is dangerous to draw too far-reaching conclusions from outward signs, but it would seem as if the Turkish star has already passed the median,' he cabled — and it was passed. 'A long and bitter struggle may lie ahead, for the Turkish infantry are stubborn fighters and gallant men.'

The pity of this is that Hamilton responded, not just by censorship and heavy-handed tactics to get Ashmead-Bartlett sacked, but also by writing his own version of battles for the media, competing directly with the correspondents. (Ashmead-Bartlett thought these were just lies.) But Hamilton never tried to harness Ashmead-Bartlett's pen to rally support in terms of reinforcements and munitions for Gallipoli — and the potential was certainly there.

After the war Hamilton tried to condemn Ashmead-Bartlett's pessimism about the campaign by citing a letter from Charles Lister, who was in Malta when the correspondent passed through on his way back to London in June 1915, after being torpedoed on the *Majestic*. The point Hamilton wanted to focus on from the letter was Lister's fear that Ashmead-Bartlett's pessimism about the campaign could turn the whole press against Gallipoli. Lister, however, also stressed Ashmead-Bartlett's potential to help the campaign, then in dire need of reinforcements and munitions after the setbacks of the early weeks on Cape Helles. Here is the relevant extract:

> Ashmead-Bartlett has been here, home bound. He was blown up on the 'Majestic' and escaped, but without his notebooks, etc, which I believe contain scathing denunciations of all those in authority, and which are just as well at the bottom of the sea. He will talk when he gets home. I hope he will get us more men sent out; but his tone is pessimistic and his statements exaggerations, which he qualifies by about 75% in his next sentence. So perhaps they will take no notice of him.

Instead of harnessing this force, Hamilton made Ashmead-Bartlett a critic and an opponent. Censorship dictated the 'positive' cables the correspondent sent through June and July, even though he inserted cautionary notes about the strength of the Turks. Privately, Ashmead-Bartlett seethed about the incompetence of continued frontal attacks on entrenched Turkish positions, and the spin put on those attacks in Hamilton's own reports for the press. On 15 July, for instance, he wrote in his diary:

> I completed what I could put together about the latest 'big victory' in front of Achi Baba. I do not know what value these accounts will be to the Press as Sir Ian Hamilton apparently now acts as his own correspondent and sends in cables a long time ahead of ours. It is almost impossible to know what to write.

Frustrated, Ashmead-Bartlett penned a satirical version of an 'official bulletin' that could apply to all the allied attacks on Gallipoli so far. It read:

> After a concentrated bombardment, our infantry advanced against the demoralised enemy and speedily captured four lines of trenches. We were on the verge of taking Achi Baba when unfortunately something (generally the French) gave way on our right, leaving us with an exposed flank. Our centre then had to retire, suffering heavy casualties. On our left something else gave way, and the enemy was unfortunately able to reoccupy his old position. We are now back in the same line from which we started this morning. The enemy's counter-attacks were most gallantly repulsed with enormous losses. At least ten thousand of his dead are lying in front of our lines and it is reported that thirty thousand wounded have been evacuated to Constantinople. Our troops are much elated by their success, and declare

themselves ready to attack again at any time. We have made a distinct advance of at least five yards in some places.

This was the 'hopeless game' that Ashmead-Bartlett believed now characterised the Gallipoli expedition. As he moved between his camp and the battlefronts of Anzac Cove and Cape Helles he found criticisms of GHQ becoming stronger, and more open. 'Those who would not have ventured to say a word a month ago now speak their minds freely and openly,' he noted in his diary in late July. Colonel Leslie Wilson, an MP commanding the Hawk Battalion of the Naval Division, told him tales of muddle and mismanagement, adding that they were trying to get rid of him because he had influential friends. Wilson claimed orders from GHQ were seldom intelligible, and always had to be changed, modified or ignored.

Another MP, Aubrey Herbert, attached to the Anzac intelligence corps, told Ashmead-Bartlett about what the journalist believed was the most serious charge of all against GHQ — the cruelty of leaving thousands of wounded to perish between the lines. The Turks were willing to give armistices to bury the dead and collect wounded, but GHQ did not arrange them. 'They [GHQ] live with a minimum of comfort, it is true, but in complete safety, at Imbros,' wrote Ashmead-Bartlett. 'One would think that it would interfere with somebody's night's rest to know that hundreds of his fellow-countrymen were lying mutilated and unattended only a few yards away from our lines, crying for water, suffering the agonies of the damned, well knowing that their end is a long, lingering death from supperating [sic] wounds, alive with maggots, or from thirst and starvation ... I can never forgive GHQ for their attitude towards this question.'

Such was the brooding anger of many officers and of Ashmead-Bartlett as Hamilton, now supplied with new divisions, prepared to launch a daring breakout from Anzac that would end the Gallipoli stalemate. It would also serve to bring his simmering relations with the war correspondent to a head.

9

'This Should Draw All the Ladies of London'

WORLD War I coincided with a popular new mass entertainment — moving news pictures. The *Animated Gazette* and other newsreels taken on 'cinematograph' machines (film cameras) became instantly popular, a growing hit in exhibition halls and theatres as war broke out. The only other method of mass communication was the print media, and it was hardly surprising that the public initially could not get enough of filmed war scenes in this new medium.

During these early days, however, it was a business beset with all sorts of problems. Covering the 1912 Balkan war, cameramen on the Bulgarian side had been thrown into a concentration camp, while the large newsreel group Pathe received the following cable from its cameraman with the Turkish army: 'Very difficult getting pictures, no correspondents at front, have to dodge. Cannot get servants stay with me, run away when shelled. Camera body draws enemy's fire, mistaken for Maxim.'

Two years later, in World War I, film companies also confronted censorship as they rushed to cover the German invasion of Belgium and the advance of the British expeditionary army in France. Initially a total film ban was ordered, but this was later relaxed. The censors did not at first understand the potential of war footage. Meanwhile, cameramen in the field grappled with bulky cinematograph cameras, ran the risk of arrest, and were even shot at by Germans. Tripod-mounted heavy cameras also made them easy targets.

British Army Lieutenant Geoffrey Malins was one of the earliest and best cameramen. Offered the job in Belgium and France by Gaumont Graphic, another of the early newsreel companies, because their best operator was 'too valuable' to lose in combat filming, Malins returned with great material. His 12-minute *Brilliant French Victory in the Vosges* was declared the 'real thing' by *Kinematographic Weekly*.

Malins's 1914 film of soldiers knee deep in snow as shells burst around them, some dropping away wounded, was too graphic for the *Weekly Dispatch*, which condemned it as 'unfit for display', arguing pompously that only pictures that told intending recruits there was a cheerful side to war should be shown in public.

Cinema — and the accompanying growth of 'illustrated' newspapers, heavy on photographs — had immediate and significant impact on media coverage of the war. 'The newspaper may and often is coloured according to its prejudice ... The only real and incorruptible neutral in this war is not the type, but the films,' wrote W. Stephen Bush in *Moving Picture World* in September 1914.

Yet film coverage, as we have already seen, was also technically difficult. Cameras in particular posed a real problem; they were mostly fixed-tripod based with hand-cranked film mechanisms, allowing little close-up intimacy or panoramic or flexible tilting shots. The breakthrough in hand-held cameras came just before the war, with Kasimir de Proszynski's invention of the smaller Aeroscope — a cinema camera seen originally as ideal for travel and natural history filming. The Aeroscope did away with an outside handle to drive the film through the camera, replacing it with a compressed-air motor that could be charged up by an ordinary bicycle pump. By pressing a button (instead of using a crank handle) the film moved through the lens and the camera, which gave the operator freedom to accurately position and move the camera during filming. An internal gyroscope gave the cameraman a more stable picture from a hand-held position.

The Aeroscope was a remarkable invention — a revolutionary machine compared, for example, with the camera being used by the brilliant young Australian filmmaker, Frank Hurley, on his epic journey with the Shackleton expedition to the South Pole, and then his later amazing film from the Western Front. Hurley used a Box Prestwick, a tripod-fixed cinematograph. In contrast, the Aeroscope was small, weighing less than 20 pounds, and it could take 450 feet of film at a time, which meant about 8 minutes of filming.

Early film, mostly Eastman, was extremely expensive (almost 3 pence a foot) and made from celluloid, which was fragile and highly inflammable. Ashmead-Bartlett wasted much of his film stock because of his inexperience, while Lieutenant Malins improvised by designing a pocketed full body belt into which he inserted numbers of 450-foot rolls of film. If he had been shot, he would have gone up like a firecracker.

The lightweight Aeroscope may have been clumsy and bulky by today's standards, but it had already enabled Malins to shoot his dramatic footage. And it was an Aeroscope that Ashmead-Bartlett's agent, Hughes Massie, handed him in London in June 1915 and asked him to take back to Gallipoli and provide action film.

Massie was apparently acting on the suggestion of Alfred Butt, the theatrical entrepreneur who saw huge profits flowing from the new popularity of war films. Apart from the camera, Butt wanted Ashmead-Bartlett to take back 10 000 feet of film, which he would supply. 'This will be an immense load to lug around, but it will repay us, if only we are able to get some really valuable pictures and at the same time are allowed to use them,' thought Ashmead-Bartlett.

Censorship aside, taking silent film footage that satisfied public demand was already facing 'technical difficulties' just a few months after war broke out. The public, it seems, thought battlefields were all smoke-covered bayonet charges. But modern weapons were largely smokeless. Even film of an ammunition round being fed into a machine gun did not seem to have the same emotional appeal. As well, film cameras just could not easily pick up the effect of a shell explosion. Moreover, modern trench warfare was all mud and bleak, shelled landscapes, with little appeal to the new filmgoers. As Malins noted of his early experiences in Belgium, filming the fighting:

> If I had filmed this scene, all that would have been shown was a dreary waste of mud-heaps, caused by the explosion of the shells, and the graves of fallen soldiers dotted all over the place. As far as the eye could see the country was absolutely devoid of any living thing. Thousands of people in England, comfortably seated in the picture theatre, would have passed this scene by as quite uninteresting.

Film, however, continued to draw crowds, with its capacity to shock through realism and to bring home the human side of war. To meet the public demand for action footage, one newsreel company even faked the shooting down of a Zeppelin. It is easy to imagine Butt's requirement for Ashmead-Bartlett: 'Get me action and human interest!'

Ashmead-Bartlett, as always looking for new revenue streams to finance his lifestyle — and pay creditors — was 'struck' with the film proposal. But what would the authorities at Gallipoli think? First, however, he had to learn how to operate the Aeroscope. Although the 'machine' appeared very neat and compact, the difficulty was to load and unload the very volatile film. Otherwise, it worked automatically with its little air engine. 'However, for better or worse, I shall take it,' he decided. 'At any rate, it costs me nothing.'

The business deal with Butt was favourable. The theatre owner would provide the camera and film, while Ashmead-Bartlett would receive 45 per cent of the profits from screenings. Butt, Ashmead-Bartlett and Alfieri, the London photographic processing company, had also negotiated a potentially lucrative US screening contract.

The prospect of such returns might have been worth the hassle of lugging the camera and film back to Gallipoli, but Ashmead-Bartlett quickly found filming far trickier than just taking photographs, which he already did quite well. The 'infernal thing' could turn out to be the death of him, he declared. The camera was continually mistaken for either a machine gun or a patent gas machine. And the prospect of chemical warfare was a real worry on Gallipoli.

Then came the problems of operating it. The valve in the pump blew out one day 'with a terrific explosion'; and the film tins were old and the lids fitted badly, making it difficult to close them in the dark. Ashmead-Bartlett didn't know which of the two lenses to use, so he first settled for the 'big lens'. Unfortunately this was the wrong one. Initially he wasted a lot of the expensive film.

Holding the camera steady also proved a challenge, and in learning he suffered a lot of film failures. Using the Aeroscope, he found, was not like pointing his camera through a glass lens, but more like pointing a rifle through upright sights. Initially he had no darkroom, and this created the further problem of damaging film in reloading. Because the film was highly inflammable he just buried it in boxes in the ground to store them, and keep them as cool as possible.

Still, he felt he could really achieve something new by filming, and doggedly persisted. 'I should be able to get a wonderful historical record of the Expedition provided I have sufficient skill to take the pictures and the machine does not crack up, and the film does not get spoilt in placing it in the boxes without a darkroom,' he wrote in his diary.

Some relief came when he struck a deal with the expedition's official photographer, Ernest Brooks, who had some experience in cinema work, to film for him for a short period. As a sideline to his official work, Ashmead-Bartlett paid him £25 a month plus 10 per cent of screening profits, with the prospect of a deal lasting until the capture of Constantinople. Brooks, however, was soon called away on other duties (he returned later) and Ashmead-Bartlett, much to his annoyance, was thrown back on his own resources to operate the camera. He determined to conquer its mysteries:

> I sat up all one night in my tent and finally without the assistance of a red lamp or anything I got the film in the lower box, threaded it successfully and also placed

the top take-up box in position. I then managed to pump it out and put right several pieces of mechanism which had got loose or gone wrong.

Thus armed I sallied forth to the Australian position at Anzac and took a series of pictures. I stayed there three days and each night I took out the used film in a darkened dug-out and placed a new one in position with endless difficulty.

At Quinn's Post, one of the most dangerous positions on the Anzac line, the 'support cast' for this early venture into filming proved a little tetchy. Colonel William Malone, whom Ashmead-Bartlett described as a 'hardy old New Zealand officer', thought the journalist seemed 'a bit swollen headed and full of his own importance'. Malone took him to a section of the trench often hit by Turkish fire, to 'give him a thrill'.

Ashmead-Bartlett did not seem to mind, and happily filmed. His surviving film shows men in skimpy 'Anzac uniform' delivering messages in deep dugouts, which historians believe was shot at Quinn's Post. It may be grainy and somewhat stilted, but it is the only surviving footage of this historic Anzac position.

Colonel Malone aside, Ashmead-Bartlett found the 'Colonials' keen to be filmed, and have it screened back home. The film, they said, should stimulate recruiting. Ashmead-Bartlett was also keen: he saw that the constant bursting shells on Anzac beach provided dramatic footage, and spent endless hours trying to capture it on film.

The other drawcard was film of 'naked bathers running in under shell fire'. Swimming was the main relaxation for the Anzacs, and they hit the water in typical Australian style despite the shellfire. One officer joked that after all 'we have got hold of all the fashionable bathing resorts along the coast!'.

'They are a magnificent crowd these Colonials and a few hundred of them naked under fire ought to draw all the ladies of London who are not shell making,' wrote Ashmead-Bartlett in his diary. 'I did not know if you can exhibit such things in a theatre but no doubt the resources of civilization are not exhausted and your expert will be able to shove in a few faked fig leaves.'

While Ashmead-Bartlett saw them as an opportunity to arouse the ladies of London, naked Australian soldiers appealed to some in the British Army as well. The novelist Compton Mackenzie wrote this passionate prose: 'Their almost complete nudity, their tallness and majestic simplicity of line, their rose-brown flesh burnt by the sun ... all these united to create something as near to absolute beauty as I shall ever hope to see in this world'.

The real worry for Ashmead-Bartlett, however, was wartime military censorship, not nude scenes. The War Office soon began questioning his rights to take both photographs and films. As he started to send film back to London from July — he had actively filmed at Anzac and also Cape Helles — he worried not only about censorship, but what his newspaper bosses might think of his new enterprise. They knew nothing about it. 'This experiment may land me in hot water,' he fretted. 'However, there ought to be a record of events out here, and if the authorities will not send out an operator I shall carry on in my own amateurish way.'

Hamilton generously gave permission to film on the proviso that the film was censored back in England. Ashmead-Bartlett wrote to Sir Reginald Brade, Secretary of the War Office, trying to strike a deal. He wanted Brade to send the film on to Butt who, he said, would be willing to abide by any conditions. 'If they are any good as an aid to recruiting please make use of them,' he told Brade (the War Office was then using film for recruiting). 'Under no circumstances must the boxes be opened at the War Office. Otherwise the film will be all spoilt.'

The other main message Ashmead-Bartlett wanted to convey was: don't tell the newspaper proprietors. This was a private business, something Ashmead-Bartlett had going on the side — like books and possible lecture tours — that might make money. 'I am not particularly anxious they [Newspaper Proprietors Association] should be informed as some of their representatives who do not know me personally will probably say I am neglecting their interests, which is absolutely absurd because I only take these pictures to pass time in the intervals when there is little doing in the same manner in which I can take camera photographs,' he told Brade.

This is a little disingenuous of Ashmead-Bartlett, who had a potentially lucrative commercial deal with Butt for a percentage of the screening revenue. The War Office was not happy with the filming, keeping the footage sent and questioning Hamilton on what was going on. After Hamilton replied that he had given permission and Ashmead-Bartlett would be willing to come to some deal about the filming, he was told that Ashmead-Bartlett should not be allowed even to take photographs. Oddly, Hamilton told the journalist to continue.

But the sniping did not stop. In August the War Office sent Major Delme Radcliffe to the peninsula to take charge of the war correspondents, even to live with them. The outraged correspondents objected, as we shall see, but Radcliffe was soon quizzing Ashmead-Bartlett about his extracurricular activities in photography and filming. What was the carve-up of revenues on these activities?

Photography was easy to explain. Back in the early days of the expedition when he was under the control of the Admiralty, the Newspaper Proprietors Association, Alfieri Picture Services and the Admiralty had struck a deal without consulting Ashmead-Bartlett. The Admiralty took 25 per cent of sales proceeds to support the Sailor's Home, the Alfieri Syndicate took 25 per cent, and the remaining 50 per cent went to Ashmead-Bartlett. 'I do not know by what right or rule the Admiralty appropriates 25 per cent, but I have never raised any objection for two reasons, the one I am delighted to contribute this 25 per cent to some sailor's home, and the other on the general principle that it is a mistake to argue with the masters of many legions,' he told Radcliffe.

Ashmead-Bartlett was less flippant about his filming. This was purely a private concern, with none of the parties in the photography

'This Should Draw All the Ladies of London'

deal knowing about it. 'I am quite free and willing to do any equitable deal with the War Office,' he said.

But it was not to prove so simple. In August his activities were hamstrung by General Headquarters Medforce, which cabled the War Office: 'No arrangements have been made with Ashmead-Bartlett as to copyright of cinematographic films ... He [says] he was given permission ...'

The War Office replied: 'Bartlett and others should not take photographs or cinematographic films for reproduction ... no authorisation to do so was given'.

The National Press Association was incensed. Sir George Riddell pointed out: 'It was expressly arranged with the Admiralty when he [Ashmead-Bartlett] was appointed, that he should be permitted to take photos'. But the War Office was not to be deterred. It replied: 'We understand that steps have been taken to inform Mr Ashmead-Bartlett that the privileges he enjoyed have been withdrawn'.

It is clear that Ashmead-Bartlett's film footage from the Dardanelles then received a savage mauling from both the War Office and the Official Press Bureau censors. The bulk of his footage was seized and never released. Decades later, stored boxes of the film were unearthed by an historical researcher, Phillip Dutton of the Imperial War Museum, but the film had completely deteriorated.

By September 1915 the War Office censor wrote in justification to Sir Frank Swettenham of the Press Bureau: 'Recently ... certain accredited correspondents have sent back photos and cinematic films to be forwarded to individual agencies. This creates a monopoly, which is most undesirable ...' The War Office cabled Mediterranean Command, stopping all correspondents taking photos and films.

Correspondence raged between newspaper proprietors, entrepreneurs, the Alfieri film production company and other news agencies. Given the controversy and the censorship, it is amazing that any of Ashmead-Bartlett's unique Gallipoli film footage even reached the British and Australian public of the day, not to mention its survival for future generations.

Filming was not the only media activity where Ashmead-Bartlett found his own commercial deals might conflict with his newspaper masters. While he was in London in June his agent Hughes Massie struck a deal with publisher Hutchinson for Ashmead-Bartlett to write a book on Gallipoli. But as censorship tightened Ashmead-Bartlett realised that a book would not be allowed until the war ended, or the allies captured Constantinople. He began toying with a book that would have 'far greater sale', not just a rehash of his Gallipoli dispatches.

Gallipoli was too vast a subject, too great to spoil by haste, he wrote to Hughes Massie, seeking a new understanding with Hutchinson for a longer term book. The Dardanelles campaign, he felt, would arouse bitter controversies for centuries — a forecast that certainly applied to Australia, but not Britain. Ashmead-Bartlett wanted a more measured view of the campaign, not one produced 'red hot' like most war books. And he would have a lot to say as his most interesting articles had not been allowed to be published 'and even those that have bare [sic] but a very scant relationship to the bare and naked truth'.

Meanwhile, the Newspaper Proprietors Association certainly wanted a 'red hot' Gallipoli book, surprising Ashmead-Bartlett with a plan for a shilling book based on his published reports, perhaps including Sir Ian Hamilton's dispatches then appearing in newspapers.

Ashmead-Bartlett was keen to appease Hutchinson with his idea for a longer term book — eventually published as *The Uncensored Dardanelles* in 1928 — while believing the shilling book of his dispatches would help its eventual sale. But he wanted a payment for the quickie, and after a flurry of letters about the royalty rights to his dispatches, the newspaper publishers agreed to pay him a penny per copy of the book sold. It was quickly published in 1915 as Ashmead-Bartlett's *Despatches from the Dardanelles*, with no input from Hamilton.

Although he had no agreement with the War Office, Ashmead-Bartlett continued filming through the big August attempted breakout from Anzac, coupled with a new landing at Suvla Bay, just north of the Australians. It almost cost him his life.

Late one afternoon he was trying to film Turkish artillery fire on Chocolate Hill at Suvla Bay, which British troops had been fighting to take. He set up the Aeroscope above the parapet of a partly destroyed trench to get a panoramic shot of bushfires started by the shelling. Turkish gunners were on to him straight away. A shell whizzed past his head and hit the back of the trench without exploding. Ashmead-Bartlett could not believe the enemy's gunners could be so quick. Then came another. 'I saw a bright flash and found myself in total darkness,' he wrote later. 'I struggled to get clear but realised that I was buried. Shortly afterwards a spot of light appeared and I became conscious that I was being dug out. My benefactor turned out to be a soldier who had seen my mishap and immediately ran to my assistance.'

On being dug out, Ashmead-Bartlett found the fuse of a high explosive lying on his legs. Somehow, he escaped without a scratch. But not so his belongings. His small camera, walking stick, field glasses, water bottle and coat, which he had left in a pile, had been blown to pieces.

'The infernal old cinema [camera], of which I was now heartily tired, the cause of all my troubles, had, of course, survived and I was reluctantly compelled to drag it back to camp.'

The 'infernal old cinema' continued to plague him. When he returned to London in October he left the Aeroscope with Brooks, asking him to continue filming. But the War Office stalled on releasing any of the film for public exhibition. In November, when Ashmead-Bartlett sent Mrs Brooks a cheque for £25 for her husband he told her there could still be a 'lot of money' in the venture. 'I dare say you know the matter has to be kept quiet as Mr Brooks is really working for the Admiralty, so please keep this letter private,' he told her.

Eventually, the War Office released some of the film, which the Empire Theatre screened at a selected showing in early January 1916, shortly after Gallipoli was evacuated. 'Convincingly genuine,' said the Evening Standard's reviewer, remarking on the lack of official parade ground uniforms on the peninsula. The footage of Australian troops repulsing an attack 'were sights that fired the blood and made a man itch to be taking his share'.

'The lean, hard but good humoured faces of the Anzacs, the kick of the rifles, the men who are squatting down in the bottom of the trench preparing cartridge clips while the others fire, the pressing home of the clips — all this is seen as though in real life. And alas! So many of the men who figure in these pictures have now "gone west". It is a pity there is not a more complete pictorial record of their splendid work.'

The *Daily Sketch* said the obvious excitement and reality of the film brought a 'sharp thrill to the most cold-blooded'. The *Daily Mirror* said it had 'touched us deeply' to see our heroes 'at their daily avocations'.

The *Daily Express* had the most poignant comment. It said the fighting scenes were not just thrilling but real to the point where one commentator in the audience wondered whether the fighting was staged.

Thereby hangs a tale. Ashmead-Bartlett and Brooks were at the Suvla Bay fighting on 2 September. A tent they had erected near the Chocolate Hill front had been removed as it served as a rangefinder for Turkish artillery. So they carried the Aeroscope out into the front trenches, where the Turks were only about 50 yards away, looking for pictures. They almost caused a major battle. Finding what Ashmead-Bartlett said was an Irish battalion, Brooks asked them to pose as if they were resisting an attack. The men looked at the cinema camera instead. 'That's not realistic enough,' Brooks complained. 'I'll make it realistic,' shouted an Irishman, turning and shooting at the Turks. His comrades joined in. The Turks, thinking an attack was imminent after a relatively quiet day, replied with a fusillade.

'A sustained duel then began and in the excitement the Irishmen forgot all about us,' said Ashmead-Bartlett. 'Soon the Turkish artillery joined in, and it looked as if we had started a battle all along the line.'

Brigade Headquarters was quickly on the line to find out what the hell was going on. 'Oh, nothing, Sir,' replied one of the Irish NCOs, 'it is only the cinema'.

Ashmead-Bartlett had his action footage, but he was mortified. 'I thought the matter had gone far enough, so we crept away to avoid the wrath of the divisional headquarters.'

The footage, complete with a brief glimpse of Ashmead-Bartlett himself crawling along behind the firing line, remains controversial to this day. Were they Irish or Australian soldiers in the firefight? When the film arrived in Australia in March 1916 it was released by Fraser Films with the injunction in an advertisement in the Sydney *Sun*: 'Something every Australian wants to see'. *Ashmead-Bartlett's Pictures of the Dardanelles*, as it was billed, were taken, the advertisement thrilled, with no ordinary tripod camera but one 'worked by clockwork and steadied by a gyroscope'. And it showed, amongst the landing parties, trenches and dugouts 'Aussies in the Firing Line'.

The Australian War Records Section in London searched for film of Gallipoli in 1919. Brooks told them he did not know of any footage other than that taken by Ashmead-Bartlett and himself. Certainly there is no live footage shot of the landing on 25 April 1915. Ashmead-Bartlett put the Australian researchers in touch with Butt, assuring them that the footage included 'an excellent picture of fighting at close range between the trenches, which is not a fake but perfectly genuine and was taken at a distance of about 30 yards from the enemy's line'.

Ashmead-Bartlett offered to write captions for the film acquired from Butt, but the task was undertaken in 1919 by Charles Bean, by then Australia's official historian of the war. For a journalist and historian known as a stickler for facts, Bean's captions are certainly odd. They claim the footage was taken between May and August 1915. But Ashmead-Bartlett did not acquire the camera until June, so this must be incorrect.

Bean also captioned the firefight as 'Australians firing from newly won positions'. Historians are divided, while Ashmead-Bartlett's own records appear to say conclusively that the soldiers were Irish.

Other questions remain about Bean's treatment of the film. The 20 minutes held by the Australian War Memorial, titled *With the Dardanelles Expedition: Heroes of Gallipoli*, is the result of his editing as well as caption writing. Did he edit it to preserve the Anzac legend, asked George Imashev, a former curator of film and sound at the Australian War Memorial, in an article in the memorial's *Wartime* magazine. Bean suppressed material incompatible with his view of the Anzac spirit, argued Imashev, and could well have done the same with film. In the same vein, some film historians question whether Bean deliberately juxtaposed shots of English officers taking tea with 'Australians' — or Irishmen — in the firing line to underline the popular belief that the Australians were poorly led at Gallipoli. If he did, any film edited out has been lost.

One explanation for the confusion over the firefight may be that Australians, keen to see moving film of their soldiers in action, as the 1916 Sydney *Sun* advertisement shows, just jumped to the wrong conclusion. Certainly Ashmead-Bartlett's moving description of the landing created a box office boom as movie producers rushed to meet public enthusiasm for the story.

Within a few months of the landing, two locally made feature films, both featuring a re-enactment of the landing, were showing. Alfred Rolfe's *A Hero of the Dardanelles* was partly a recruitment propaganda film, shot with hundreds of troops supplied from Liverpool Barracks in Sydney, and the Army generously providing the appropriate shelling. The troops stormed ashore at Tamarama beach in Sydney in scenes that were publicised as 'most graphically and faithfully portrayed in accordance with Ashmead-Bartlett's historic despatch'. There was no doubting either the inspiration for the film or the public appeal of Ashmead-Bartlett's story.

It was quickly followed by *Within our Gates* or *Deeds that Won Gallipoli*, a J.C. Williamson drama of German agents in Australia which also featured a re-enactment of the Gallipoli landing, this time staged at Obelisk Bay near Sydney. Hundreds of bayonet-wielding troops leapt ashore and charged up the hill, attacking Turks along the way.

In the late 1920s came *Daughter of the East* (*The Boys of the Dardanelles*) and *The Spirit of Gallipoli*. The latter recycled footage of one of the earlier films, while *Daughter* featured fighting scenes shot on the sand hills at Maroubra, a Sydney beachside suburb.

It is staged landing scenes from these early feature films that television networks regularly screen with Gallipoli programs — usually with no explanation.

The early feature films were very patriotic. But by the 1980s Peter Weir's popular *Gallipoli* was seen by some critics as an anti-war film. It dramatically highlights the waste of young men's lives at the Nek, when the Australian 8th Light Horse perished in futile open charges to support the August Suvla breakout. The subtext of Weir's film is a popular angle of the Gallipoli story for Australians — the incompetence of English officers.

While Ashmead-Bartlett made a remarkable contribution to this theme in his writings, his film does not push this point, subject to any later possible juxtaposing of English officers taking tea and 'Australians' fighting. To the modern viewer its very silence comes as something of a shock that rivets the attention. Bean's captions add that silent era feel, although his actual words tell us little of what is actually happening.

The film reveals a reality of Gallipoli quite different from popular conceptions, with the Anzacs cramped in tunnelled dugouts on a hillside not unlike an old goldmining town. The everyday life, delivered messages, swimming, eating and the unloading of troops, equipment and donkeys brings home the grind of the eight-month occupation against impossible odds. The hillside 'village' created by the Australians and shown in the film has now disappeared.

Staged firefight or not, it was still a real exchange with the Turks. Whether Australian or Irish troops are pictured, it is the only close-up footage of an actual Gallipoli battle. Indeed, Phillip Dutton of the Imperial War Museum says the 18-second firefight is 'possibly the first authentic example of British Commonwealth troops in combat in the First World War'.

Myth Maker

Madeleine Chaleyer, senior curator of film and sound at the Australian War Memorial, believes she has found snippets of Ashmead-Bartlett's footage in at least one other compilation of World War I film. But the 20-minute *Heroes of the Dardanelles* — digitally remastered in 2005 by Peter Jackson's (director of *Lord of the Rings*) Weta Digital special effects company in New Zealand — remains all we have of a cinema version of Gallipoli. As Charles Bean noted, it is a 'priceless' piece of Australian heritage.

10

'They Cannot Long Conceal the Truth from the Public'

'**WENT** to GHQ. Had final row with Braithwaite. Ordered to return home.'

Ashmead-Bartlett's succinct diary entry for 28 September 1915 tells tidily how the tensions that had been building for months came to an explosive head. The consequences would help end the Gallipoli expedition and have far-reaching implications for the careers of its leader, General Sir Ian Hamilton, and his journalist gadfly, Ellis Ashmead-Bartlett.

The immediate cause was Ashmead-Bartlett's attempt to smuggle a letter to Prime Minister Herbert Asquith telling him the truth, as he saw it, of what was happening at Gallipoli, using the Australian journalist Keith Murdoch as an intermediary. Ashmead-Bartlett felt the truth was being suppressed, both by censorship of the correspondents and Hamilton's own jaunty, coloured dispatches.

Although Hamilton and Ashmead-Bartlett later became bitter opponents, on the surface relations on Gallipoli remained cordial right up until the journalist's expulsion. Hamilton, always the somewhat stiff but courteous gentleman, remained available to the small press corps, with his professed liberal views on press freedom lulling them into a false security. Yet slowly controls tightened. Apart from censorship, the correspondents discovered that senior officers had been instructed not to talk to them. 'Another petty way of annoying us,' said Ashmead-Bartlett.

Then, on 2 August, Major Delme Radcliffe had turned up at their camp, announcing that he had been sent out by the War Office to take charge of all war correspondents — and live in their camp. The correspondents were horrified. 'This is the blow I felt has been hanging over us for so long, and which may mean the curtailment of all our freedom of movement,' wrote Ashmead-Bartlett in his diary. 'If this is the case and we are made to go around in a body, I shall not stay long, but shall return home.'

Whatever the War Office's aims on Gallipoli, such cocooning would shortly become its preferred method of operating a small group of war correspondents on the Western Front. There, they were moved around in a group. They lived and worked together as a virtual propaganda unit, with censors and guides. The journalists had limited access to the front lines, always accompanied by military guides. All cabled back their censored dispatches on the same day after receiving the latest official information on battles. It was a style of 'embedded' war reporting that cut right against Ashmead-Bartlett's preference for freedom to just roll around and report on what he saw, albeit accepting some censorship.

The Gallipoli press camp held a little conclave that night — minus Sydney Moseley — with Ross, Nevinson and Ashmead-Bartlett deciding to call on Hamilton to protest the following day. 'I felt it necessary to strike before any new rules and regulations are made,' said Ashmead-Bartlett.

Censorship was not their only grievance. They all objected to Moseley, who seemed completely out of his depth, but sadly also because he was in poor health and just did not fit in. Ashmead-Bartlett rudely dismissed him as a 'terrible little Jew boy'.

The three called on Hamilton next day, with Nevinson, the senior correspondent, deputed to speak. Hamilton, then planning the big August breakout, appeared happy to see them. Nevinson told him of their fears of curtailment, while Ashmead-Bartlett added snidely, 'especially as some members of the party are not at all agreeable to us', a reference no doubt to both Radcliffe and Moseley.

Hamilton expressed surprise at Radcliffe's arrival. It was without his knowledge or sanction, he said, declaring this officer would neither take over the censorship duties nor live in the correspondents' camp. 'I will promise you [that] you shall have absolute freedom of movement and that nothing shall be done to curtail the privileges you have enjoyed in the past,' he told them. 'It is the last thing in the world I desire.'

And as for Moseley, Hamilton agreed that the Central News Agency correspondent had spent little time in the battle zones. Moseley, he said, was 'no use here so I shall send him back'. This was a shameless piece of prejudice and snobbery by Hamilton as well as the journalists.

'Absolute freedom' may have been Hamilton's public face, but in private it was different. He and GHQ kept scathing personal files on the correspondents, which were sent to the War Office. The correspondents in turn suspected they were being spied upon. GHQ files show what Hamilton really thought:

> Ashmead-Bartlett: 'A well-known war correspondent who possesses considerable gifts, and is able to write despatches on military events with great clearness and descriptive powers. Unfortunately he is not to be trusted. He has the habit of criticism and sees everything from a most pessimistic standpoint. On this account many of his despatches have had to be severely censored. Besides this, his tone when speaking to officers and men is most improper ...'
>
> Sydney Moseley: 'This gentleman is quite unsuitable to be attached to a British Army in the capacity of a war correspondent. He is unfitted to associate on terms of social equality with officers or his fellow correspondents. The latter very strongly resented his presence in their camp.'
>
> Keith A. Murdoch: 'He does not pretend to be, and would not be suitable for employment as an actual war correspondent. After he left, it transpired that he had

made himself an accessory to Mr Ashmead-Bartlett in a breach of the regulation by secretly conveying home for the latter an uncensored despatch. In view of Mr Murdoch's abuse of the trust reposed in him it appears advisable that he should not again be allowed to visit any of the Armies in the field.'

Henry Nevinson: 'May be described as a valuable war correspondent, who is at the same time a man of literary mark. Advancing age, however, has, it is believed, decided Mr Nevinson to abandon work in the field.'

As for Lester Lawrence of Reuters, Hamilton dismissed him in a letter to Kitchener as 'hopelessly inefficient'. Lawrence, he said, hardly saw anything. 'I mean he is extremely shortsighted, and has, moreover, no more understanding of military matters or the difference between a British soldier and a Turkish soldier, or between a field gun and a 9.2, than my boot.'

Apart from Nevinson, only the Australasian trio of Bean, Phillip Schuler and Malcolm Ross, with their focus of reporting on their national troops, drew any accolades. Bean, with his future history project in mind, lived more on Anzac Cove than at the press camp on Imbros Island.

For Ashmead-Bartlett the Gallipoli 'round' meant regular trips to Anzac and Cape Helles, spending a day or two there and then returning to write up his story. It was hazardous work, with the Turks shelling the supply boats as well as the forces ashore. Both Nevinson and Bean were wounded, with Ellis being buried in that one shelling incident and almost struck in another.

In contrast to the sniping at GHQ, Anzac was always a pleasure to visit. 'It is the one spot where the army has confidence in its general [Birdwood], who is immensely popular with his men,' Ellis said. It also provided great copy. In July he cabled back a long report that helped burnish the growing Anzac legend. The Australians, he wrote, had just about shed all their clothing. While the typical Tommy carried around his worldly goods, sitting in trenches with his pack on, it was extremely rare to find an Australian in anything more than a pair of shorts. 'In this primitive costume the Australians and New Zealanders live and work and fight,' he wrote. 'Their huge frames and giant limbs are now burnt by the sun to a dull brick red. Some learned ethnologist, suddenly here for the first time, would hardly classify them as belonging to Aryan stock; rather would he believe he had suddenly discovered a surviving branch of that race of red men who swarmed over the plains of America until swept away by the ancestors of the present-day shell-makers.'

London newspapers played it up. 'Nakedest army ever seen in the field' headlined one. 'The Dardanelles army in knickers' said another. In the same report, Ashmead-Bartlett discovered a Western Australian miner who claimed the countryside was so much like home that he had even found some gold. He also reported on the individualistic streak of the Australians, with one work party refusing to be relieved until they had finished their task. 'Democracy in the trenches,' one London newspaper headlined his report.

Life at the correspondents' camp wasn't all writing copy. Ashmead-Bartlett fielded a stream of letters. One woman pleaded with him to mention the New Zealanders more. There was also correspondence about his books as well as a possible lecture tour. And the London papers, as usual, chased him about his expense accounts.

Still, life was tolerable. 'But for the flies and the heat and the bad food it is not unpleasant out here,' he told Harry Lawson in July, midsummer in the Mediterranean. With typical journalistic ingenuity, he found some extra luxuries. Along with a group of officers he discovered the pleasures of a small naval monitor that arrived in early August. The shallow-draft monitors were designed to provide heavy fire support without risking battleships and their large crews. This one, captained by Philip de Crespigny, seemingly contained an Aladdin's Cave of food and drink. 'No ship ever left England so completely fitted out for a crusade,' wrote Ashmead-Bartlett admiringly. 'You could obtain everything you had dreamt about for months on board this vessel. Champagne, liquors, cocktails, port, sherry and every species of cordial for hot climates. His store-house was packed with the choicest viands, caviar in tins, foie gras, hams, tongues, potted meats, and preserves of every known brand and variety. Where the ship carries her ammunition, if she carries any at all, beats me. He is going to see plenty of me this summer.'

It was on a visit to Anzac that Ashmead-Bartlett heard for the first time of Birdwood's proposed plan for the new invasion, using the divisions Hamilton had wrung from Kitchener. A great fan of Birdwood, the English general in charge of the Australasians, Ashmead-Bartlett saw him showing exactly the leadership that Hamilton lacked. 'He is a remarkable man, for he sets his troops a personal example in everything; bathing with them, living among them, visiting the trenches, eating their food, undergoing inoculation against every species of complaint as an example for others to follow.' Later, in a long article on Birdwood, he styled him as the 'soul' of Anzac. In early July Birdwood confided in him the scheme he was working up for a breakout from the enclave. Pledging Ashmead-Bartlett to secrecy — Hamilton had not yet accepted it — Birdwood said he envisaged a left hook out of Anzac, coupled with a fresh landing at Suvla Bay just north. These two thrusts would then get astride the Sari Bair ridge that dominates the peninsula, and advance on the Dardanelles Strait to capture the forts and allow the allied navy to pass through to take Constantinople.

Birdwood conceded the difficulty of the Australians getting out of Anzac with the Turks right on top of them. It could not be done by a regular attack. The Australians and New Zealanders would have to first move along the shore and then scale their craggy objective.

Ashmead-Bartlett was horrified. 'How can the Australians successfully debouch from a position like Anzac and storm these hills?' he puzzled. 'To me it is an utterly impracticable operation of war and one which will only lead to fresh reverses and enormous losses. I have never heard of troops being asked to perform such a strange feat of arms before.' With the Turks now reinforced, he felt that 'man for man' they were the equal of the allies. A landing place in Suvla Bay would only provide a fresh beach, and a new bathing place. With the Suvla hinterland broken and unknown country, all the old difficulties would repeat themselves in an advance inland. 'After two or three days a complete stalemate will arise,' he forecast.

Such gloomy prescience proved chillingly accurate, unfortunately at the cost of thousands of casualties. But Hamilton embraced the plan, dismissing a Bulair landing, as Ashmead-Bartlett passionately advocated, as 'absolutely out of the question' from a naval or military viewpoint.

Hamilton, incidentally, also dismissed a really quirky Ashmead-Bartlett idea: bribing Turkish soldiers to desert by offering ten shillings and a pardon. 'This makes one wonder what Ashmead-Bartlett himself would do if he were offered ten shillings and a good supper by a Mahommedan when he was feeling a bit hungry and hard up amongst the Christians,' he angrily wrote in his diary. The very idea of a bribe seemed to unsettle the very proper Hamilton. It would 'rebound in shame upon our heads,' he said.

For Hamilton, the breakout plan arrived as he appeared to be going through a Pauline conversion against the old-fashioned concept of frontal assaults right along a line. 'The old battle tactics have clean vanished,' he wrote to Kitchener a month before the breakout. 'I have only quite lately realised the new conditions . . . To attack all along the line is perfect nonsense — madness.'

On the eve of the breakout in early August Radcliffe, still in charge of the correspondents although now located at GHQ, sent Lawrence and Moseley to Cape Helles to witness the diversionary attack there, assigning Nevinson and Ashmead-Bartlett to the Suvla Bay landing. The essence of the attack was speed. The troops of Kitchener's 'New Army' would come ashore at Suvla, protected in new bullet-proof 'beetles', and quickly advance towards the Anafarta Hills.

Aboard the liner *Minneapolis* off Suvla Bay, Ashmead-Bartlett indulged his flair for reporting the bizarre. Going down to breakfast he found an old steward carefully vacuuming the stairs. 'How strange that the stewards should clean the carpets of an Atlantic liner when the fate of Constantinople was hanging in the balance,' he wrote in a long feature article for the British press. 'But such is the force of habit and discipline on the humble mind.'

At a breakfast of iced melons, fish, eggs and bacon, the mood was quiet except for the roar of the guns. One gunnery colonel, whose men and artillery were already ashore, broke the silence. 'This is a strange way of carrying on war,' he said. 'Here I am sitting eating my breakfast, and at the same time watching my batteries going into action.' It was a metaphor for the failed invasion. Its commander, the ailing Lieutenant General Sir Frederick Stopford, took it upon himself to change the priority to securing the landing, rather than hastening inland to capture the Anafarta Hills. In an incredible lapse of leadership Hamilton turned a blind eye until it was too late. By the time he forced Stopford into action the Turks had rushed in reinforcements and the allies never captured the hills.

For Ashmead-Bartlett the writing was on the wall from the beginning. 'There seemed to be no decision or life about the movement of our men, even at this early hour,' he wrote in his diary after the landing. 'Instead of advancing, the army was crawling parallel to the Anafarta Hills, as if loathe to seize its objectives. At every halt the men fell asleep in spite of the shells and snipers. Exhaustion and thirst were already beginning to tell on these new formations. No firm hand appeared to control this mass of men suddenly dumped on an unknown shore.'

Going ashore, Ashmead-Bartlett tapped out his first dispatch of the Suvla Bay landing with his typewriter perched on ammunition boxes on the beach, using other ammunition boxes as a chair. A picture of him working away on his ammunition box furniture while soldiers look on must rank as the quintessential snap of a war correspondent. He was initially fairly upbeat, concentrating on the success of the actual landing rather than the failure to push inland. He ended his cable, however, on an ominous note. 'The Turks were taken by surprise,' he said. 'Their reserves have not yet come up and their main position is still intact.'

Stopford was soon headquartered on his sloop offshore. More delay followed. 'The atmosphere became depressing,' said Ashmead-Bartlett privately. 'One could not help feeling that the offensive had suddenly come to a standstill, that the "punch" had gone out of the attack.' The British occupied some early points such as Chocolate Hill, but appeared disorganised by thirst, Turkish shellfire and snipers, mounting only spasmodic attacks on the major objective of Scimitar Hill.

Nevinson, who covered the new landing in tandem with Ashmead-Bartlett, returned from a scouting mission very discouraged. 'Our infantry are demoralised, weary and absolutely refuse to advance,' he told Ellis. 'The muddle is beyond anything I have ever seen.'

Ashmead-Bartlett witnessed thirst-maddened troops rushing into the sea and swallowing sea water. 'The troops were hunting for water, the staffs were hunting for their troops, and the Turkish snipers were hunting for their prey,' he wrote. Late one evening he found Hamilton standing all by himself, worriedly looking at the piles of smoke arising from smouldering fires along the Anafarta front. 'To the commander-in-chief it must have been obvious at this hour that his final effort to reach the Narrows had failed.'

Hamilton finally raised Stopford's force to action and, after they had occupied points such as Chocolate Hill, an attack was eventually launched on Scimitar Hill. Watching from a vantage point on Chocolate Hill, Ashmead-Bartlett noted that where the day before he had seen one Turk now there seemed ten, crowded into trenches.

The British attack advanced quite well, forcing the Turks to evacuate some trenches. But concentrated Turkish artillery stopped them. The mass of British troops 'wavered, began to move in circles, and finally to disintegrate and rush back down the slope,' he wrote in his diary. The surprised Turks quickly reoccupied the trenches.

Ashmead-Bartlett rushed back to his Imbros camp to write a new dispatch. 'I spent the whole day trying to minimise our defeat at

Myth Maker

Suvla, an almost impossible task,' he wrote. It is a revealing line. For a correspondent classified as untrustworthy by Hamilton, Ashmead-Bartlett had known about the Suvla attack for some weeks without writing about it, and then tried to gloss over the disaster.

On Imbros he caught up with the news about the Anzac breakout and the diversionary attack on Achi Baba at Helles. The latter had failed, while at Anzac he learnt the dominion troops had 'fought splendidly ... but have lost out of all proportion to the results achieved', as he wrote in his diary.

In a lucky break, Malcolm Ross, the New Zealand journalist, had left him a spirited account of the actions of his own countrymen. Crediting Ross fully for the information, Ashmead-Bartlett penned a stirring report on how the New Zealanders reached near the crest of Chunuk Bair on the vital ridge.

'Although few in numbers they closed on the Turks with fury, using their rifles as clubs, swinging them around their heads and laying out several with each sweep', his dispatch read. 'The Turks could not stand this rough treatment, and those who were not killed or wounded fled, and the New Zealanders began hastily to dig themselves in. So far this was the finest feat in the fighting, and the highest point yet gained by any troops in the peninsula.'

The London papers played it up. 'Maori warriors charge the enemy with clubbed rifles and bayonets' headlined one, splashing the 'thrilling despatch' across its front page. Charles Bean later questioned the accuracy of the club-wielding Maoris report, which Ashmead-Bartlett said he had picked up from New Zealand officers to add to Ross's account.

On Imbros, Ashmead-Bartlett found depression reigned amidst reports of colossal losses on all fronts. He fretted about heightened censorship. 'There is great difficulty in getting off our despatches,' he wrote. 'No one knows how much of the disaster should be allowed to pass and how much be suppressed. I admit that it is very difficult for the censors, but they cannot long conceal the real truth from the public.'

Some newspapers in London were beginning to think the same. The *Times* acidly noted the difference between an Ashmead-Bartlett censored account and an earlier rosy Press Bureau report that had led the public to believe that the new landings threatened the Turks and left them in a critical position. Yet there was nothing in Ashmead-Bartlett's report or subsequent official statements to justify this. The only conclusion to be drawn was that nothing had changed on Gallipoli after the new attacks. 'Why is it that the general effect of [the censor's] handiwork is to suppress the disagreeable truth and to pass the cheerful falsehoods?' the *Times* asked.

After a quick return visit to Suvla, where he learnt that Stopford had been recalled, Ashmead-Bartlett and Nevinson went to Anzac to glean first-hand details of the failed breakout. Anzac had now changed, Ashmead-Bartlett reflected. Before it had been like a 'gay, heavily populated city full of life and hope'. Now, with nearly half of Birdwood's army melted away from death, wounds and disease, the men's physiognomy seemed to have changed.

'They no longer carry themselves with that confident air of assurance formerly so marked amongst the men from "Down Under",' he wrote. 'Anzac seems to have gone through some terrible illness and to have aged. Everyone looks older and drawn. They have the air of men resigned to their fate, but who are determined to see the matter through. There is still the grim decision, but the hope and expectancy has altogether vanished.' The hard reality facing the Anzacs was that they had pushed the Turks higher up the craggy hills only to have the enemy still looking down on them from impregnable lairs. The feeling was that so much sacrifice had been made in vain and that no hope remained. Now the troops were faced with weary months in winter trenches.

'No wonder that mysterious moral force no longer sustains the Dominion troops,' he wrote in his diary. 'Before the last advance hardly a man reported sick. Now hundreds daily pass before the doctor and have to be evacuated from the peninsula. The fifth act has ended in tragedy after the splendid opening and months of fierce combat to consolidate the position. Where is it all going to end? That is what everyone at Anzac is asking today. To this question no one can reply.'

If these were Ashmead-Bartlett's private thoughts — and after the terrible losses in attacks on Lone Pine and the Nek the mood among the Anzacs would be understandable — they did not appear in his censored dispatches. Indeed, in a new report describing how the New Zealanders and Gurkhas reached some of the heights but were driven back, he said the men did not seem at all downhearted. They claimed they were willing to have another go, he reported.

Ashmead-Bartlett's analysis of the Turkish counter-attack against the Anzac flanking movement received a huge play in the London press. 'Generals fight with rifles' said several headlines as Ashmead-Bartlett reported how the allied forces were forced back after capturing new ground. The Turks, he said, had fought with desperate courage, realising the precariousness of their position if the allies gained the ascendancy between Chunuk Bair and Q Hill. Only the 'magnificent conduct' of the allied officers saved the situation:

> Generals and Colonels fought with rifles and bayonets alongside their troops in the firing line. It was a fierce hand-to-hand struggle among the scrub through broken ground, in which no man knew how his comrade was faring. Many commanding officers were killed, including General Baldwin, who had throughout these four days set a splendid example to his men. Gradually the enemy was driven back and the ground we had been obliged to abandon regained.

Ashmead-Bartlett's prose reached a new level when he described how the Empire's soldiers were lying dead between the lines at the highest point yet reached on the peninsula:

> Thus closed for the time being amid these blood-stained hills the most ferocious and sustained soldiers' battle since Inkerman. But Inkerman was over in a few hours,

whereas these Englishmen, Australians, New Zealanders, Gurkhas, Sikhs and Maoris kept up this terrible combat with the Turks for four consecutive days and nights amid hills, dongas, and ravines 900ft above the sea, to which point all water, rations, and ammunition had to be borne along paths which do not exist except on the map and down which every man who fell wounded had to be borne in the almost tropical heat of August in the Mediterranean.

Hamilton and his chief of staff Braithwaite were much subdued when they met the three remaining correspondents — Ashmead-Bartlett, Nevinson and Lawrence — back on Imbros after both the Anzac breakout and the Suvla landing had stalled. Finding them 'particularly amiable', Ashmead-Bartlett noted that generals often felt the need of friends after setbacks in the field.

Success had 'almost been in our grasp' Hamilton told them, maintaining an outward upbeat appearance. The Gurkhas had actually reached the summit of Chunuk Bair and were chasing the Turks down the other side when they were driven off by the fire from British warships. The Navy later hotly disputed his claim. This was the second time Hamilton had given the press his 'near success' line. Following the disastrous attacks on Krithia in June Hamilton had said, 'we came within an ace of victory'.

Ashmead-Bartlett found Hamilton's contention of near success amazing, and tried to pin him with a question: Could the Anzacs have held the crest of Chunuk Bair if the enemy maintained his artillery on W Hill in the Anafarta heights, which the British at Suvla failed to take? It was a pertinent question, pointing up the failure of the British to take the Anafarta Hills and stop some of the artillery fire as crucial to the collapse of the Anzac breakout. 'No,' Hamilton replied, telling him that the Turks actually withdrew their guns from W Hill when the British landed at Suvla, but returned them when the advance failed to develop.

The generals then surprised the correspondents. Be ready for further movements, they told them, indicating a fresh attack on the Anafarta Hills. 'They do not stand a dog's chance,' thought Ashmead-Bartlett privately.

It was the last great attack of the Gallipoli expedition, summed up in the *Daily Express* headline of Ashmead-Bartlett's report: 'Splendid failure at the Dardanelles, Hill-top positions won and lost because a corps arrived too late'. Hamilton threw whatever remnants of his new divisions he could cobble together into this last major attack on the Anafarta Hills. The much punished 29th Division was even brought up from Cape Helles. Ashmead-Bartlett thought this 'really beating a willing horse to death'.

The attack was almost as disastrous for the correspondents as it was for the British Army, which was pushed back after initially appearing to hold Scimitar Hill. A final charge of yeomen (rural volunteers), who had just arrived, also failed after a promising start. Watching from Chocolate Hill, Ashmead-Bartlett was buried when a shell exploded nearby as he was trying to film, and Nevinson was wounded in the head by shrapnel, saved only by the thickness of his Indian helmet. Ashmead-Bartlett was pulled free, but he left the battlefield dressed only in his shirt and trousers.

'Life out here is becoming hell,' muttered Ashmead-Bartlett as more gloom descended on the correspondents and senior officers. Censorship increased. Even a reference to the use of the 29th Division at Suvla was blue-pencilled out of an Ashmead-Bartlett dispatch by the censors. 'My cable is quite ruined,' he said.

As he tried to summarise the lost August offensive, Ashmead-Bartlett became depressed about what would get through. 'I made it pretty hot,' he wrote, 'doubting whether much of it will get through'. In spite of censorship, he managed to convey in his last major battle dispatches a sense of the failure that now pervaded the five-month-old Gallipoli expedition. 'If our plans did not succeed in full it is certainly no fault of the troops who advanced from Anzac,' he wrote. And on the final charge on the Anafarta Hills, he was allowed to print this: 'If we have failed in the great strategic theme of getting astride the peninsula north of Anzac by seizing the hills round Anafarta and forcing the enemy to abandon his positions before Achi Baba and on the Kilid Bahr salient, it was certainly not through want of trying'. His theme was that the Anafarta attack 'just' failed because Stopford's force did not take the initiative and seize the hills before the Turks rushed in reinforcements.

Later, Ashmead-Bartlett argued that the whole August offensive never stood the smallest chance. The Anzacs were given an impossible task to attack in darkness through what his colleague Nevinson had described as a 'labyrinthine region'. If the battle-tested Anzacs had been given the easier job of taking the semi-circle of hills at Anafarta instead of untried new British troops, it might have been a different story, he argued.

Tackling Major Guy Dawney, one of Hamilton's aides and a friend of the King's, immediately after the failure, Ashmead-Bartlett received a reply that stunned him. 'Had we succeeded it would have meant a marquisate for Sir Ian,' Dawney told him. 'What on earth does a marquisate for Sir Ian matter one way or the other?' thought the incredulous journalist.

Dawney later turned on Hamilton and, like Ashmead-Bartlett, was instrumental in his eventual recall. Meanwhile, the journalists found many senior officers on the peninsula in a state of near sedition about their leadership. 'The feeling of discontent throughout all ranks grows in intensity every day, and it is obvious that the morale of the army can only be restored by a change of leadership,' Ellis said. 'GHQ has not got a single friend left. Never have I heard such outspoken criticism on all sides. If they intend to carry out their threat of sending anyone home who ventures to criticise their conduct of the campaign, they will be obliged to evacuate the whole Peninsula, as every general and private says exactly what he thinks.'

Indicative of such discontent, the military brass began to leak. Birdwood handed Ashmead-Bartlett a 27-page report by General Godley, the officer in charge of the New Zealanders, analysing the latest actions. Birdwood complained bitterly to him about the failure of Stopford's 9th Corps to take the Anafarta Hills, claiming that without this it was impossible for his own troops to remain on the crests of Sari Bair. Birdwood told him to be careful with Godley's report as Hamilton would want to use it in his official reports.

Lieutenant Colonel Lord Grenard also showed him a letter from Lawson of the *Telegraph* — Ashmead-Bartlett's boss — stating definitely that Hamilton had written to him trying to have the journalist sacked. Ashmead-Bartlett, Hamilton told Lawson, was unsuitable as a war correspondent. 'This is quite true,' said Ashmead-Bartlett, who in typical journalist fashion took criticism by authorities as a compliment. 'I have always refused to write to dictation what I do not believe to be true, at anyone's request.'

Grenard wanted Ashmead-Bartlett to write a private letter to Lawson telling him the truth of what had happened at Gallipoli. Impossible, owing to the regulations, he replied. General Mahon, who at one stage refused to serve under Major General de Lisle, Stopford's replacement, complained bitterly to Ashmead-Bartlett how his division had been split up at the Suvla landing, and parts of it he had not since seen. 'He declared that both Hamilton and Braithwaite ought to go, and only this could restore the confidence of the troops. Never, in fact, was an army in a more deplorable state of moral disintegration.'

Summoned to GHQ one evening in late August, Ashmead-Bartlett was told that his cable detailing the attempted Anzac breakout had been delayed so that a paragraph could be added telling how one officer had repulsed Turks with machine guns. In the face of such army interference with his copy, he repaired to Captain Philip de Crespigny's amply stocked monitor to enjoy a good dinner.

In fact, Ashmead-Bartlett was so disconsolate about the barriers to getting the truth known that he contemplated resignation. But he could not leave without the permission of the London newspapers. He stayed in his camp writing and his diary for 27 August to 1 September captured his mood. 'Very weary and dispirited,' he wrote. 'No one seems to know what is going to happen. It is obvious that the army can do no more fighting, and unless Bulgaria comes in we shall be stuck here for the winter.'

Winter presented a real danger for the allies, occupying trenches lower down the hills than the Turks. 'We are more likely to be driven into the sea by the [combination of] storms and enemy's artillery fire,' he wrote.

Just then an opportunity presented itself in the form of Keith Murdoch, the well-connected Australian journalist who was passing through Gallipoli on his way to run a cable bureau in London. Murdoch had lost out to Charles Bean in an Australian Journalists' Association ballot to accompany the Australian troops abroad. Appointed now to the London post, his friend Andrew Fisher, the Australian prime minister, had given him a semi-official job en route to check up on mail delivery for the Australian forces — a source of many complaints in Australia.

While investigations for government might seem a strange job for a reporter, Murdoch took it up with gusto. From Cairo, he wrote an ingratiating letter to Hamilton seeking permission to visit Gallipoli. 'I should like to go across in only a semi-official capacity, so that I might record censored impressions in the London and Australian newspapers I represent,' he told Hamilton. 'But any conditions you impose I should, of course, faithfully observe ... May I add that I had the honour of meeting you at the Melbourne Town Hall, and wrote fully of your visit in the Sydney *Sun* and Melbourne *Punch*; also may I say that my anxiety as an Australian to visit the sacred shores of Gallipoli while our army is there, is immense.'

Hamilton rightly thought the letter 'wheedling', but agreed — a decision he would live to regret. Murdoch duly signed the official form for all correspondents, binding himself to all the censor's rules, and pledging not to attempt to correspond by any means other than that officially sanctioned.

Arriving at Gallipoli, Murdoch had what he called the 'conventional ideas' — that the expedition was almost successful, and the peninsula would shortly be in the possession of the allies. This is not surprising, even for an astute journalist like Murdoch. Hamilton's official reports for the press were full of breezy optimism, as the historian Robert Rhodes James called it, often with Turks 'beating a retreat', or a 'successful attack' by the British. One official report claimed Turkish losses in the August offensive were far greater than the allies, a claim few on Gallipoli believed. Hamilton had stressed to Kitchener how close the August offensive had been to success. Both Ashmead-Bartlett's and Bean's censored reports lavished praise on the actions of the Australians, undoubtedly adding to the public belief that things were going well.

A few days at Gallipoli, however, opened Murdoch's eyes. He told the Dardanelles Commission in 1917: 'After conversing principally with Australians — I think I saw almost all the Australian Generals on the spot and also a number of Australian friends, officers and men, and also some British officers on the left flank — I became strongly impressed with the fact that the expedition had wholly failed, that the armies were in a parlous position, and that the situation was not receiving due consideration in London.'

If this was his impression from four days of talking to generals, Ashmead-Bartlett's equally gloomy assessment came as a real call to journalistic arms. At the press camp, the two swapped notes. 'Murdoch the Australian sailed today' reads Ashmead-Bartlett's laconic diary entry of 8 September 1915. 'I gave him an important letter of introduction to Mr Asquith. He promised to get it through.' Behind this brief diary entry was a journalistic plot to get the truth out. Ashmead-Bartlett actually briefed Murdoch carefully on the 'essential points' of the disaster, but the Australian wanted more. They wouldn't believe him back in London, he said. He'd only been at Gallipoli a few days. But they'd believe Ashmead-Bartlett if he were to write a letter.

From his talks on Anzac, Murdoch told Ashmead-Bartlett that the Australians dreaded a winter campaign above all else. More of their positions would become untenable. 'He declares, and I think quite rightly, that unless someone lets the truth be known at home we are likely to suffer a great disaster,' Ashmead-Bartlett wrote later.

But a letter home was not only risky, it breached the conditions correspondents had signed to work with the expedition. Or did it? Ashmead-Bartlett had heard that anybody in the military — and the press were attached to it — was entitled to write to their prime minister. Still, he agonised. He had already asked the London newspapers if he could return home, but what if they refused? He would lose his last chance of getting the truth out if he didn't send this letter via Murdoch. His London bosses, in fact, did ask him to stay on.

'Even if I am breaking the censorship, that is beside the point,' he rationalised. 'The issue now is to try and save what is left of the army.'

Ashmead-Bartlett says he was influenced by other 'cogent reasons'. Many senior officers had begged him to do something to get the truth known to the British government. All believed a further offensive was out of the question, although they had heard requests had been made for more troops. Hamilton had indeed sought more reinforcements after Suvla. Medical officers also told Ashmead-Bartlett that losses from sickness would be heavy. Another factor, as he told the Dardanelles Royal Commission in 1917, was that Murdoch informed him he would write a report back in England, and Ashmead-Bartlett worried he might make mistakes. 'Under these circumstances I finally came to a decision to give Murdoch [a] letter and to risk the consequences to myself.'

The fateful letter was fairly dispassionate, but nonetheless direct in its assertions. The August offensive was a 'ghastly and costly fiasco' he told Asquith, in language the prime minister was unlikely to read in any other communiqué that came to 10 Downing Street. The Army at Gallipoli was incapable of a further offensive. Losses in August alone totalled almost 50 000 dead, wounded and missing. To hear officers talk you would imagine there was an open state of mutiny. Only traditions of discipline were keeping the force together. 'One hates to write of such matters, but in the interests of the country at the present crisis I feel they ought to be made known to you,' he told Asquith.

Ashmead-Bartlett tried to look at the wider strategic considerations that Asquith would obviously have before him. The only justification for holding on, or even reinforcing Gallipoli, was if Bulgaria came in on the allies' side. Otherwise he was convinced the force could be evacuated 'without much loss'. This was an eerily accurate prediction. The military advice, including Hamilton's, was that losses would be heavy, possibly up to half of the force.

If the troops had to be left on Gallipoli to bring Bulgaria in on the allied side, Ashmead-Bartlett tried to set out some other options for the prime minister. The confidence of the troops could only be restored 'by an immediate change of supreme command'. This was his most direct hit on Hamilton so far, but it was a lethal one. Any fresh landing on a grand scale should be north of Bulair, Ashmead-Bartlett's pet theory. If a stay through winter was necessary, the 'colonial' troops should be taken off. 'With their active minds, and the positions they occupy in civil life, a dreary winter in the trenches will have a deplorable effect on what is left of this magnificent body of men, the finest any Empire has ever produced.'

Ashmead-Bartlett obviously believed a full evacuation was the right move. England's greatest asset against Germany was its superior financial strength, and in Gallipoli 'we are dissipating a large portion of our fortune, and have not yet gained a single acre of ground of any strategical value'. The futile expedition could ruin England's prospects of wearing down Germany's colossal military power.

'I have taken the liberty of writing very fully because I have no means of knowing how far the real truth of the situation is known in England, and how much the military authorities disclose,' he said, signing off. 'I thought, therefore, that perhaps the opinion of an independent observer might be of value to you at the present juncture. I am, of course, breaking the censorship regulations by sending this letter through, but I have not the slightest hesitation in doing so, as I feel it is absolutely essential for you to know the truth. I have been requested over and over again by officers of all ranks to go home and personally disclose the truth, but it is difficult for me to leave until the beginning of October. Hoping you will, therefore, excuse the liberty I have taken.'

Asquith certainly never objected to the liberty when he eventually saw the letter. But Hamilton did.

Handing Murdoch the letter, Ashmead-Bartlett felt the first relief for some time. Coaching Murdoch as well with some notes and memos, he felt that at least the Australian government would get to know the truth. And England could hardly afford to ignore Australian opinion.

As Murdoch pocketed the envelope clearly addressed to 'The Rt. Hon. H.H. Asquith, 10 Downing Street' and headed to England he had no idea what a storm it was about to unleash.

11

'I'm Glad We're Dyin' Game'

AFTER the failed August offensive the correspondents were all exhausted. Some were ill, with Bean and Nevinson recovering from injuries. Ashmead-Bartlett was depressed, and had contracted 'stomach trouble'. At least he and most of the others had the relative comforts of their Imbros camp. Bean lived in a dugout on Gallipoli, from which he had doggedly pounded out thousands of words for the Australian papers.

Captain William Maxwell, their censor and himself a former correspondent, arranged for them to take a break at Mitilini, a pretty village on the island of Lesbos to the south. The correspondents booked into the Hotel Grande Bretagne, but Ashmead-Bartlett complained of the fleas at this 'vile hole', saying that life would be more comfortable back at their camp. The tall, skinny Bean said he hadn't noticed any fleas. 'Well, you know, Bean, even a flea won't bite a bone,' flashed back Ashmead-Bartlett, the master of the swift retort.

With Mitilini's cafes and hot baths the correspondents rediscovered a touch of normal life for a few days. But Ashmead-Bartlett's 'stomach trouble' persisted, and he claimed his 'sole amusement' on the island was the company of a woman he met, a Mrs Quincy Adams, the wife of an American naval officer. 'She was both gay and amusing, and not having spoken to a lady for three months, her society was extremely agreeable,' he wrote.

While the correspondents were relaxing at Mitilini, the real drama of the Gallipoli expedition was unfolding in London. Murdoch's trip to London aboard the SS *Moolton* took him via Cairo — where

Ashmead-Bartlett said later he had let slip that he was carrying the letter to Asquith — and then called at Marseilles.

Somewhere along the way Hamilton heard that Murdoch was carrying a secret letter. Suspicion as to the source of his information initially settled on one of the camp orderlies, whom GHQ used to spy on the correspondents. Had an orderly overheard Ashmead-Bartlett and Murdoch conspiring, and reported it to GHQ? Certainly the initial information that the letter was addressed to Harry Lawson of the *Daily Telegraph*, and hence might be for publication, was incorrect and could have come from a garbled version of an overheard conversation.

Hamilton, however, later revealed that he had received a letter from one of the other correspondents who 'felt obliged, for the honour of the journalistic profession, to inform GHQ that Mr Ashmead-Bartlett had smuggled an uncensored letter out of the war area through the agency of Mr A.K. Murdoch [sic]'.

Most writers and historians have since nailed Henry Nevinson as this informant. Certainly the 59-year-old Nevinson was a friend of Hamilton's from Boer War days. And he took his job and its military overtone seriously, even wearing a row of ribbons on his tunic. But the case is unproven and one historian, Nicholas Hiley, believes an argument can equally be made that the New Zealander, Malcolm Ross, was the informant. Bean said Ross admired Ashmead-Bartlett to the point of toadyism, but even Bean was staggered to hear Ross 'giving away' Ashmead-Bartlett behind his back. Ashmead-Bartlett said it was only when he read Hamilton's *Gallipoli Diary* in 1920 that he learnt there was a 'Judas in our camp who had betrayed me to GHQ'.

Whoever his informant, Hamilton quickly cabled Kitchener to have Murdoch apprehended on arrival. 'Meanwhile, Ashmead-Bartlett is away,' he told Kitchener. 'I shall at once sever his connection with this force and send him home if, on inquiry, I find my information regarding this incident to be correct.' Clearly Hamilton was itching to be rid of his journalist critic.

Myth Maker

As the press censorship system in England geared up to stop any publication of an uncensored dispatch, the British military met the *Moolton* when it docked in Marseilles on 19 September. 'I have a wire from Lord French [Field Marshal Sir John French] to ask you if you are carrying any letters,' the officer said. Murdoch did not try to dissemble. 'Yes, I have one,' he admitted. 'It is for the Prime Minister of England.'

After the officer outlined his authority to command the letter, Murdoch surrendered it. The officer then rummaged through his other papers, confiscating the report Murdoch had prepared for the Australian government on mail for the troops. From here, the fate of the letter descended into farce. The War Office must have been mortified to discover it had a letter not to a newspaper editor, but to the prime minister. Despite initial assurances that it was delivered, the letter in fact was 'lost' somewhere in Whitehall; likely just destroyed by the War Office to hide its embarrassment.

Back in his cabin as the *Moolton* steamed towards England Murdoch resolved to draft his own letter, based on his impressions of a few days, but also drawing largely on the now lost views of Ashmead-Bartlett. He drafted 8000 words, addressing it to his own prime minister and friend, Andrew Fisher. Like Ashmead-Bartlett, Murdoch agonised that the letter could break the terms of his censorship commitment given to Hamilton to enable him to visit Gallipoli. But he also believed censorship still gave him the right to correspond to a cabinet minister, and Fisher was certainly that.

While he was typing up his draft in the London office of the *Times*, where his cable service was situated, Murdoch lunched with Geoffrey Dawson, the well-connected editor of the *Times*. Sitting in the 'olde worlde' chintz of Simpsons in the Strand, where frocked waiters carve beef on silver trolleys alongside the table, Murdoch outlined the horrors of Gallipoli. Dawson was clearly shocked, later asking if Murdoch would repeat his story to a British cabinet minister.

Over the next few days Murdoch was passed along the line of ministers hostile to the Dardanelles expedition, including Lord Carson, chairman of the Cabinet's Dardanelles Committee, and Lloyd George, Minister for Munitions. The journalist and historian Les Carlyon notes Murdoch might just as well have had the sign 'pawn' on his back.

Lloyd George directed him to Asquith. Why not send a copy of the letter to the English prime minister, the very intention of Ashmead-Bartlett? Murdoch obliged, telling Asquith that while the letter was intended for Commonwealth ministers, 'if it adds one iota to your information, or presents the Australian point of view, it will be of service in this most critical moment'. Amazingly, Asquith almost immediately had it printed on the duck-egg blue stationery of the Committee of Imperial Defence and circulated to the Dardanelles Committee. Overnight it had become a State Paper. Why Asquith took such an extraordinary step, virtually guaranteeing Murdoch's letter legitimacy, remains a matter of conjecture. Was he also now disillusioned with the Gallipoli expedition? Or was he trying to appease Lloyd George, a Gallipoli sceptic, to keep him in the Cabinet? Perhaps he felt that as Murdoch's paper was addressed to the Australian prime minister it would be impossible to suppress anyway. When he eventually read it, Hamilton was staggered by what he saw as the falsehoods and half truths involved. But he was really wounded by Asquith having it printed it on the famous blue stationery of the Committee of Imperial Defence and circulating it to all of his peers, without Hamilton seeing it or having a chance to comment on it beforehand.

Murdoch's letter was scathing, living up to his warning to Asquith that it was meant for Australian eyes. Whereas Ashmead-Bartlett's original letter was cool, analysing the current stalemate and building up to a series of options to put before the prime minister, Murdoch flayed about, pushing every nationalist hot button he could find.

The Australians at Gallipoli now loathed and detested English officers for their conceit and complacency, he alleged. The new Kitchener divisions were 'merely a lot of childlike youths without strength to endure or brains to improve their conditions'. But there was a 'grandeur' about the Australians, 'swinging their fine limbs as they walk about Anzac'.

'I do not like to dictate this sentence, even for your eyes, but the fact is that after the first day at Suvla an order had to be issued to officers to shoot without mercy any soldiers who lagged behind or loitered in an advance,' he told Fisher about the new English divisions.

No such order existed, at least on paper. There were isolated cases of Australian and English soldiers being threatened with execution. Turkish historians tell how Kemal Atatürk witnessed officers beating Australian soldiers with sticks to get them to charge at the murderous battle for the Nek. Atatürk himself had no hesitation in ordering his men to die for their country. Murdoch said later that his information for the order came from the diary of an English officer that he read. Hamilton said it was just a lie.

Murdoch, however, was spot on about the failure of GHQ and Hamilton, and one could almost hear Ashmead-Bartlett talking when he wrote to Fisher: 'But for the general staff, and I fear for Hamilton, officers and men have nothing but contempt. They express it fearlessly. That however is not peculiar to Anzac. Sedition is talked around every tin of bully beef on the peninsula, and it is only loyalty that holds the forces together. Every returning troopship, every section of the line of communications, is full of the same talk. I like General Hamilton, and found him exceedingly kindly. I admire him as a journalist. But as a strategist he has completely failed.'

Murdoch was best in his peroration. 'I hope I have not made the picture too gloomy. I have great faith still in the Englishman. And, as I have said, the enemy is having his own troubles too. But this unfortunate expedition has never been given a chance. It required a great leader. It required self-sacrifice on the part of the staff as that sacrifice so wonderfully and liberally made on the part of the soldiers. It has had none of these things.'

The 29-year-old Murdoch became much in demand as his letter did the rounds. He met most of the Cabinet, and many senior officials. Winston Churchill told him the contents were 'lurid'. The War Office assured him Ashmead-Bartlett's seized letter had been delivered to

Asquith — a lie. When he read Murdoch's letter a few weeks later Hamilton was astounded. It contained, he said in the language of his circle, information that no gentleman would say, or believe.

But the Murdoch letter was unknown to Hamilton in late September as he chased the War Office for information on the seized Ashmead-Bartlett letter, which he still thought was addressed to Harry Lawson. The war correspondents were due back from Mitilini, and Hamilton was anxious to send Ashmead-Bartlett packing. On 21 September the War Office confirmed that a 'despatch answering the description' was seized from Murdoch, but specifically warned Hamilton not to take any action until they sent him further details.

Ashmead-Bartlett returned to the Imbros camp on 27 September to find some of the servants had drunk all of the journalists' liquor supplies and disappeared back to their units. He sacked his Australian servant. The corporal in charge had fled, preferring, said Ashmead-Bartlett, the dangers of the trenches to the wrath of the correspondents. 'Lawrence's Irish servant has at last succeeded in the fulfillment of his one ambition, namely, to drink himself comfortably into hospital,' he wrote.

Oblivious to a trap that was being set, Ashmead-Bartlett went over to GHQ the following day, taking up with Colonel G.E. Tyrrell, the intelligence chief, the continually vexed issue of censorship. Ellis had known Tyrrell from his days as British military attaché in Constantinople during the Balkan wars. Tyrrell had only just arrived on the peninsula, and Ashmead-Bartlett was surprised by his frank admission that the campaign had been wrongly handled from the start. Ashmead-Bartlett, however, wanted to talk about specific issues of censorship, some of which Tyrrell had handed over to Radcliffe, whom the correspondents detested. Bean called him a 'little whippersnapper' who was angry with the journalists because Ashmead-Bartlett had him removed from the press camp. Radcliffe had also complained to Hamilton that Nevinson was inventing material for articles. He regularly sent orders to the press camp via a soldier who also acted as a spy for him. Now he was censoring their letters as well.

Tyrrell told Ashmead-Bartlett he had handed Radcliffe the job because he was too busy. He had a lot more important things to do than worry about censorship, and it was a secondary matter for him. The exchange became heated as Ashmead-Bartlett pointed out that correspondents were officially attached to the Army and had a right to be 'properly treated'. Tyrrell cooled down, and left the tent for a while, returning to ask Ashmead-Bartlett to see Braithwaite in another tent.

It was here that the trap was ready to be sprung. Hamilton's GHQ had somehow learnt that the letter was addressed to Asquith, not a newspaper editor, but were determined in any case to rid themselves of the correspondent despite being told by the War Office to stay their hand. In fact, the War Office did not officially tell Hamilton that the letter was actually destined for the prime minister until the following day. With several officers present, Braithwaite, whom Bean and others regarded as the power behind Hamilton, asked the journalist to sit down, and said: 'When I had a talk with you in June last you promised not to criticise the leaders of the army or to break regulations again'.

'I consented to certain things, and as far as I know I have kept my agreement,' Ashmead-Bartlett replied.

'On September 8th you sent out an uncensored letter by Murdoch, who was leaving, addressed to the Prime Minister?'

'I did. I consider I have a right to write to the Prime Minister.'

'You know you had not. That letter has got Murdoch into serious trouble.'

'How did you find out I had sent the letter?'

Braithwaite turned evasive, merely saying it had been seized at Marseilles. Ashmead-Bartlett then asked him: 'Has the Prime Minister received it?'

The question took Braithwaite by surprise, and he hesitated before saying: 'I do not know'. Ashmead-Bartlett believed GHQ was severely embarrassed at having stopped a letter to the prime minister. But Braithwaite quickly recovered to say: 'As you have again broken the rules of the censorship, you will no longer be allowed to stay with the Army and must sever your connection with it at once and return home.'

If Braithwaite intended this as a knock-out blow, he seemed taken aback when Ashmead-Bartlett jumped to his feet and asked: 'May I leave at once? I have long been anxious to be relieved of my post, and have in fact applied to the Newspaper Proprietors Association to be allowed to return.'

Clearly Hamilton and his chief of staff had not thought through the disciplining of a troublesome correspondent. Ashmead-Bartlett on Gallipoli was certainly a nuisance, but let loose back in London with his impeccable political contacts, he could be positively dangerous. Having laid down immediate expulsion, however, Braithwaite now had no alternative but to agree.

'For the first time for days I felt in high spirits,' said an elated Ashmead-Bartlett. 'Colonel Tyrrell expressed his regret. I said good-bye to a few officers and then left GHQ for ever without a single regret. Never have I seen such a collection of mediocre minds, chronic muddlers, and such an atmosphere of petty jealousies and intrigues.'

The 'sacking', with its prospect that he would now be able to tell the real story of Gallipoli, immediately put Ashmead-Bartlett in high spirits. He told a few of the officers that they would also be on the way home shortly as GHQ could hardly expect to survive once the truth was known. And Ashmead-Bartlett made it clear he intended to tell it. 'I am now absolutely free,' he rejoiced. 'I can say what I like, I can write what I like, and I can see whom I like.'

Back in the press camp, however, colleagues were upset about his forced return. Nevinson wanted to return with him. 'Poor devils!' wrote Ashmead-Bartlett. 'They will have a poor time now that I am gone. At least I fought for their rights, and but for me they would have been completely crushed beneath the iron heel.' Ashmead-Bartlett may have been exaggerating his role, but there was no doubt he was the camp leader. Bean described him as not just a manager,

Myth Maker

but overbearing. 'Things always go his way when he's about.' Even Hamilton's diaries contain references to him accommodating requests from Ashmead-Bartlett — before relations soured. Certainly he was a ringleader in getting Radcliffe removed from the press camp.

'Lucky beggar,' thought Bean when he first heard the news that Ashmead-Bartlett was going home. When Bean read a copy of the letter to Asquith he felt it put things at Gallipoli in a crude light, but was brilliantly written. However, it rather overstated the case 'as Bartlett always does'. 'But a great deal of it was absolutely unanswerable and badly needs understanding,' he said.

Bean, who would go on to write the benchmark history of Australia in World War I, disagreed with two of Ashmead-Bartlett's assumptions: that the Suvla landing and Anzac breakout would never have succeeded; and that any landing should have been up at Bulair. The first he regarded as false, and the second he believed was dubious. 'However, that is a matter of detail,' he wrote in his own diary. 'Bartlett's letter was worth the consideration of any man, and I've no doubt it will be considered in time. Several members of the Cabinet asked him to write to them privately — which was not a very loyal thing of them to do, but then politicians are not loyal.'

Ashmead-Bartlett had made one mistake, Bean believed: he should have taken the letter home himself. But Bean conceded it was a difficult decision. Ashmead-Bartlett could hardly have left his employers in the lurch, and it was doubtful that he would have been allowed to return. Certainly the letter would not have passed the censors. 'So he decided that the object was worth the cause,' he said.

The press camp was in a state of high drama over Ashmead-Bartlett's sacking. He told them that his career as a war correspondent was probably over. Bean's hatred of Radcliffe deepened. He now described Radcliffe as a 'little worm', blaming his spies for finding out about the Murdoch letter. Bean also had his own session with Tyrrell about censorship, which provoked the view from the intelligence chief that war correspondents were a dying profession. In a 'properly organised' nation, Tyrrell believed, government could do away with war correspondents by simply telling the people what it believed was necessary to win the war, whether that be truth or lies.

'He thinks we're dyin', does he?' said Ashmead-Bartlett when Bean relayed him the story. 'Well, I'm glad we're dyin' game!'

The departure provoked ruminations about Ashmead-Bartlett's character among his colleagues. A 'strange chap', said Bean. Nevinson had always likened him to Byron. Bean described him as a tremendously fast and hard worker whose 'stuff' was easily the most vivid of any living war correspondent.

'He's extraordinarily brilliant in conversation,' said Bean. 'I never heard anyone who could approach him in unexpected retort — in turning every sentence he speaks into a brilliant paradox to point some very incisive argument. He thinks very straight and his written dispatches are full of life and colour, hit hard, and give a brilliant idea which is remarkably true. He exaggerates a bit to make his points but the general result is a pretty accurate description of what had happened, and always vivid.'

'A splendid companion — when in the mood — but an upbringing that had made him selfish,' Bean continued. 'A good friend, who had been anxious to stay on Gallipoli out of fairness to his employer, Harry Lawson. Plucky, but a correspondent who didn't believe in exposing himself more than necessary to get the story he wanted. The camp life of a king, and a man with half a dozen thoughts in his head about making money — like spending hours on end trying to get film of a shell burst.'

While the journalists reminisced, Hamilton was laying false trails about the sacking. He told Nevinson that the War Office had instructed him in a cable to send Ashmead-Bartlett home. This was sheer invention. Hamilton also offered to suggest to the London papers that Nevinson take Ashmead-Bartlett's place. Nevinson flatly refused.

The Gallipoli commander, damaged by successive disasters on the peninsula, realised he had created a powerful enemy, and moved to cover his tracks. In letters to Asquith, Lawson and Windsor Castle —

Myth Maker

obviously for the attention of the King — Hamilton painted a 'woe is me' picture of falling foul of the press. Dealing with the Murdoch uncensored letter incident he told Windsor Castle: 'supposing information gets into the wrong hands, the whole of the army might suffer'.

True enough, but in none of the defensive letters home did Hamilton reveal that the offending Ashmead-Bartlett letter was addressed to the Prime Minister of England, the political commander of that army. Hamilton, however, seemed to admit he had blundered. 'I know I make a dangerous enemy, who, stating his own story, may gain powerful supporters,' he told Windsor Castle. Quite so.

'My luck is dead out,' he told Lawson. 'I, of all men, have just been forced to take an unpleasant decision regarding Ashmead-Bartlett.' Hamilton prepared the ground by praising Lawson's correspondent before putting the boot in. 'I regard Ashmead-Bartlett as of real good value to this force,' he said. 'He handles his pen like an artist and, beyond doubt, he has interested the people of the United Kingdom and Ireland in our progress ... the public were indebted to him ... we were indebted to him ... ordinarily I should have been the last man in the world to wish to sever our associations.'

If Ashmead-Bartlett had just contravened War Office regulations again he probably would not have been 'sent away', said Hamilton. 'He was writing first-class stuff, and one is always prepared to make allowances for the artistic temperament. But when he broke his word of honour in so deliberate a manner I could not get over it at all.' Hamilton was basing his case on 'honour', hoping to appeal to a man who would shortly become Lord Burnham, that nothing was more important than a gentleman's word. Yet it would later come out at the Dardanelles Commission that what Ashmead-Bartlett told Braithwaite was entirely correct — everyone in the military, and correspondents were attached to it on Gallipoli — had the right to write uncensored to a member of parliament including, obviously, the prime minister.

While the Army was sending him home in disgrace for breaching his word of honour, the Navy gave Ashmead-Bartlett a rousing

178

send-off. Inter-service relations were strained, with the Navy furious over Hamilton's allegations that naval shelling had driven the Gurkhas off Chunuk Bair. At a farewell on HMS *Cornwallis*, the crew sent up a delegation to thank Ashmead-Bartlett for what he had written. Bean was there, and described it as 'extraordinary' to hear the Navy praising the correspondent's writing in terms critical of GHQ, such as, 'we all know ... the way in which the army had been thrown against impossible positions'.

Steaming out of Mudros Bay on 3 October, six months after he arrived, Ashmead-Bartlett felt pangs of regret. 'How many tragic events have happened since I first entered its waters in the first days of April of this year?'

Arriving in London on 14 October he set up home again in the Carlton Hotel, where Gina was there to meet him. 'Managed to smuggle in my precious cinematographic films,' he confided in his diary. That night he sat up until the early hours discussing with his agent and friend from school, West de Wend Fenton, his plans to launch a 'great campaign'.

These were tumultuous times. Zeppelin airship bombers were raiding London. One crashed in Essex. The Western Front continued in costly stalemate, although the allies had some small gains in the Champagne region. The Russians remained under enormous pressure on the Eastern Front. Before he left Gallipoli, Maxwell told Ashmead-Bartlett that the news from the Russian Front was too bad to print in his 'Gallipoli Liar' news sheet. Bulgaria had just come into the war on Germany's side, attacking Serbia. France was pressing England to join an expedition to land at Salonika on the Greek coast to aid Serbia, pulling some troops off Gallipoli.

On top of these pressures, Asquith's Cabinet was hopelessly divided on the future of the disastrous Gallipoli expedition, undertaken at the start of the year with high, unrealistic expectations that 'Johnny Turk' would soon be knocked out of the war. The Turk had proved a stubborn and effective fighter, whom the Australian troops in particular had grown to respect.

Cabinet was split between the 'Westerners', who felt military resources should be concentrated on the main battle against Germany in France, and the 'Easterners', who believed Russia and Serbia must be supported. The pressures pulling Cabinet asunder were aided by the lobbying of two new arrivals: Murdoch, armed with his emotional, and in places factually incorrect, report against the Gallipoli expedition; and Major Guy Dawney.

Hamilton had sent Dawney, one of his well-connected senior staff officers, to London to lobby on his behalf, realising that the sacked Stopford was already campaigning against him. But Dawney was part of a small clique of staff officers who, although loyal to Hamilton, believed the campaign had gone hopelessly wrong and the 'truth' needed to be known. This was the message that had been poured into Ashmead-Bartlett's ear as well. Dawney became another of the extraordinary facets of Gallipoli — a senior officer telling everyone from the King down that Hamilton, although a great general, was too optimistic.

While Murdoch and Dawney lobbied behind closed doors, Ashmead-Bartlett planned something quite different — high profile and uncensored press reports, coupled with a major lecture tour with photographs. Fenton said he would organise a syndicate for the lecture tour, and wanted Ashmead-Bartlett to charge £100 a performance. 'A large sum,' thought Ashmead-Bartlett, 'but still warranted by the extreme state of public interest in everything to do with the Dardanelles'.

Within a few days the lecture tour was arranged. Jack White, who managed the affairs of Sir Joseph Beecham, the patent medicine entrepreneur who also dabbled in theatre, was in the syndicate, along with the Berry brothers, proprietors of the ailing *Sunday Times*. Fenton took a commission. Ashmead-Bartlett was hopeful of also stitching up a commercial release of his Gallipoli films, providing the War Office agreed. This, however, did not happen until early 1916.

The lecture circuit, with prospects to also go to Australia and America, meant he was on his way to realising at least one of the commercial dreams he had outlined to colleagues back on Gallipoli. The deal, for 25 lectures with an option for 75 more, was signed over champagne. 'This looks like being good business,' said the prospective lecturer.

Events moved quickly as Ashmead-Bartlett now threw himself into the task of getting the troops evacuated from Gallipoli, convinced that to leave them there would risk a 'disaster unparalleled in English history'. He did the rounds of newspapers and ministers, catching up with Keith Murdoch in the process. The Australian told him of the Marseilles incident, but said Asquith had told him that Ashmead-Bartlett had the right to correspond uncensored with his prime minister. Asquith also told Murdoch that he would send for the letter.

In a subsequent meeting with Lawson, however, he learnt that Asquith had never seen the letter. No problem. Ashmead-Bartlett simply handed over a copy to Lawson, who sent it to the prime minister. He also lobbied Lord Northcliffe, whom he called a 'Napoleon' of the press. Northcliffe, who had extraordinary political influence via his newspapers, not only embraced evacuation, but threatened a sustained press campaign if Cabinet did not agree. 'There is a great responsibility on your shoulders,' the press baron told the correspondent after they lunched at the *Times* building. 'Only you are in a position to bring home to the Government and country the true state of affairs in the Near East.'

Two new press allies proved invaluable. The Berry brothers, William and Gomer, were trying to build up the *Sunday Times*, and told him they were prepared to defy censorship to run his views. But the censors could move to close down the paper, so they devised a stratagem to present Ashmead-Bartlett in interview form, believing this committed no breach of censorship.

Churchill, however, proved a tougher nut to crack. Ashmead-Bartlett found to his amazement that, despite the big setbacks of the August attacks, Churchill's views had not changed since he last saw him in June. He continued with his obsession that the fleet should have forced the Narrows, asserting that another attempt could succeed. Then he set the normally unflappable journalist with the question: 'If you were suddenly appointed commander-in-chief, what force would you regard as a minimum to have any hope of taking Constantinople?'

Ashmead-Bartlett thought quickly. Bulgaria's entry into the war on Germany's side had changed the equation. Greece and Romania were hedging their bets.

'Even if these two countries declare in our favour, I should require the existing forces on the Peninsula, 100,000 men landed in Asia Minor, and another 200,000 constantly kept up to full strength in Thrace and Macedonia,' he replied.

The figures stunned Churchill. Ashmead-Bartlett left the conversation convinced that Churchill knew nothing of modern warfare; that he jumped to absurd conclusions and suffered from extraordinary illusions. 'In fact I now regard him as a grave danger to the country,' he said. This was not one of Ashmead-Bartlett's better predictions.

Churchill, however, confided in him a hot piece of news: Cabinet had decided to recall Hamilton, along with Braithwaite. The fact that Churchill would tell a journalist of the withdrawal of a field commander — a highly sensitive military move — spoke volumes for the trust politicians put in Ashmead-Bartlett, whatever Hamilton may have thought about his breaching his word of honour.

Ashmead-Bartlett made no attempt to report this startling news, although the newspapers immediately ran the story. The pressures of the Murdoch letter and Dawney's campaign had become too much. Hamilton had been offered a lifeline by ditching Braithwaite, but in the best traditions of his brand of honour, refused. Hamilton also vehemently opposed evacuation, claiming that half the force could be lost.

Acting under instructions from an exasperated Cabinet, where 'Westerners' such as Lloyd George were threatening resignation, Kitchener sent Hamilton a secret cable that had to be personally decoded. It must have been a heartbreaking task for Hamilton, sitting alone in his tent, to pick his way through the message letter by letter to find out he was being recalled.

Prayers for victory aboard HMS *London*, April 1915

Men with full kit from 11th Battalion AIF preparing to land at Anzac Cove: many lost their lives.

Wounded soldiers from the Gallipoli fighting returning to ship

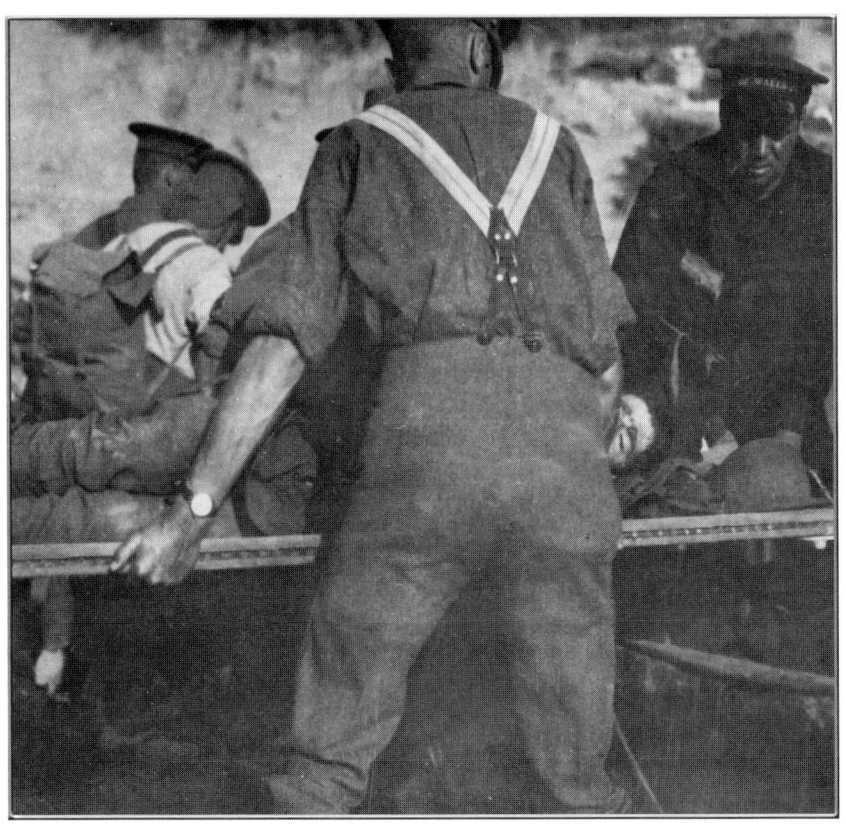

A sailor from HMS *Prince of Wales* assists in the rescue of Anzac wounded at Gallipoli.

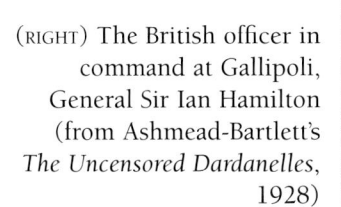

(RIGHT) The British officer in command at Gallipoli, General Sir Ian Hamilton (from Ashmead-Bartlett's *The Uncensored Dardanelles*, 1928)

(BELOW) Anzac Cove, April–May 1915: a Royal Navy signaller is sending a message back to the troop ship; a steam pinnace is at right

Shock public impact of Ashmead-Bartlett's vivid press reports: the Brisbane *Courier* front page, 8 May 1915 (NLA)

SATURDAY, MAY 8, 1915.

OUR NOBLE BOYS.

HOW THEY FOUGHT AND DIED.

A GREAT TRIBUTE TO THEIR VALOUR AND RESOURCE.

THEY LAND IN THE DARK AND SCALE THE HEIGHTS.

IN THE TEETH OF A MURDEROUS FIRE.

HOLD POSITIONS FOR FIFTEEN HOURS UNDER INCESSANT SHELL FIRE.

UNEXAMPLED COURAGE OF THE WOUNDED.

AUSTRALIANS, WITH BLOOD UP, SPURNED COVER.

THE BLAZE AND RATTLE OF THE COVERING WARSHIPS' GUNS.

THE ALLIES ADVANCING STEADILY ALONG THE PENINSULA.

DESPERATE FIGHTING IN PROGRESS.

BOTH SIDES LOSE HEAVILY.

CONSTANTINOPLE BOMBED BY RUSSIAN AIRMEN.

LATEST COMMUNIQUES FROM BOTH FRONTS.

JAPAN PRESENTS AN ULTIMATUM TO CHINA.

The sinking of HMS *Majestic* by the German submarine *U-21* off W Beach, 27 May 1915: Ashmead-Bartlett survived this incident. (IWM Q22836)

The by-line 'Ellis Ashmead-Bartlett' became famous through his Gallipoli reports — especially in England, Australia and New Zealand: a copy of the *Sketch*, London, 2 June 1915.
(NLA)

The Dardanelles, 1915: Australian war correspondent C.E.W. Bean, front, and Ellis Ashmead-Bartlett
(AWM A05382)

Three of the other war correspondents at Gallipoli: Henry Nevinson (English provincial press), Malcolm Ross (New Zealand) and Lester Lawrence (Reuters) photographed by C.E.W. Bean
(AWM G01411)

A youthful Keith Murdoch, who visited Gallipoli for four days
(AWM A05396)

(RIGHT) Correspondents in Anzac trenches: Ashmead-Bartlett, foreground, and Nevinson, rear

(BELOW) At Gallipoli Ashmead-Bartlett learnt to use the recently invented, revolutionary, hand-held Aeroscope cinematograph camera to produce the only surviving live record of the conflict. (National Museum of Photography, Film & Television/Science & Society Picture Library)

The Aeroscope was later used to great effect on the Western Front by expert cameraman Lt Geoffrey Malins.
(IWM HU64116)

Lt Malins demonstrates his improvised method for carrying into battle his highly volatile reels of film.
(IWM HU64116)

Bean watched him go, recording that 'the poor chap looked to me very haggard — almost broken up'. In London former friends cut him in the street, and a bitter Hamilton would spend years fighting for his reputation.

'At least that is a step in the right direction,' wrote Ashmead-Bartlett of the sacking. 'It saves me agitating any further on that score. I [am] determined to go on making exposures of their deceitfulness and incompetency until matters [reach] a crisis.' The sacking was slightly painful for Ashmead-Bartlett, however. He had bet Malcolm Ross £10 that Hamilton would leave the peninsula by the end of September, with a week's grace — and he lost the bet by a few days.

All fired up from his Churchill discussion to disclose the facts about the situation in the East, he gave a *Sunday Times* reporter some strong statements. The 'interview' appeared on 17 October, causing what Ashmead-Bartlett called 'a tremendous sensation'. Northcliffe rang, wanting to run the interview in the *Times* or *Daily Mail*. Murdoch called to say he had cabled it to Australia. Other papers began quoting it. The editor of the *Sunday Times* began to fear he would be locked up.

Under the innocuous headline of 'The Near East Situation' the interview blasted English military policy. On the Dardanelles, he thundered: 'There is no getting away from the fact that apart from the question of its conception and doubtful paternity we have committed every conceivable blunder in our methods of attempting to carry it out'.

His message was that England was now at the crossroads of the war, and had to make some hard choices. Any good gambler who had spent as much as he could afford stopped and waited the turn of his luck. The reckless ones (some might say including Ashmead-Bartlett) lose everything they had. It was up to the politicians to see that lives were not thrown away recklessly.

With his press campaign warming up, Ashmead-Bartlett embarked on the lecture circuit, but in considerable physical pain. The stomach trouble he had contracted in Gallipoli returned with a vengeance, and doctors advised him to rest. The day of his first lecture, which was a sell-out at Queen's Hall in London, he could hardly stand up in his hotel room. But his agents told him it was impossible to call off the lecture — people were already being turned away. Telling his doctors to 'go to the devil', Ashmead-Bartlett staggered down to the Carlton Grill Room to see if he could eat some boiled sole for sustenance. His friend, the actress Marie Lohr, arrived for dinner before her evening performance and Ashmead-Bartlett told her of his plight.

'The only thing for you to do,' said the actress, having some experience of performing while ill, 'is to drink half a bottle of champagne. That will probably carry you through the evening but make you worse tomorrow, which won't matter.' Needing little encouragement to drink champagne, Ashmead-Bartlett followed her instructions. 'Now,' continued the actress, 'have a glass of old brandy and you will probably feel alright'. The would-be lecturer again followed orders, and believing he now felt 'a bit better', although somehow he could not get his head clear, staggered off to the Queen's Hall.

By the time he arrived Ashmead-Bartlett was seeing everything in a haze. A worried Fenton, unaware of the actress's potent elixir, poured a tumbler of port down his throat and left another 'huge tumbler' on the lectern.

'I was then half pushed onto the stage, really not knowing what was happening,' recalled Ashmead-Bartlett. 'I remember seeing an immense sea of faces.' Fortunately he knew the subject, and launched into it. Half way through he thought he could not finish, but remembered Fenton's second tumbler of port, and drank it straight off. '[It] put new life into me, and I was subsequently told that I finished in grand style, in fact much better than I had started.' In fact he had spoken for two and a half hours which, given the mixture of champagne, brandy and port he had consumed, was an amazing feat.

Uncle Willie, who was in the audience, wrote to him the following day. Admirable in many respects, he said, but marred by Ashmead-Bartlett spending too much time with his back to the audience pointing to slides and maps. As well, he arrived on the platform too late, irritating people. Uncle Willie, of course, was unaware of Ellis's alcohol-laden path to even make the platform. And both were unaware that in the audience was a censor sent to keep an eye on the journalist. Apparently the censor was not sufficiently irritated to close down future lectures.

Uncle Willie added a postscript: Ellis must stop calling the Australians 'colonials'. They did not like it. As well, said Uncle Willie, he might word this praise for the 'colonials' differently to avoid indirectly disparaging the English troops.

The alcohol, unfortunately, did not kill off the illness, and it worsened as Ellis's writing and lectures gathered pace. At one stage he had to be admitted to the Harold Fink Private Hospital. Run by an Australian, a Dr Shields, Fink's was an expensive and fashionable nursing home with a reputation for dancing and theatrical performances. 'It was said you could be entertained right up to your death,' said Ashmead-Bartlett, who found the nurses and upper-class lady volunteers there quite diverting.

The public campaigning continued as Cabinet agonised over the future of Gallipoli. The new commander, General Munro, advised a pull-out, but his tenure was cut short by being posted to head the new Salonika force. Kitchener himself toured the front, and at one stage even advocated the Ashmead-Bartlett solution, a fresh landing at Bulair. But the new commander, Birdwood, was opposed, and the idea died. Eventually, under the weight of a divided military, freak winter storms which were killing troops, and the pressures of other fronts, Cabinet pulled the plug.

On the night of 19 December the troops were withdrawn from Anzac and Suvla, remarkably with no casualties. The Turks were taken by surprise. Three weeks later Cape Helles was also evacuated without any losses.

Ashmead-Bartlett was furious that it had taken five months from the failed and costly August offensive for Cabinet to remove the troops. 'The Army was left to rot in the trenches,' he said.

Had his campaign shortened the agony? Given the various forces at work it is impossible to attribute credit to any one person or factor. As the novelist Compton Mackenzie felicitously noted, Ashmead-Bartlett was just one more load of coal on a Newcastle of ill-will.

The more pertinent issue is not so much the credit due to Ashmead-Bartlett as a war correspondent prepared to risk the wrath of authority by revealing military bungling and acting to save further losses, but the attitude of his fellow journalists. They not only refused to detract from the censor's line, but deplored Ashmead-Bartlett's breach of censorship by sending the letter to Asquith. Both Bean and Nevinson believed any dissenting war correspondent should resign. Bean argued that while war correspondents should be given considerable freedoms, if they didn't think truth was getting 'a fair show' they should resign and give the authorities the responsibility of 'muzzling them'.

Nevinson said he would have urged Ashmead-Bartlett to resign and go home had he known about the attempt to smuggle out the letter with Murdoch. 'It might be argued that a correspondent is justified in breaking his pledge word for what he considers the highest interests of the country, but there is no question that the man who is discovered doing it has to go,' he wrote. In other words, the crime may be permissible, just don't get found out!

Compton Mackenzie said that whether Ashmead-Bartlett's criticisms were right or wrong, he must have known he could not persuade Hamilton to change his mind. 'If [Ashmead-Bartlett] wished to remain . . . it was his duty to sacrifice his opinions.'

Such opinions seem quaint in an era where the whistleblower is now revered, and journalistic freedom hailed. As historian Nicholas Hiley, who has made a detailed study of early World War I censorship, concluded:

> The strongest impression left by the story of the war correspondents on Gallipoli is not that a minority attempted to criticise events, but that the majority believed firmly

that the war belonged to the military staffs. It was generally accepted that if an official correspondent disagreed with his military censors it was his duty to resign, in order that they might find someone with more acceptable opinions.

Ashmead-Bartlett was from a different school, one that believed that, like William Howard Russell and the Crimean War bungling, it was the duty of war correspondents to get the truth out and known.

12

In the Antipodes: 'Horrible–Horrible–Horrible'

IF Ashmead-Bartlett found censorship tough at Gallipoli, it was even worse in Australia. Indeed, it almost prevented him visiting the country to lecture in 1916.

His British lecture tour in late 1915 had drawn good crowds and generally favourable press reaction. 'Mr Ashmead-Bartlett ... as a platform speaker has quite the popular style,' said the Sussex *Daily News*. 'Extremely frank and straight-spoken,' said the Bournemouth *Gazette*. 'A critic of Government's conception of the Gallipoli Expedition and also of the military tactics in carrying it out,' said the Brighton *Herald* after hearing his lecture.

Perhaps too frank a critic for some. *London Life* magazine posed the question: 'Whatever does the Censor think of the nasty remarks Mr Ashmead-Bartlett persistently makes in his lectures on the Dardanelles debate?' Whatever the British censor thought, Australia certainly took a dim view. In early November, as the Asquith Cabinet struggled with the evacuation of Gallipoli, Andrew Bonar Law, Canadian-born banker turned politician who was now colonial secretary, summoned Ashmead-Bartlett to his office. Law came straight to the point: The Australian government had heard he was going out there to lecture, and was anxious to know what attitude he would adopt. 'They were afraid I might do a great deal of harm if I criticized affairs too severely,' said Ashmead-Bartlett.

'They' were the new Australian government led by the fiery William Morris Hughes, who had replaced Fisher when he resigned to become Australia's high commissioner in London. Hughes championed the war effort. He offered 50 000 more Australian troops even as Asquith's Cabinet considered evacuation. Hughes had been told some weeks before the evacuation to expect up to 50 per cent casualties. Australia's army was a volunteer force, and doomsayers could wreck recruitment rates. For Hughes, who would shortly propose conscription to further boost numbers to fight the war, Ashmead-Bartlett posed a real threat.

Ashmead-Bartlett told Law that he was likely not going out to Australia for two or three months, and events could easily change by then. 'In any case I should do my best to put the best construction on a bad case,' he said. This was an extraordinary statement by the avowed anti-Gallipoli campaigner. Just what had Hamilton passed up by not cultivating the basically sympathetic military correspondent in his requests to the War Office for more resources to be devoted to the Dardanelles campaign? From initial enthusiasm, Hamilton's abject failure of leadership had actually turned the journalist completely against the expedition.

There was an added factor behind the remark. Ashmead-Bartlett was going to Australia as a commercial venture. The agreement then being negotiated with J&N Tait, a Melbourne-based theatrical management firm, proposed to pay him £100 for each of 25 lectures in Australia and New Zealand. Fenton, his old school chum, again acted as his agent — £2500 plus first class expenses was a tidy sum for a journalist who had been in the bankruptcy court only a few months before.

Law was a sharp politician who would become British prime minister seven years later. He readily saw the makings of a deal that might solve his problems both with Australia and Ashmead-Bartlett. 'Perhaps I can arrange to settle your quarrels with the War Office so as to enable you to go to the Western Front instead of going to Australia?' The *Daily Telegraph* wanted Ashmead-Bartlett to cover the Western Front, but his poisonous relations with the War Office over the letter to Asquith were a handicap to gaining accreditation.

Ashmead-Bartlett, however, did not bite. He was then already committed to his British lecture tour, at £100 a performance. Besides, his current poor health meant he was too ill to 'take to the field'. He also believed the War Office would never forgive him — a belief that turned out to be absolutely correct.

Australian gripes aside, the two fell to talking about Cabinet's dilemma over Gallipoli. Law confided that he agreed with Ashmead-Bartlett, and that he had constantly argued for withdrawal in Cabinet, but other ministers could not make up their minds. Ashmead-Bartlett warned him that unless Cabinet made a decision to avoid disastrous winter losses, both he and the press baron Northcliffe were prepared to make a bigger public issue of it.

Although on the lecture trail, Ashmead-Bartlett maintained a lively social life and a keen eye for political gossip. His diary is sprinkled with references to dinner at the Ritz with the fabulously wealthy Aga Khan, the powerful Mrs Astor and the Duchess of Sutherland. Watching Asquith deliver a speech in parliament, Ashmead-Bartlett thought him unwell, perhaps drinking too much. Everyone knew the prime minister enjoyed a drink or two, and Ellis believed his bold statement that he was not going to change his habits because of the war probably did him more good in the eyes of the country than anything else. Kitchener's declared abstinence, however, had not improved his war strategy; while the King's great resolution to drink water until Germany was defeated only resulted in him falling off his horse while on parade in France.

In the October meeting Law extracted from Ashmead-Bartlett a promise that he would not go out to Australia without reporting back to the colonial secretary. As the lecture tour deal was signed, with the first talk to be given in early February, the prospectively troublesome speaker kept his promise. He told Law his lectures would be narrative and not critical. Law seemed only partially comfortable with that, giving Ashmead-Bartlett a letter of introduction to the governor-general of Australia, Sir Ronald Munro-Ferguson, in the hope that this link might help keep the journalist to his word, and 'avoid difficulty'.

But 'difficulty' still loomed. New Zealand told Downing Street that Ashmead-Bartlett would be allowed to land, but his lectures would be censored before he was allowed to deliver them. A flurry of official cables accompanied Ashmead-Bartlett's media circus through America to Australia, as the Hughes government agonised over whether to even allow him into the country.

Ashmead-Bartlett left England on 23 December, armed with letters of introduction from Law, Northcliffe, Keith Murdoch and even the former New South Wales premier, George Reid, after giving farewell interviews to the Australian press on the withdrawal from Gallipoli. An American press pack met him in New York on New Year's Day. With his reputation as a whistleblower spreading, the *New York Times* correspondent in London had cabled over saying Ashmead-Bartlett would be making 'sensational revelations'.

'Of course I had no intention of doing [so],' he noted in his diary. Press reports next day of his arrival interviews were more or less accurate, thought Ashmead-Bartlett, but 'some had put in anything they liked'. Sections of the American press were then pro-German, and happy to play up the journalist's criticisms of the British military over Gallipoli.

These twisted reports of Ashmead-Bartlett's interviews and lectures sent the wires crackling back to London. British ambassador Sir Cecil Spring-Rice cabled that Ashmead-Bartlett was doing 'much harm' in the US, and would do more in Australia. Best warn the Australian governor-general, he urged. He cabled again a few days later, saying the naval attaché, an Australian, believed it would be 'wiser' to dissuade the journalist from going on to Australia, and this action should be taken from London. Even Ashmead-Bartlett was becoming concerned. He wrote to Lord Burnham saying that he had tried to be 'very moderate' in his American lectures, but the coverage in the 'yellow press' was awful, including invented interviews. 'I am afraid that if some of these accounts reach England that my friends would think I have gone mad,' he wrote. He even asked Uncle Willie to put in a good word for him if he heard him criticised for 'wild utterances' in the United States.

Myth Maker

Ashmead-Bartlett certainly needed a good word or two. The rattled Australian government again cabled Law, this time asking that the tour be stopped. Law had already advised that, like New Zealand, Australia should vet his speeches. But the colonial secretary was sufficiently worried to ask Lord Burnham if he could call off the tour. 'Not my responsibility,' replied the newspaper proprietor. Ashmead-Bartlett then had no connection with the *Daily Telegraph*, and the lecture tour was purely his own venture. Ashmead-Bartlett had told him the American press was grossly distorting his words, something Burnham himself had warned him about. The only way to stop him, said Lord Burnham, would be for the Australian government to refuse him permission to lecture.

Oblivious to this frantic cable and letter exchange, Ashmead-Bartlett savoured New York's social life, dining with the daughter of Pierpont Morgan and lunching with the 'sinister' press baron William Randolph Hearst. Hearst was rumoured to be pro-German, but denied this to Ashmead-Bartlett. One friend was keen to introduce him to a young heiress, a Miss Miller, who had US$16 million. 'Alas,' said Ellis, 'she is not very beautiful, and as far as I am concerned she could stick to her money and do what she likes with it'. Money was never everything for him. It was all about living an exciting life.

Although he did not stay at his usual haunt, the Ritz, because it was then under German management and regarded as a propaganda centre, he lunched there. The Ritz managers reproached him for not staying at the hotel, while in the dining room Ashmead-Bartlett found himself surrounded by German and Austrian waiters from the Carlton, Ritz and Savoy hotels in London who had fled to America. All professed to hate their own country and were eager for news of London.

Ashmead-Bartlett was intrigued not only by the Ziegfeld Follies, where beautiful women danced between tables, but by bumping into a group of 'cinematographic artists' — film actors — all in various stages of intoxication at a New York supper club. 'I am told that some of the best of them only put up their best performances when they

In the Antipodes: 'Horrible–Horrible–Horrible'

are drunk,' he said. 'There is a tremendous field for such artists now in New York and very large sums are paid for the first class ones. I sincerely hope that this phase of acting will die out as soon as possible.' The Gallipoli would-be cinematographer clearly had a lot to learn about the film business, and considering his own lecture tour debut in an alcoholic haze, his comments smacked of hypocrisy.

Ashmead-Bartlett's two New York lectures involved more hurdles than just the pro-German press. He could not get his slides and maps through Customs. And once again he fell ill on the vital opening night, this time with influenza. A specialist worked on him with sprays and 'all sorts of patent cures', guaranteeing he would have Ashmead-Bartlett speaking that night. It worked, but only just. Ellis spoke for an hour and a half, but he was feeling 'more dead than alive'.

Trailing yellow press reports of his activities — the Hearst papers were the worst, he felt — Ashmead-Bartlett was relieved to leave for the Pacific coast to board a ship in Vancouver for Australia. Fearing more twisted reports in the press, he cancelled a Pacific coast lecture. 'It is no use explaining the position to a few hundred people in lecture and then having several million read something absolutely different in the papers,' he told Lord Burnham in a letter.

Perhaps just as well. The Hughes government in Australia had decided that it was probably too late to stop Ashmead-Bartlett from landing, but Hughes moved to see that his tour was subjected to the 'most strict censorship'.

This was evident from the day he stepped ashore in Sydney from the steamship *Niagara* on 11 February 1916, coincidentally Ashmead-Bartlett's 35th birthday. Frank Tait, one of the managers of his tour, was on hand to meet him and had arranged for a group of returned soldiers to also attend. The *Niagara* was late docking and only Tait was there. Too late for the soldiers, said Tait. But Ashmead-Bartlett learned later that the government had stopped the welcoming, although it was filmed by a newsreel company, the *Australian Gazette*, as a news item.

Myth Maker

After checking into the Australia Hotel, reputedly Sydney's finest, he was whisked off to a reception from the Returned Soldiers Association at Baumann's Café, in between giving an interview to the *Sydney Morning Herald*. 'A brisk, breezy conversationalist,' commented the *Herald*, after Ashmead-Bartlett urged its reporter to get the interview over quickly.

In the *Herald* interview — repeated later in his lectures — Ashmead-Bartlett rammed home the message that he was not in Australia to create trouble. 'I have not come here to harp on the mistakes of the past, and I want to make that clear at the outset,' he said. 'I would rather dwell on the great and grand future that I am fully confident is in store. What I have come to tell is the story of the courage and heroism, and the truly wonderful work of those brave fellows who have made so great a name for Australia. We are all proud of them.'

It was what Australians wanted to hear, and Ashmead-Bartlett played to his audience. His initial dispatch had given the small, fledgling nation something to be proud of. At lectures and speeches Ashmead-Bartlett found that references to the bravery at the Anzac landing always drew applause. But by the time his tour was winding up, he became quite blasé, even perhaps cynical about it. Interviewed by reporters in Brisbane, he noted in his diary, 'I had to give them the usual tale about the glories of their country etc'.

Back at the Australia Hotel, the high-living Ashmead-Bartlett was puzzled. Was this really a hotel? It was little more than an 'enlarged public house' he believed. 'The rooms are small, the food very bad and the [service] practically non-existent,' he declared. It was the start of the author of the *Hero of the Dardanelles* story falling out of love with the homeland of his legendary fighters.

Worse was to come. The next day, as Ashmead-Bartlett prepared for an afternoon rest before his evening lecture at the Sydney Town Hall, the local military censor, Major L.F. Armstrong, who was also a barrister, summoned him. Armstrong informed him that, acting under instructions from the Ministry of Defence in Melbourne,

Ashmead-Bartlett would not be permitted to say a word until his entire lecture had been submitted in writing.

Nothing would be said that could possibly do any harm, Ashmead-Bartlett assured him. Besides, he never wrote out his lectures and had nothing prepared in advance. It would be impossible to do this before that evening. Armstrong appeared sympathetic. He apologised personally, saying he felt heartily ashamed of the role he had to play. But telephoning through to Melbourne, he was told the instructions had to be carried out. No relaxation was possible.

There was more. Armstrong confided that he also had orders to attend the lecture with four policemen. If Ashmead-Bartlett departed from the submitted script he had orders to stop proceedings and clear the hall. 'I think he had orders to arrest me, but was too tactful to say so,' said Ashmead-Bartlett.

Armstrong gave him until 6 pm to produce a manuscript of his evening lecture. He would call around to the Australia Hotel to read it. Ashmead-Bartlett was in a fix. Maybe he should call off the lecture? But his agents had told him it looked like being a packed house. Advertisements in the *Sydney Morning Herald* that very day offered seats at prices ranging from two shillings to five shillings each.

The advertisement had tried to ward off fears that Ashmead-Bartlett was a troublemaker. The lectures were 'not in the nature of criticism' it said, but describing Ashmead-Bartlett as the 'official War Correspondent of the British Government at the Dardanelles', went on to declare unabashedly:

> Mr Ashmead-Bartlett's Brilliant Pen Pictures of the marvellous achievements of the ANZACS have conveyed to the Mothers, Fathers, Wives and children and relations and friends of our gallant lads something of the dash and bravery of the Australians and New Zealanders. But now the great man is here amongst us. He will tell you in his wonderfully convincing manner the history of the ANZACS from the very date of the memorable landing on April 24th [sic] last.

Whether or not he was convincing, Ashmead-Bartlett was certainly fast on his feet. Leaving Armstrong's office he immediately devised a plan. Returning to the hotel he collected carbon copies of all the articles and telegrams he had ever written about the Dardanelles — some 150 000 words in all. When Armstrong arrived he handed him the sheaf of papers. 'I am going to lecture on all that, but I cannot say until I have felt my audience which parts I shall use,' he told the censor.

Armstrong's face fell when he realised he would have to read through the mass of documents in just two hours. After reading a few pages he flung the rest on a table and said, 'I am sure it will be all right, and that you will refrain from any kind of criticism'.

Just as he was leaving, Armstrong turned and said, 'I have forgotten something. My instructions are to send a copy of the lecture to Melbourne. How can that be done?'

'Oh that is quite simple,' replied Ashmead-Bartlett. 'I will have a reporter make a verbatim copy tonight and you can send it to Melbourne first thing in the morning.'

The ruse, said Ashmead-Bartlett, was how he defeated the War Office campaign against him in Australia. However, he would have to learn to live with the fact that he could not beat it in England.

Sydney's Town Hall that night was crowded. The *Herald* reported an 'overflowing attendance' with a liberal sprinkling of khaki, while the *Daily Telegraph* said the huge auditorium 'was not exactly crowded, but there were few vacant seats'. Ashmead-Bartlett, said the *Herald*, eager and alert, bounded up the steps to the stage and launched into a 'vivid description' of the invasion 'with rapid and incisive utterances'. The *Telegraph* complained that he had a chronic habit of dropping final *g*s.

In truth, with censors and police on hand threatening to close the lecture at any stage, Ashmead-Bartlett dropped more than *g*s. Starting with a declaration that he was not there in any 'carping spirit, and that any errors belonged to the past', he took his audience through a routine description of the invasion. The campaign's conception was 'undoubtedly very great' but its conduct was 'open to criticism'. The

Australians 'proved themselves' in the field. And so on. The fire-breathing Ashmead-Bartlett of recent months in England was clearly very much under the censor's hammer. Moreover the journalist, still recovering from his second bankruptcy only the year before, would have fully appreciated that the future of his lecture tour, and its fee of £2500, was in the balance. The historian Kevin Fewster says the Australian government worried unnecessarily about the tour — Ashmead-Bartlett tempered his comments to placate the authorities and ensure a commercial success.

The *Herald* report captured the subdued meeting, although it did not know of the underlying reasons. Ashmead-Bartlett, it said, did not court applause, and it was some time into his speech before the audience cheered. Ashmead-Bartlett began to play on the patriotism of the audience. Armed with the names of members of the First Brigade (NSW), he extolled their deeds and his audience responded. 'The house warmed to the narration of heroic deeds of kinfolk even dearer to their hearts,' said the *Herald*. 'In this way Mr Bartlett "made good" with the audience.'

The censorship, however, still chafed at the naturally rebellious Ashmead-Bartlett. Three days later at a luncheon in his honour given by the local journalists' association he lashed out. It was a surprise, he said, after breaking down the censorship system in England — no doubt a reference to his letter to Asquith and subsequent media campaign against Gallipoli — to find 'that I am handicapped here far more by the censorship than in England'.

The *Herald* declared that Ashmead-Bartlett as a luncheon speaker was in fine form, without any of the nervousness and apparent searching for the right word he had displayed in his lectures. Journalists might have liked his anti-censorship rhetoric, but the Australian censor was not amused. Armstrong visited him the next day, saying 'Melbourne' — where parliament and the bureaucracy operated until Canberra was built in 1927 — was 'incensed'. So incensed, in fact, that all future Ashmead-Bartlett lectures would have to be written out and submitted in advance of delivery.

Another stratagem was quickly devised as a lecture was due that night. Ashmead-Bartlett suggested Armstrong read a copy of the lecture he had given on Tuesday, and then send it to Melbourne as that night's lecture, while the transcript of the one he would actually deliver that night would do for Saturday's lecture. 'In this he kindly acquiesced,' he said. Armstrong actually believed that Ashmead-Bartlett's lectures boosted recruiting for the war.

Negative censors aside, Ashmead-Bartlett's public receptions were very enthusiastic. Between lunches, receptions, drinks with the staff of the Sydney *Sun* at the Rose Bay Golf Club, and speeches at intermission of the new play *Under Fire*, the author of the Gallipoli landing legend was in great demand. An old school friend even turned up at his hotel to borrow money.

An unusual incident occurred in the first few days of Ashmead-Bartlett's arrival in Sydney. Army recruits mutinied over being ordered to train for an extra hour a day, broke camp and seized trains and tramcars. Shots were exchanged. The *Herald* somewhat delicately noted that Ashmead-Bartlett, having seen the Australian soldier at the top of his game now saw him 'on strike, occupying the town and [making] a horrid nuisance of himself generally'.

Ashmead-Bartlett was horrified, citing it as showing the Australian concept of discipline. The soldiers, he said, having all come from trade unions, could not accustom themselves to the discipline of an army. 'They think they have the perfect right to go out on strike at the smallest pretext,' he said. 'There is no question that the Australian character is sadly lacking in any sense of discipline and obedience to senior authority.'

Coming from the man who cocked a snoot at British military authority this might seem a trifle rich. But it was indicative of Ashmead-Bartlett's emerging view of the land he had extolled. The more he saw, the less he liked.

There was one aspect of Australia, however, that he very much liked — the women. 'The ladies of Sydney are pretty and very free, independent and have the reputation of being extremely immoral,' he said with glee. Establishing that their 'great resort' was the Winter Garden at his hotel, he set out to test his conclusions. In their pretty summer frocks it was impossible to tell which of the female crowd in the Winter Garden were 'genuine ladies with virtue above suspicion' or which, in the local vernacular, were 'sports'. But the hall porter knew their 'form' and quickly arranged an introduction to two that Ashmead-Bartlett selected, a Mrs Ritchie and a Miss Parnell. Hiring a car, he took them for a drive to Rushcutter's Bay, and then back to the Australia Hotel for supper before motoring Miss Parnell home to Manly. He did not 'return until 3 am', his diary records in his usual discreet manner.

Australian women quite fascinated Ashmead-Bartlett, as they enjoyed freedoms he had seen in no other country. They appeared 'especially pretty' between 17 and 25, although they matured extremely quickly, owing, he felt, to the hot climate. But it was their freedom that amazed him, going about unaccompanied to hotels and dances, and on motor trips; meeting men friends and returning home at all hours of the night.

'They are for the most part very lax in their morals, all of which makes Sydney such a delightfully free and easy place to live in,' he said. 'But no-one seems to care, and the old free and easy life goes on from year to year.'

Sydney was Australia's other saving grace. The city made travellers from Europe feel less unfamiliar than anywhere else in Australia or New Zealand. Although woefully designed, the city seemed 'drunk with the joy of living and the joy of sport'. Sydney Harbour at night, with its twinkling lights, reminded him of Constantinople.

Australia as a whole, however, was deeply flawed, he thought. The 'besetting fault' of Australians was their childish belief that everything in their country was perfect, with the grandest cities, unsurpassed theatres and the best libraries, galleries, hotels and standards of culture in the world.

'Now of course all this is the height of absurdity and nonsense,' the elitist Englishman wrote. 'Australia and New Zealand are a very long way behind almost every other portion of the Empire. There is little or no culture — in our sense of the term — in the country. There are but few people with whom an agreeable intellectual exchange of ideas can be maintained. The conversation at dinners and parties is usually extremely banal and the mass of the population ill educated.'

Ashmead-Bartlett complained about lining up to use the hotel bathroom 'with the other inmates'. Food was a 'terrible trial', and it was practically impossible to get a decent meal. Food was just flung at patrons by waiters. Servants were almost impossible to find. Those brought out from England were speedily 'got at' by trade unions, charging prohibitive rates or finding other jobs.

The dominance of trade unions and their stifling effect of slow work and uniformity really got up the nose of the conservative Ashmead-Bartlett. 'It is difficult to understand how Australia will ever become a tolerable country for those accustomed to European civilisation, unless the tyranny of the trades unions is broken and the labour laws are altered,' he said. Wages were enormous compared to England; hours and conditions regulated; and Asian labour banned. It couldn't last, he thought, and the pressures of postwar settlement in a single empire would 'oblige' the unions to take in many new settlers. That eventually happened, but only really after World War II. Ashmead-Bartlett was before his time. 'White Australia' was not killed off until the 1960s, and union dominance lasted well into the 1980s and 1990s.

Postwar development, and intake of new settlers, became something of a theme. He raised it in speeches, and with politicians. 'You are a wealthy community . . . [yet] the population of Australia [then about 4.5 million] does seem to me to be ludicrously small,' he told a luncheon of the Millions Club in Sydney, urging a generous intake of British ex-soldiers after the war. Canada was preparing to do it, he warned. An imperial parliament, with elected representatives from Australia and the other dominions, was another issue he trotted out.

The low standard of political discourse was certainly an Australian characteristic he deplored. Politicians attacked one another and in turn were attacked in the press 'in a manner which would be considered absolutely indecent in [England],' he said. The best Australians did not go into politics, 'where the abuse is great and the rewards extremely small', preferring to make money and live well.

However, while Australians held their own governments in contempt they had extraordinary respect for the 'home country' government, implicitly believing it contained the best brains in the Empire, incapable of mistakes in policy or strategy. 'They therefore never questioned the wisdom of the Dardanelles Expedition or the methods of carrying it out, and the same spirit caused them to acquiesce in the evacuation without a murmur,' he said.

Melbourne was the next city on the tour, a journey in that era broken by the change of trains at Albury for the different rail gauges. The train he found uncomfortable, the food inedible and the attendants uncivil. 'They are of course all trade union officials,' he complained.

At the Oriental Hotel he was given a suite of rooms and proudly told that a previous inhabitant had been Sir Ian Hamilton. Ashmead-Bartlett made no comment. He called on the governor-general, Sir Ronald Munro-Ferguson, whose chief claim to fame, he sniffed, was his marriage to one of Lord Dufferin's sisters. Sir Ronald appeared friendly, and showed him around the garden. It was not until later that Ashmead-Bartlett learned how hard he had fought to stop the tour.

'I never saw him again during my stay in Australia,' he huffed. A call on Defence Minister Senator Sir George Pearce was unsuccessful. He was busy. 'In consequence of the spirit of hostility all round I shall bother no more with official people, but just get the tour through and then shake the dust of the country from my feet forever,' he said.

Ashmead-Bartlett seemed to blow hot and cold on his reception in Australia. After the cold shoulder from officialdom he acted like a wounded member of the establishment, resenting the lack of attention. Then, a few days later, after a well-attended lecture plus a civic reception complete with champagne, cakes and official thanks from the lord mayor, followed by a dinner at the Overseas Club at which the lady mayoress led a crowd in patriotic singing amidst 'much bad tea drinking', he was complaining about 'cursed public functions' and crying out to be left alone.

'How I long for some privacy and a rest from this constant publicity,' he wrote. 'It gets on my nerves.' So bored did he become by Melbourne that he started playing poker again, usually losing heavily. 'I am a fool to play,' he kicked himself. 'But being bored to death by the life, I simply have to do something to prevent suicide.' This was journalistic hyperbole, of course.

His first Melbourne lecture was well attended, although Ashmead-Bartlett felt he let down the audience by not making any sensational disclosures. 'I am of course prohibited from doing so by the censorship,' he said. The Melbourne *Age* disagreed that the audience was disappointed, reporting a 'most cordial' reception. Ashmead-Bartlett, the *Age* said, performed in a free, deliberate manner 'which returns the listener to his word pictures of his cable despatches written with so much force and vigour that were widely circulated over Australia'.

The defence minister finally granted him an audience. A 'typical Laborite', Ashmead-Bartlett declared, although believing he was also a man of intelligence and 'some education'. The lecturer complained to Pearce about the heavy censorship and 'how badly and discourteously I had been treated'. Adopting the opening message of his lecture tour, Ashmead-Bartlett gave Pearce assurances that he would say nothing that could possibly do any harm, and expected in turn to be treated 'in a reasonable and proper manner'.

It was another cry from the heart. Ashmead-Bartlett had been giving out these messages ever since his meeting with Law in London back in November, yet censors hounded him around the globe. He might have had one lapse, but he still regarded himself as a member of the military establishment. Back in London, he would promise again to live by military censorship. It would take a complete blackball by the War Office for him to appreciate just how deeply he had offended by his Gallipoli letter.

But in Melbourne, Pearce was quite accommodating, no doubt realising how the popularity of the journalist and his writings had already sparked the Gallipoli legend. Even as the two spoke, moves were afoot for an annual celebration of the Gallipoli landing, not yet a year old, that would later evolve into Anzac Day. Pearce promised to 'put matters right', and Ashmead-Bartlett said he kept his word.

After his first Melbourne lecture crowds began falling off. Expensive seats were filled, but not the cheaper ones. 'I am afraid the great public do not care any more for lectures out here than they do at home,' he complained. 'Cinema–cinema–cinema; that is the incessant demand of the lower intellectual orders.'

A worried Taits, the tour organiser, now proposed that he do a regional circuit as well. Ashmead-Bartlett reluctantly agreed. 'Whilst undergoing such misery one might as well try and make all the money possible,' he consoled himself.

As he toured regional Victoria, then Tasmania, Adelaide and Brisbane, Ashmead-Bartlett began to count the days before returning to England. 'I cannot stand this life, it drives me to despair,' he wrote. 'The absence of all culture and comfort, beautiful women and congenial friends gets on my nerves. It is horrible–horrible–horrible.'

In Sale and Ballarat in regional Victoria the halls were only half full. A local barmaid warned him 'they couldn't fill the hall these days with Harry Lauder'. The boat to Launceston was 'intolerably dirty', with people fighting over 'horrible food'. In Hobart he had to sign a document saying he would not say anything he had not said in 'Australia'. Not surprisingly, Ashmead-Bartlett believed Tasmania was a separate dominion.

In both Adelaide and Brisbane the local governors told him they were not permitted to attend his lectures by order of the governor-general, Sir Ronald Munro-Ferguson. 'This is assuredly the limit,' Ashmead-Bartlett moaned. He took to playing poker again, with more losses.

While the food, tea and coffee at receptions was generally 'horrible', there was one exception. In Adelaide, he motored out to Hyland

Penfold's winemaking estate to sample the local vintages. Ashmead-Bartlett thought that some of the light hocks and clarets were fine, but the rest of Australian wines were 'filthy in the extreme'. Local winemakers didn't appreciate that to follow the French in making champagne, port, sherry, hock and claret they needed different soils under different growing conditions miles apart. 'Such considerations matter not to the confident Australians,' he said, consoled by the fact that Penfold gave him a case of good port. 'Very acceptable,' he declared it, saying he needed some port for his lectures. Of course Australian winemakers would eventually make their international mark precisely by not strictly following French traditions.

Returning to Sydney, he found the delightful Miss Parnell was waiting for him, but there was trouble brewing with Taits. Ashmead-Bartlett's Gallipoli film had finally been cleared by the censors and was now showing in England. The Fraser Film Company in Australia had bought local screening rights and was preparing to screen it. The film was being advertised as 'something every Australian wants to see', and Taits were blaming the fall-off in lecture audiences on this. The lecture contract specifically provided that the film would not be shown while Ashmead-Bartlett was touring, but the timing was out of his hands. Besides, Ashmead-Bartlett believed the film boosted his lectures.

Just as he left for New Zealand, Taits relented and the film was finally screened in Australia. Miss Parnell saw him off on the SS *Riverina*, a 'dirty old tub', but Ashmead-Bartlett was glad to leave. 'I feel I am one days march nearer home at least.'

New Zealand, however, proved worse than Australia. An English officer of the Imperial Staff serving in New Zealand met him, telling him not to mention 'certain things' in his lectures. 'None of which I ever had the least intention of referring to,' he said. Nevertheless, an officer was assigned to accompany him everywhere he went in New Zealand. Once again, the fear was that he would say something to damage recruiting, although he had done everything to boost the numbers in Australia.

'You speedily grow tired of New Zealand,' he wrote. Australians were far more intelligent, he felt, despite the fact that New Zealanders looked down on them because of the convict settlements. A terrible wave of 'wowserism' (the anti-alcohol movement) was sweeping the country, with parts going totally dry. The sleepiness of the place was extraordinary, he said, with little or no intellectual life. 'Someone described the people as farmers out of servant girls,' he wrote cuttingly in his diary.

Even a week in Auckland, where he met a family containing some pretty young women who hospitably escorted him to the races, picnics and a round of golf, failed to lift his spirits. Rainy Christchurch on the South Island was endured in a fit of depression in his hotel room. 'I really wished myself dead,' he declared. He resorted to poker again, with further losses. 'My luck seemed to be dead out.'

On 16 March he sailed from Auckland for America aboard the SS *Macura*. 'Thank God I shall soon see America and England again.' Sailing across the Pacific his luck seemed to turn and he won £200 at bridge. 'It may help to balance the long line of lost quids,' he said.

In America, he stopped in Wyoming where some society friends were on a hunting trip. While the scenery and relaxation were enjoyable, the camping party was rent by lovers' tiffs. On leaving, Ashmead-Bartlett was presented with a grizzly bear cub, whose mother had been shot. In typical fashion, he decided to take it back to London. The bear proved a shocking travelling companion, downing copious quantities of milk, honey and meat every day. At the Ritz in New York the hotel management charged him US$4 a day to house the bear in a cage on the roof.

New York contacts opened up a new reporting opportunity. The Wheeler Syndicate, which had employed the late Richard Harding Davis, wanted him to take up where Harding Davis had left off — reporting the war from the Western Front. But how much would the military authorities let him see after the Gallipoli episode, Ashmead-Bartlett worried.

Very little, was the answer.

13

War Office Blackball

THE long arm of the War Office — in the form of a young officer — was on hand to meet Ashmead-Bartlett on his arrival in Liverpool aboard the SS *Baltic*. What had he been doing abroad? 'As they had followed me all round the world, never letting me out of their sight, the absurdity of all this is apparent,' said Ashmead-Bartlett.

The officer told him he had instructions to seize Ashmead-Bartlett's papers. Military authorities wanted to examine them. 'This was going too far,' thought Ashmead-Bartlett, whose dander was now well and truly up. He refused to hand over any papers except by force. In truth, he had little to deliver except some private diaries, letters and a large swathe of his original material on the Dardanelles campaign, most of which he was already negotiating to sell to the State Library of New South Wales to ease his chronic money shortage.

As the officer insisted, Ashmead-Bartlett realised the young man was actually quite embarrassed, as he was obviously unsure how far he could go in using force. Eventually the subaltern begged Ashmead-Bartlett to give him something so that he could show he had carried out his instructions.

Ashmead-Bartlett finally took pity on him. 'Here are some duplicate copies of documents connected with the Dardanelles,' he said. 'Take them. I don't want them.' The relieved officer left, and Ashmead-Bartlett hastened back to London together with his recent travelling companion, the grizzly bear cub. After donating the bear to the London Zoo, he applied for the return of his papers from the War Office, which had to hand them back. 'I then restarted my campaign against them in the English press,' he said triumphantly. But by mid-August 1916, six weeks after his return, Ashmead-Bartlett was in limbo. Lord Burnham at the *Daily Telegraph* wanted to send him to report on the Western Front. The new era of cocooned correspondents was in full swing, with the journalists housed together, fed a diet of official information, allowed to see only certain things, and then having their cables censored before dispatch. The well-connected newspaper proprietor discussed it with Lloyd George, who indicated that Ashmead-Bartlett should be allowed to go. But the War Office played mute and, with the nation suffering heavy casualties in trench warfare against the Germans, no politician was going to buck the military for the sake of one journalist.

Ashmead-Bartlett began to worry about the 'mystery and vagueness' of his position. One night at the theatre he met Sir Reginald Brade, the powerful secretary of the War Office who, when asked if it was alright for the correspondent to go out, replied vaguely that he 'thought so'.

Still nothing happened. Ashmead-Bartlett asked Lord Burnham to officially submit his name to the War Office to replace Philip Gibbs, the *Daily Telegraph*'s man in the small group of accredited correspondents on the Western Front. 'The War Office will then be obliged to give you a definite answer, and if by chance this is unfavourable I shall then bring the whole matter forward myself and fight it out to the finish,' he told Burnham with his usual bravado.

Ashmead-Bartlett believed he was on firm ground. William Maxwell, the Gallipoli censor and an old war correspondent, dined with him one night, telling him of an incident after Ashmead-Bartlett's departure. Maxwell had looked up the regulations, finding a War Office memo that authorised officers, and anyone attached to the Army, to write to cabinet ministers without submitting their letters to the censor.

Maxwell showed it to Colonel Tyrrell, the intelligence head who had been present the day the correspondent was booted out. 'Then we had no right to dismiss him,' Maxwell reported Tyrrell as saying.

When he showed Braithwaite, who had ordered Ashmead-Bartlett off the peninsula on Hamilton's instructions, he was told: 'For Heaven's sake, Maxwell, keep this dark for we haven't a leg to stand on, and he can get us all'. Hamilton made a similar comment.

'I really must know where I stand,' Ashmead-Bartlett fretted to Burnham, who promptly submitted his name to go to France. But as the silence dragged on Ashmead-Bartlett wrote to the War Office himself, seeking not only to accompany the Army in France but also to wear his old Boer War medals. He was rejected on both counts.

The French, however, proved more accommodating, and he gained accreditation to report from the French General Staff Headquarters. General Joffre, the French commander-in-chief told him: 'I want you to see the truth and to tell the world. It is the only reason you are here.'

Perhaps, but Ashmead-Bartlett still found it difficult to get to 'the only place of interest' — the Somme — where major battles were being fought. And he grew frustrated at the controls. 'I am afraid we are destined to play the role of historians rather than war correspondents,' he said. Nevertheless, the French earned his praise for selecting their best officers to show war correspondents around — unlike the English, whose military guides were 'a wretched crowd of narrow minded, ignorant and self important' officers.

Although writing long dispatches about Verdun, Ashmead-Bartlett was restless in the new controlled environment, and quite unhappy with his treatment in the *Daily Telegraph*. In October 1916 he complained to Lord Burnham about the placement of one of his articles on page three, and the small size of his by-line. The article should have been on page one and the by-line larger — the sort of treatment his reputation deserved, he complained to Burnham in petulant tones.

'Either I have some reputation as a war writer or I have not,' he wrote. 'If I have, the public should know I am writing for you again. If I have not, why trouble to send me out here at all?' If his work was not considered of equal importance to that of other correspondents, he wanted to come back to London.

Ashmead-Bartlett's sensitivity was no doubt due to the fact that, as he was stationed with the French forces, his copy was seen as of less importance than that from the five 'official' correspondents embedded with the British troops — a position he was denied by the War Office.

Lord Burnham replied, quite rightly, that Ashmead-Bartlett's letter had an 'intemperate tone'. Yes, his article should have been on page one, but the size of by-lines was all the same. Lord Burnham said he was not taking the letter as any serious intention to quit. But Ashmead-Bartlett was serious, and on 6 November he resigned. The real reason, he told Lord Burnham, was not the placement of his articles but being herded across battlefields with other correspondents. He felt he was 'no longer the man for the job'.

'It was probably a mistake my ever coming out again,' he told his proprietor. 'I have always been accustomed to work on my own and to roam at large over battlefields and to gain my impressions for myself and then to submit them to the censor. But now all is changed. We go around together in batches led by officers, and our very numbers prohibit visiting at the psychological moment the points which are of interest to the public, except on rare occasions.'

After 11 campaigns, Ashmead-Bartlett was finding it difficult to work in the new environment of total war. He could not get the 'interesting impressions' he had thrived on. Somehow, the romance seemed to have gone out of war reporting. In a speech after the war, Ashmead-Bartlett elaborated, saying the new Western Front war writers were as different from their predecessors as chalk from cheese. The new breed was part and parcel of the Army, and wrote purely in the interests of the Army. 'There is no rivalry and there are no scoops to be made,' he said. 'The very men themselves, have, for the most part, never been engaged in war before.'

But Ashmead-Bartlett was a star writer for the *Daily Telegraph*, and Lord Burnham was appalled at the resignation. He tried the old editor's trick — flattery. Ashmead-Bartlett's latest dispatch on Verdun was 'magnificent', Burnham told him. 'I regard it as the greatest

Myth Maker

achievement in journalism during the war — certainly on the Western Front,' he said. Yes, Lord Burnham conceded, the war correspondents' game had changed, and was now 'most unsatisfactory'. The liberty of criticism had gone, and all the authorities wanted was realistic and impressionistic descriptions of attack and defence, 'mainly when the advantage is on our side'.

Lord Burnham counselled him against a hasty decision. 'You cannot alter the conditions of modern warfare, and you are making, continuing and confirming your name as a war correspondent,' he said. As a further temptation to stay, he offered Ashmead-Bartlett a chance to report on the Russian Front.

A jaded Ashmead-Bartlett quite liked the Russian idea, but nevertheless returned to London to 'take a break'. Was there another reason behind this sudden move? From France, Ashmead-Bartlett had written to friends about plans by his old friend Fenton to launch a new Sunday newspaper 'run on business lines'.

Then, just a few weeks after returning, he suddenly wrote to a friend that he was off to America on business for Uncle Willie. 'If I bring the deal off I have nothing further to worry about for a long time to come,' he said. Ashmead-Bartlett wanted the friend to help him 'pitch a tale' to Inland Revenue, which must have been chasing him for tax. 'I am now engaged on the biggest deal of my life and I am determined to see it through,' he said. Whatever the deal involved, it fell through — another of the many dreams of wealth that Ashmead-Bartlett chased endlessly. Much bigger ones would come.

When he returned from the United States in April 1917 the War Office was waiting for him again at the Liverpool docks. This time his bags were searched and documents inspected. When an outraged Ashmead-Bartlett complained about an officer tearing pages from his diary, he was told: 'You ought to be flattered. We only examine the papers of well-known people. The others don't interest us.'

With the business deal off, Ashmead-Bartlett wanted to go back to war reporting. But the War Office would still have none of him in the tightly controlled news flow from the Western Front. The entry of the

Americans into the war, however, showed the real determination of the War Office to keep Ashmead-Bartlett out of war reporting at all costs.

By early 1918 the Newspaper Proprietors Association tried a new tack. Why not get Ashmead-Bartlett to write about the Americans in the war? But this quickly fell through when it was decided to group the Americans together with the British and French forces, meaning they could be covered by the already tightly controlled reporting flow. Trying again, the Newspapers Proprietors Association offered Ashmead-Bartlett the job of war correspondent for the British Sunday newspapers, sending him to Paris where he languished in the Ritz Hotel awaiting War Office accreditation.

Not surprisingly, the War Office turned him down. 'My hopes of getting to the front are once more blasted,' he told friends. Even the NPA wanted to know what was going on. Sir George Riddell, one of the proprietors, asked Ashmead-Bartlett what was happening. 'You had better get this matter cleared up as no doubt the same difficulty would occur if and when the question of your appointment as Correspondent with the American Forces arises for decision,' Sir George told him.

From the Ritz, Ashmead-Bartlett tried to do just that. He bombarded his friends and contacts with appeals for help. Lord Northcliffe; his old friend F. E. Smith, now Lord Birkenhead the attorney-general; and Uncle Willie were all asked to exert whatever influence they had to change the War Office's mind.

His appeal over vindictive treatment by the War Office was the same to all, but the actual message varied. Of course, it all went back to the Dardanelles and his letter to Asquith, he told them. 'Whether I was justified in my action or not, I only acted as I did because I felt it my duty to do so, and my views have been amply vindicated by subsequent events,' he told Northcliffe. 'It seems very unfair that I alone should bare [sic] all the blame for what happened at the Dardanelles, when there were so many others who played a far more prominent role than myself.'

And one of those, he told Birkenhead, was Northcliffe himself. It was Northcliffe and his influence that really brought about the withdrawal and saved what was left of the expedition, he wrote to Birkenhead. And since then Northcliffe's newspapers had attacked the military authorities many times while Ashmead-Bartlett 'had never written a word against any of them'. 'But he being too powerful to attack they concentrate on the lesser fry like myself and prevent me carrying out my profession,' he complained.

All appeals to the War Office fell on deaf ears. Indeed, as Ashmead-Bartlett then tried to gain American accreditation to work with their forces the War Office raised the stakes. Ashmead-Bartlett, it alleged, had shared a flat in Paris with a correspondent of the *Manchester Guardian*, Robert Dell, who was later expelled from France. Worse still, he associated with a Russian suspect. This, of course, was just after the Bolshevik revolution, and the clear implication was that Ashmead-Bartlett was sympathetic to the communists, perhaps a spy himself. This was an absurd suggestion given the journalist's conservative politics. He had already stood twice for parliament as a Conservative candidate.

Ashmead-Bartlett was furious. He wrote to the War Office claiming untrue charges were levied behind his back. He had never met Dell or any Russian spies. He wanted a full court of inquiry.

'I have been the victim of this ceaseless persecution ever since the Dardanelles campaign,' he told Sir Reginald Brade at the War Office. 'In America, in Australia, in New Zealand, on my return home, and subsequently in Paris. No one has ever dared yet to bring a single charge of any description whatever against my loyalty and patriotism. I may not always have seen eye to eye with the authorities, but I have always advocated the most vigorous prosecution of the war.'

Lord Burnham came in on his side, telling Brade that if the matter was not settled he would take it to the prime minister. At one point, the War Office appeared to lift its objection, saying Ashmead-Bartlett should ask the Americans. If they said OK, nobody would have any objection. But the American military replied that it would be 'indelicate' to authorise him to work with their troops, a clear indication that the War Office was working against him even in Washington. 'You will have to fight the matter out with your own people,' the Americans told him.

For weeks the matter flew between Paris, London and the staff of General Pershing, commander of the US Expeditionary Force in France. Eventually the American high command said 'No'.

Ashmead-Bartlett was disconsolate. 'I shall abandon war correspondents work altogether now and devote myself to other things,' he wrote to an officer friend. 'I am busy at the present moment negotiating for a seat as I intend to stand at the next election. If you want to have any power or influence in England you must be in Parliament. Then you can do what you like. I have been outside too long and I intend to make a great effort to get in this time.'

It was almost as if he was determined to get even, and with good reason. Ashmead-Bartlett may have helped save a lot of lives by campaigning for Hamilton's removal and the evacuation of Gallipoli, but he had destroyed his own career.

14

Seven Marriages, One Legal

IN the immediate aftermath of war, the old Hapsburg Empire, which had been part of central Europe in one form or another since the 12th century, collapsed. Its dual monarchies, Austria and Hungary, were in turmoil, rent by nationalists, communists and a rapid influx of speculators trying to snap up bargains in everything from real estate to art as local currencies collapsed.

The allied leaders, in Paris to thrash out a peace deal with Germany, were trying to draw new national boundaries for central Europe as Romania, Serbia and the Czechs sought to carve off pieces of the crumbling Hapsburg Empire. And in both Hungary and Austria the spectre of communism reared, fanned by Vladimir Lenin's new Bolshevik regime in Moscow.

At the *Daily Telegraph* in London, Lord Burnham sniffed a major new crisis right on the heels of the war, dispatching Ashmead-Bartlett to cover it from Vienna, the Austrian capital. For Ashmead-Bartlett it was chance to re-invent his career as a global roving correspondent after the frustration of sitting out the final war years under the War Office blackball. Ashmead-Bartlett, long a political conservative, was also drifting to the right wing of conservatism. His new assignment would take on more significance than just filing a few articles. He developed a passion to save Europe from communism, and was prepared to again sacrifice his journalistic career for the larger cause. But this time the cause included the Holy Grail of his life — money to pay for his high adventure lifestyle — as he became embroiled in events he could never write about, playing some extraordinary roles as a counter-revolutionary, speculator, food relief organiser and even a modern day Scarlet Pimpernel, saving women and children from communist terror.

By January 1919 Ashmead-Bartlett was in Vienna, staying at the Hotel Bristol and making regular trips into Hungary, where Count Mihaly Karolyi had just set up a leftist government, promising general suffrage and land reforms. But the eccentric Karolyi was threatened not only by attacks from neighbouring Romanian and Serbian forces, but also internal insurgency organised by the militant journalist Bela Kun, a soviet agent of Hungarian-Jewish origin who was close to Lenin.

Initially, Ashmead-Bartlett's main concern was a new Austrian alliance with Germany; he wrote in newspaper articles that it would enable Germany to control all the new republics formed out of the collapse of the Hapsburg monarchy. 'They will have the gateway to the Balkans and on to the East,' he said, arguing that Britain might just as well have not fought the war. 'These people must be fed,' he implored, becoming involved in the allied food relief effort. 'Send them food and they may keep quiet.'

Deepening unrest, however, quickly riveted his attention on what he saw as the communist menace. 'Personally I fear above everything else an outbreak of Bolshevism in these parts,' he told Lord Burnham. He saw Bolshevism as 'threatening the entire civilization of Europe'.

Budapest was in turmoil. Karolyi was out of his depth, trying to create a government from a leftist coalition of his own Independence party, the socialists and the radical communists. The coalition government was joyfully welcomed by revolutionaries, soldiers and sailors. Ashmead-Bartlett lunched with President Karolyi and some of his supporters, including sailors of the fleet. 'We all dined at the same table, with the president sitting at one end and a sailor with his low neck and red shirt at the other,' he said. 'I never thought to find myself in such strange company, but misfortunes make strange bedfellows.'

In March 1919 Karolyi's government fell, swept away by Bela Kun's forces. Ashmead-Bartlett was in Vienna, but hurried to Budapest. On the train he met a Hungarian countess returning home with her children. Both she and her husband were on the communists' suspects list, and she handed Ashmead-Bartlett 80 000 Hungarian crowns and all her jewels, pleading with him to help her children out if she and her husband were arrested. They were, and Ashmead-Bartlett promised 'by hook or by crook' to help the children. He did, smuggling them out to Vienna. It was the start of a brief conversion from journalist to counter-revolutionary. In Budapest, he teamed up with a British diplomat, Sir Thomas Cunningham, to revive the Karolyi government, but in vain. Cunningham fled to Vienna, while Ashmead-Bartlett wrote articles for the *Daily Telegraph* warning of the spread of communism across all of Eastern Europe. 'Life is rotten here,' he told Lord Burnham. 'There is nothing to eat and nothing to smoke and very little to drink. I would starve but for the British mission who supply me with tinned stuff.'

Back in Vienna, he and Cunningham were prime movers among a growing band of Hungarian counter-revolutionaries who had fled Budapest. Ashmead-Bartlett asked Baron Rothschild to help finance the counter-revolutionaries, and the financier promised a million crowns. The journalist's life became a heady mix of guns and conspirators. He wrote that he had to 'drink champagne in the middle of the morning' to settle down.

The Bolsheviks in Budapest were reportedly furious with him for writing in the *Daily Telegraph* that they were just a Jewish mafia who could be knocked over by a single British division. But that did not stop him making another visit, this time attempting what he thought would be a 'pleasure trip' down the Danube.

'I was arrested three times, remaining a prisoner in the hands of the Red Guard for a day, and was shot at by every Bolshevik with a rifle from both banks,' he wrote. Most foreigners had fled Budapest by the time he eventually arrived. 'I think I am the last Englishman left in the place and you can rely on me [to] keep up the fight against Bolshevism to the bitter end,' he wrote to a friend.

Angered, he watched as the Bolsheviks confiscated money, houses, jewellery, antiques, furniture and even stamp collections. Ashmead-Bartlett was convinced Bela Kun was channelling the loot back to his

Moscow masters. Such was his growing hatred of communism that he vowed in a letter to a society friend: 'You shall never see me in Paris until I have helped to destroy and wipe this gang off the face of the earth'.

He certainly tried. The 'terror' of the next fortnight must have equalled the French Revolution, he believed. Ashmead-Bartlett threw himself into saving friends. 'Forged passports, forged marriage certificates, strange disguises all have to be utilized,' he wrote to Lord Burnham. 'At least six ladies have left the country as my wife and I cannot yet make out whether I am legally married to any one of them or not. I realize this is outside my work, but it is impossible to leave anyone to the fury of the gang in Budapest who rob them of all their money and jewellery and starve them unless they consent to work practically as slaves in any sort of job the government thinks fit.'

Red Guards raided the Ritz Hotel where Ashmead-Bartlett was staying, hunting for jewellery. Hungarian guests quickly gave their valuables to the Englishman. 'In a quarter of an hour I must have been worth about five hundred thousand pounds,' he said.

Censorship by the Bolsheviks forced him to devise a new code system with the *Daily Telegraph*. If he could write uncensored he would sign it 'Ashmead-Bartlett'. If censored by the Soviets he would sign 'Ellis Ashmead-Bartlett'. He warned Lord Burnham that cables signed with his full name were only to throw dust in the eyes of the Bolsheviks. 'If you get cables that would otherwise cause you to think I have become a Bolshevist myself, you will understand I am obliged to send them either through motives of policy or to protect myself,' he told his newspaper proprietor.

Amidst the turmoil a small delegation from the Peace Conference at Versailles arrived in Budapest, led by General Smuts, the former Boer War leader who had served in the Imperial War Cabinet during the war. Ashmead-Bartlett and the counter-revolutionaries were appalled. They had hoped for an armed force to fight the communists. Instead, said Ashmead-Bartlett, only an 'ancient Boer general' arrived. And he was prepared to talk with the communists!

The delighted communists called the two-person foreign press brigade to a special dinner at the Ritz, later moving to Ashmead-Bartlett's room, where the entire party drank copious quantities of wine and champagne. 'I had to drink about six bottles of champagne so as not to arouse their suspicions,' he told Lord Burnham. 'They disclosed to me their innermost secrets. At three a.m. they left me, swearing eternal friendship and offering me 10,000 pounds in English money if I would only join their cause and get the *Daily Telegraph* communized.'

There was little chance of that. Burnham was just about to become a Viscount, while Ashmead-Bartlett was busily advising the new Hungarian conservative forces of Count Karoly Huszar on how to topple Bela Kun, and writing negative articles about the regime in the *Daily Telegraph*. In late April the communists ordered Ashmead-Bartlett to leave the country. 'They were absolutely rabid with rage at the attacks I have made on them,' he said.

Back in Vienna's Bristol Hotel his determination to topple the communists increased. 'This business has ceased to be for me a purely newspaper one,' he told Lord Burnham. But all his schemes had a comic opera touch. A planned 'uprising' on the border failed when Austrian police arrested the counter-revolutionaries. Then came his maddest scheme of all — the capture of the Hungarian embassy on the Bankgrasse in Vienna, a bizarre venture in which Ashmead-Bartlett would play a journalistic version of Indiana Jones.

Hungarian counter-revolutionaries occupied the communist embassy one night, 'arresting' the 16 inhabitants and setting a trap for an expected Bolshevist official. Worried about a reprisal attack from communist sympathisers, they sent a messenger to Ashmead-Bartlett with a request for more guns. The messenger found Ashmead-Bartlett dining with counter-revolutionary leaders. They all celebrated with champagne, sending the messenger back with a few bottles — and two more guns.

Later that night he went to the captured embassy to take charge, first organising the trap to capture the visiting Bolshevist official, and then the 'serious business' of counting the huge stash of cash the Bolshevists had smuggled into their Austrian embassy to finance local propaganda. For Ashmead-Bartlett and his fellow conspirators it must have been a bit like stumbling into Aladdin's Cave as they rummaged through the bags of cash. One hundred and thirty-five million crowns and 300 000 Swiss francs was the final count — a huge sum of money in the days before the value of the crown slumped. Counting it, he said, 'You will experience emotions you have never known and will excuse every crime that was committed against the sacred laws of property'.

With the counter-revolutionaries left to guard their captives, Ashmead-Bartlett organised the money into two huge bags and headed back to the Bristol Hotel, arranging for his driver to drop him a short distance from the door to avoid suspicion. But he had not calculated on the sheer weight of the paper money and arrived at the hotel's front door about 4.30 am, puffing and dragging the bags.

'What have you got there?' inquired the old night-porter.

'Oh, I have a lady friend, a Miss Wood, who has just escaped from the Bolshevists, and she managed to bring out some of her belongings in these bags. I have promised to take care of them for her. Will you carry them upstairs to my room?'

The night-porter strained to lift them. 'Isn't it astonishing what women can find to put in bags,' he said. 'My wife fills hers up like this whenever she travels.'

In his room Ashmead-Bartlett stuffed the bags under his bed, and kept two pistols handy as he tried to sleep. Given the excitement of the night and the stash of money under his bed he could not doze off. 'Uneasy lies the head that wears a crown,' he punned in a letter to a Countess Catya. To another he said: 'I don't suppose so much money has ever been taken in the history of the world. It was a great night, the best I ever had and the most amusing.'

Some of the amusement quickly faded when the newspaper *Der Neue Tag* featured a story naming Ashmead-Bartlett as a ringleader in the embassy attack. The report said he had handed the money to

219

Cunningham to give to the allied powers — a doubtful proposition, although he was deeply involved with the British embassy. So deeply, in fact, that both of them issued denials, but the press kept hounding Ashmead-Bartlett. 'Really, this publicity is most trying, but I suppose one could hardly expect the greatest burglar the world has ever known not to come out sooner or later,' he said, obviously relishing his new role.

Ashmead-Bartlett soon found himself in police custody, along with his co-conspirators. A police interrogator pointed to the newspaper report, saying: 'Well, Mr Ashmead-Bartlett, it is stated that you were the ringleader of this raid on the Hungarian embassy the other night.'

'I assumed a most innocent air and replied, "I have the reputation of being one of the most foremost journalists of England",' Ellis replied. 'What would my paper have said had I not been present at such an interesting and entertaining evening?'

The police inquiry was as comic as the raid itself. Ashmead-Bartlett and his fellow conspirators were all released, despite the fact that several of those arrested had implicated the journalist. Bela Kun lifted diplomatic immunity and the embassy captives were liberated.

Undeterred by such publicity, Ashmead-Bartlett resumed his lead conspirator role, organising events from the Bristol Hotel, ducking more police inquiries and playing ringmaster to the counter-revolutionaries squabbling over their sudden pile of cash. He worked up a proclamation for a democratic Hungary, which he had printed. It read as if it was straight out of a revolutionaries' manifest: 'Hungarians! Will you remain a race of ruined slaves or will you choose your own government and your own leaders? The time has come to strike.'

Dual lives as correspondent and counter-revolutionary collided, however, when Bela Kun was toppled in Budapest after just 133 days in power, and Lord Burnham now wanted Ellis to go to Russia to report on the new Soviet government instead. 'Vienna is finished,' Burnham told him in a cable. 'Go to Petrograd.' Ashmead-Bartlett was shocked. The situation in Hungary and Austria was more critical than ever for the peace of Europe, he told his boss. The Hungarians were trying to form a new government under Count Karoly Huszar, swept to power as a nationalist army under Admiral Horthy entered Budapest. 'The leaders in all this have been Cunningham and myself but his name must never be mentioned,' he replied to Lord Burnham. 'We have organised the whole counter revolution against Bolshevism and we have brought all the conflicting interests together and united them with a definite policy under Count Karoly.'

What a turnaround. Only a year or so before the British government was blackballing Ashmead-Bartlett from his job as a war correspondent. Now here he was acting as a British agent provocateur, working hand in hand with the Foreign Office to topple a regime in central Europe. Ashmead-Bartlett spelled out to Lord Burnham his plans to 'run through' to Paris to plead with the allied leaders then thrashing out the peace plan to send support forces into Hungary to defeat communism. If he was withdrawn everything could collapse again into disorder. He wanted release from his contract, promising Lord Burnham he would continue to both fight the Bolsheviks and file reports for the *Daily Telegraph*.

Lord Burnham was unimpressed. His star journalist had gone native. The paper could get a Reuters wire service coverage of Austria–Hungary, he replied. What he really wanted was a good coverage of the Russian Front, from which there had been very little reliable news. 'But I can see that what you want to do is to stay and continue your political work in Austria and Hungary,' he told Ashmead-Bartlett. While this was valuable it was not the newspaper's business. This was a job for the British government, not a newspaper. Lord Burnham accepted his resignation. 'Come and see me when you return,' he said.

Ashmead-Bartlett cabled in his formal resignation, but he was very disappointed. The newspaper had failed to print some of his stories, and now it was prepared to let him go. 'I have had quite enough of them as they have no courage and no appreciation of one's work,' he wrote. This was unfair. The paper wanted a correspondent, not a political agitator.

He hurried to Budapest, travelling in the same carriage that Archduke Ferdinand took on his fatal trip to Sarajevo in 1914, where his assassination sparked World War I. The new Karoly government handed him an extraordinary assignment — to take their case to the Peace Conference at Versailles.

Ashmead-Bartlett rushed to Paris, and through British diplomatic contacts arranged a meeting with the British prime minister, Lloyd George, who was then negotiating the postwar carve-up with Prime Minister Clemenceau of France, President Wilson of America and Prime Minister Orlando of Italy. The meeting was opportune as the Big Four were just about to consider Hungary.

Surrounded by officials and maps of Europe, Lloyd George listened as Ashmead-Bartlett made the Hungarian case for both self-determination and support from the allied powers. As they talked, Ashmead-Bartlett felt the prime minister and his advisers showed a 'painful ignorance' of the situation in Hungary.

Perhaps that cut both ways. Pressed by Lloyd George about the aims of the new Hungarian regime, Ashmead-Bartlett said that what they really wanted was to be a self-governing country within the British Empire. And they wanted an English prince for their throne. Could they borrow one of the King's sons? 'I doubt whether one of them would be willing to go,' laughed Lloyd George. The prime minister also pressed Ashmead-Bartlett on communism. Wouldn't it die out by itself? Surely Europe was strong enough to resist it? Ashmead-Bartlett replied that a firm hand would be needed to destroy it in Hungary. If left alone, it would spread through all the neighbouring countries.

After handing the new Hungarian government's policy declaration to Lloyd George, who promised to take it to the Peace Conference that afternoon, Ashmead-Bartlett felt satisfied he had done everything he could to brief the allies about Hungary. That night he played bridge with friends, losing 2000 francs.

But his real 'Waterloo' came in Paris in June. At a party, some of the women guests played a game of throwing small sticks and feathers at each other. Ashmead-Bartlett 'amused' himself by pulling the sticks from the hair of a Mademoiselle Marie Alejandrina Elizalde, known as Nina — a smallish, dark-haired, pretty Argentinian woman with deep brown eyes. He arranged to call her. His diary of two days later, 17 June, reads: 'This is the anniversary of Waterloo and likely to prove mine as well, for it was during the course of the evening that I proposed to Mlle de Elizalde, and was accepted by that lady — or at least provisionally so for I do not know to this day exactly how it all came about.'

They had gone to a ball, dancing together most of the night. It was love at first sight. Later, as he took her out into the garden, Ashmead-Bartlett found he had grown 'extremely fond' of her, and proposed. Nina did not answer, but on the drive home they had a long discussion, finding that they were both similarly smitten. In the end, she said yes. They had known each other just 48 hours.

Ashmead-Bartlett was stunned by the sudden turn of events. 'Of all the pieces of unadulterated folly of which I have been guilty in my life, this is assuredly the greatest, and God alone knows into what unhappiness and trouble it may lead me in the future,' he confided in his diary. 'I know little or nothing of my future wife and she knows absolutely nothing about me, otherwise she would never have accepted my premature proposal in the way she has done.' Still, he could not deny that Nina was a woman of extraordinary charm and beauty, and also of excellent character. There was no hint of slander about her in Paris, where she was staying with her mother. Nina's family was part of Argentina's aristocratic landed gentry, with large property holdings.

Ashmead-Bartlett found her 'the embodiment of oriental grace and calmness'. She told him she had Moorish blood and that she was the laziest woman on earth, only ever playing two holes of golf and spending hours lying in a hammock reading. She did not even know how to write a cheque, much less cash it, he exclaimed.

Still, he worried that his 'peculiar temperament' would not permit him to appreciate her affectionate nature. Ever the rhyming wordsmith, however, he was amused to think that after having girlfriends called Lena, Edna and Gina he would now have a wife called Nina.

While Nina worked on winning her mother over to the marriage — she had wanted Nina to marry an Italian — Ashmead-Bartlett went off to the signing of the Versailles Treaty in the ornate Hall of Mirrors, buying a top hat and hiring a car for the occasion. He was delighted to meet Lester Lawrence and Keith Murdoch from Gallipoli days. But another Australian connection left him unimpressed. 'There was an ungainly scramble for autographs, led by the Australian Mr Hughes,' he noted in his diary. Billy Hughes, the irascible Welsh-born Australian prime minister, had been an unlikely star at the Peace Conference, often a thorn in the side of President Wilson.

Hughes's autograph-seeking performance aside, Ellis, in a cabled report for the *Daily Telegraph*, declared that the peace ceremony was 'a feeble and unsatisfactory ending to the greatest drama in history'. None of the German leaders who had brought on the conflict were present.

Nina now wanted them to marry immediately. 'I think she imagines I may never turn up again,' he said. But local protocol dictated a civil ceremony at the Mairie before a church wedding, and this would take a few weeks to organise. Nina's mother, a wealthy member of the de Ramos Mejia family, meanwhile tried to dissuade him from the marriage, telling him her daughter was 'quite useless as an assistant to any man'.

Ashmead-Bartlett awoke in Paris one morning determined not to marry, but then quickly changed his mind. But business in central Europe was pressing, so he left for Vienna, losing 2700 francs at the casino in Geneva on the return trip. In Vienna, his 'old gang' told him not to get married. He sent Nina a long letter which effectively amounted to delay unless she could arrange the paperwork and come to Vienna.

Ashmead-Bartlett's personal letters to Nina at the time reveal a man torn between the pressing prospect of big business deals in

Vienna and his marriage in Paris. At the time he met Nina, Ashmead-Bartlett was desperately juggling his part of the loot from the raid on the Hungarian embassy. An incident revealed in his diary confirms how he held on to a pile of the Hungarian crowns. The counter-revolutionaries asked him to part with some of the loot still in his charge. 'I absolutely refused,' he said, 'declaring it must be kept to save those who may find themselves stranded without funds unless the Entente cares to intervene'. They reluctantly agreed.

But he was only rich in Hungarian crowns, and they were rapidly falling in value. Attempting to launder the crowns into 'real' money, Ashmead-Bartlett appears to have taken some of the loot across to Paris when he met Nina, and even on to London. Certainly he made a mysterious business trip to London while in Paris. Uncle Willie wrote to him in late June 1919, saying he didn't like carrying 'this paper money' around. 'I have great doubts as to its value, at any rate for a long time to come,' he told the budding entrepreneur. Why not deposit it somewhere, and keep your name out of it, Uncle Willie advised him. Better still, thought Ashmead-Bartlett, why not buy assets. Through this period he engaged in a blizzard of investments, from mines to railways in Eastern Europe, Hapsburg Empire jewellery and share deals with Uncle Willie. He put three million crowns into railway options, and sent experts to inspect coalfields for investment. At one stage he was in deep negotiation with the Karoly Hungarian government to bring in a British syndicate to set up a new currency bank. The British embassy backed him, seeing it as a way for England to gain some control and to counter growing French influence.

Deals for icing wine, buying Chinese figurines and Persian vases, leather and even gambling concessions all absorbed him. 'All through the week I became obsessed with a mania for buying things, and seriously alarmed Nina, who thought I had gone mad.' He bought a diamond necklace for 90 000 francs, and then began to dabble in pearls. At one point an art deal was offered that would make modern collectors weep. A dealer told him about a secret warehouse stash of

Hapsburg art and furniture. An inspection of the two-acre warehouse blew his mind. 'From floor to ceiling the rooms were packed with priceless furniture, tapestries, porcelain, bric-a-brac and bronzes, not to mention imperial cradles, historic benches and summer house furniture on which numerous emperors, kings and queens have disported themselves in the past.'

Vienna was effectively 'sacked' in those years, as the fall of the crown produced panic selling of assets. Speculators piled into the city from all over Europe, fighting for places on all available trains. Every foreigner in Vienna was stricken with speculative fever — even the press, heads of diplomatic missions and their staffs. Ashmead-Bartlett described the atmosphere in his later book, *The Tragedy of Central Europe*:

> The moment official hours were over for the day, the whole of the staffs of the missions rushed into the streets, tumbled over one another in the shops and held receptions in the hotel corridors, receiving anyone who had anything to sell, buying, buying, buying, anticipating their salaries and sending home their purchases in the care of venerable, hoary-headed Kings messengers, at the Government's expense and under Government seals. What a life!

A passage in his 1923 book on central Europe is almost a self-portrait. 'With the government turning out millions of kronen per week, it was extremely easy to acquire an immense fortune in kronen, but extremely difficult to turn it back again into pounds sterling, francs, dollars, or any of the more stable exchanges of Europe,' he wrote. 'Thus only an infinitesimal proportion of the speculators really made money in the end, and the majority of them must now be starving in Vienna or else have taken to other more profitable fields of activity.'

The kronen, or crown, was hammered from many directions. It was issued at slightly higher than par to the Swiss franc, but by the end of 1918 it had already lost 60 per cent of its value. The combination of communist terror followed by invasions from neighbouring states (Romanian troops reached Budapest) sent the Austro-Hungarian currency reeling. Then the allies at Versailles imposed the punitive Treaty of Trianon on Hungary, extracting gold and appropriating land and people to neighbouring states. Hungary was reduced to its Magyar rump and excluded from international trade.

The Hungarian government printed more and more notes. Although the currency and inflation stabilised briefly in 1921, from 1921 to 1924 both were in overdrive. By 1924 the paper Hungarian crown, par with the Swiss currency just a few years previously, was worth little more than 0.0070 Swiss francs, or 0.001 American cents. This would have reduced the 135 million crowns looted from the communists in Vienna to just a few thousand dollars. Inflation tells the other side of the story. From a cost of living index of one in 1914, Hungary's index rose to 70 in 1920, settled back to 42 in 1921, and then roared away to reach 21 817 by 1924. Hyper inflation just wiped away personal savings and the value of assets. Ashmead-Bartlett softened this fall by investments and switching what he could into other currencies.

'My money will always be of value in Hungary,' he wrote in self-assuring terms to Uncle Willie in August 1919, from Paris. He admitted, however, that he was worth a lot of money in Hungary, but little in Paris. 'I am not a seller at the present time as the crown is very low, but I am quite convinced that things will improve, but it may take time. Acting on the best advice I have made certain investments in Poland which cannot fail and which may turn out valuable in the future.'

But most of his deals petered out. Like his Moroccan mining rights in the wrong country, Ashmead-Bartlett had again secured a prize, but it was the wrong money in the wrong place. Just how much survived is unclear. Later he would invest in real estate in southern France, but when it came to yet another bankruptcy in England he went under, at least in that country.

Nevertheless, his determination to remain in Eastern Europe, helping the anti-communists and playing the markets caused friction with Nina, still waiting patiently in Paris to be married. At first there were doubts that the marriage would even go ahead. Nina penned him what was apparently a sharp note after he had sent her some typewritten letters from Vienna. Ashmead-Bartlett's long response revealed a man riddled with doubt about marriage, about his future wife and whether she could cope with his lifestyle, and about their finances. He wanted to get the issue of typewritten letters out of the way first.

'If yu [sic] wish the engagement to continue, and I am sure you would not break it for such a trifling cause, we must come to an immediate understanding that you always allow me to write to you on a typewriter,' he told Nina. Handwritten letters caused him agony, he said, reducing him to such a state of nervous depression that he began to feel annoyance with the person he was writing to. The vexed issue of typed letters disposed of, he went on to tell Nina he was going through some 'bad moments' over the marriage. Would she be happy with him? They had led such different lives, belonging to different races. As well, he had 'suffered' so much in the past two years that he no longer had any faith in himself or the continuity of love 'or of anything for that matter'. Would Nina be able to support the life that he led, and that he would be obliged to lead before he settled down? It was one long round of adventures and excitement that might lead to temporary separations. 'You must in fact dearest Nina clearly understand that I cannot abandon the role I am playing at the present time under any considerations.'

Nina was put on notice that, if married, he would not change his career. 'With me my career is bound to be my first consideration and there is no disguising the fact that it involves risks and discomforts such as no man has any right to ask a woman to share with him unless she is first made aware of all the facts,' he told her. 'You will never be able to domesticate me to the extent of making me abandon the life I have led in the past and it would be a fatal mistake for you to attempt to do so because I would at once become the most miserable person in the world.'

Money also worried him. Things were not turning out as well as he expected in raising French and English money, an indicator that converting his crowns into real money was more difficult than he thought. But this was not a vital obstacle, and if he could get through the next year 'we ought to be right for the future'.

'Now having read all this you are probably of the opinion that I am trying to break off our engagement,' he told her. Not so. He simply wanted to be frank with her. 'I remain of the belief that I shall steadily love you more and more. But in one way I am peculiar. No one really has any influence over me unless I am actually with them. I might leave you for a year but the moment I return you would find me exactly the same.'

Nina had been warned. Long absences became the norm for their 12-year marriage.

One other thing worried him — their ages. He was 38 and she 32. He forecast that he would die about the age of 53 or 54 — an optimistically accurate prediction as he actually died aged 50. 'We shall at least have ten good years and if we are happy during that period we have not done so badly out of life.' The age question worried him, however, as many 'kind friends' had told him he was a fool to marry a South American or a Spaniard as they all became old and ugly at age 40. 'You must promise me dearest Nina never to do this. At the same time I probably would never notice it if I love you.'

Assuring her that he would never raise these subjects again, he told her that he could not break off the engagement even if he wished. As she had written to him: 'You are mine and I am yours'.

Nina was obviously upset, for his letter had added to a bout of illness and she suffered from delicate health. 'I will promise you never to write another line about myself,' he said, seeking to mollify her. But he had some more bad news. He could not make it for the planned wedding day. Urgent business in Poland could not be delayed. 'So much depends for your future welfare on the development of events out here that I cannot, either in my own, or your interests act otherwise than I do,' he said in a clear reference to his new investments. But he was arranging their marital home, an apartment in Vienna, with a butler for himself. He would get her a maid and a cook. And friends had loaned him a castle for their honeymoon if she came to Vienna.

Privately, Ashmead-Bartlett was quite frustrated by the delay and the paperwork. 'Getting married is the most infernal nuisance I have known,' he confided in his diary. 'You can run away with another man's wife or sleep with any woman without the slightest bother or interference from anyone. But directly you try and make a person an honest woman, the difficulties are almost insuperable.'

After some weeks delay they were married in Paris. At the civil ceremony in the Mairie he felt the French motto of 'liberty, equality, fraternity' mocked him. 'What irony these words at the hour of your wedding,' he said. 'Liberty mocked down at me; equality possessed a sarcastic smile; and fraternity seemed to whisper a long, last, agonising farewell.'

The new couple honeymooned at fashionable Trouville on the French coast. Ashmead-Bartlett's gambling luck turned as he won 2000 francs at chemin de fer in the casino. Nina did not approve of his gambling at first, but finally agreed, provided he gave her half the winnings. There was no mention of sharing losses.

Back in Vienna Ashmead-Bartlett resumed his investments, buying 40 per cent of options in a railroad for three million crowns, dabbling also in foreign exchange. 'I am anxious to invest some of my money in good things because the crown is falling lower and lower,' he complained. Hyper inflation was yet to come. Some investments started to turn sour. The mine was a dud, while the principals of the railway tried to blackmail him out of his investments.

Nina joined him for a while, but became ill, recuperating at a nursing home. As the deals began to peter out Ashmead-Bartlett took up writing again, sending in articles to the *Daily Telegraph* and beginning work on his new book *The Tragedy of Central Europe*.

The early 1920s saw Ashmead-Bartlett moving between Vienna, Budapest and Paris; then, increasingly, located in the French capital and Biarritz, where he became involved in real estate development. Their first son, Francis Ellis, was born in Paris in November 1920. Ellis wrote that his wife suffered terribly in the birth, and was only saved by the skill of the doctors. Another son, John, followed in April 1922, and a daughter, Madeleine, in September 1923.

Uncle Willie's death in 1921 raised the vexed issue of the inheritance of the Burdett-Coutts money, property — and name. Family folklore has it that Ellis refused to change his name to Burdett-Coutts, so the inheritance, and the name, went to his younger brother Seabury. Ellis received a gift of £30 000 from the will, providing him with an income of some £1300 a year. The inheritance created some bitterness. Ellis had always been close to Uncle Willie, even living with the Burdett-Coutts at different periods, yet it was Seabury who was willing to accept a name change to take the major inheritance. In 1929, when Nina visited England with the children, Ellis warned her against accepting any invitations from Seabury who, he said, had always behaved in the 'dirtiest way' towards his siblings.

As central European prospects soured in the early 1920s, Ellis resurrected his political career. Operating from Paris, but commuting regularly to London, he sought Conservative nomination for a seat in parliament. But he was fussy, not wanting to again contest hopeless campaigns in strong Labour seats. 'I cannot accept any constituency which does not offer me a sound and genuine chance of success, having already contested two forlorn hopes.'

North Hammersmith appealed. But after a lifetime of adventure he found its constituency politics boring, to say the least. He withdrew his candidacy in a hail of invective, telling his sister Audrey, who helped him in the campaign: 'I am by nature and temperament peculiarly unfitted to associate with the petty trivial weaklings who compose the vast majority of the inhabitants of North Hammersmith.' Of the local Conservative Party members he was even more scathing. 'Give me real men and women and I can do a lot with them. Give me these invertebrates and I am wasted.'

Ashmead-Bartlett loathed and detested 'middle class social orgies', telling Audrey he could not face a long campaign of tea and garden parties, dances and whist drives. 'This constituency needs nursing by a very rich man with a wife who finds the fulfillment of her marriage vows towards her husband can be best carried into effect by pretending to take an interest in other peoples offspring.'

After resigning from the contest, he noted in his diary: 'A great weight has been lifted from my soul and a still greater weight of bad whisky from my stomach. I would in fact sooner be a dog and bay at the moon than stand for North Hammersmith again.' But become a dog he did, and within a short time he was telling the Conservative hierarchy that there was a 'much better spirit' in the North Hammersmith association. He secured Conservative nomination for the electorate although Winston Churchill had been listed as a possible wildcard contender. Ashmead-Bartlett lost in the 1923 election, but was finally elected in late 1924.

Parliamentary life meant leasing a home in London, adding to his financial pressures as Nina and the children remained in Paris. Ashmead-Bartlett also confessed to Nina some early nervousness about speaking in the House of Commons, finding the solution in alcoholic fortification, as he had in his earlier Gallipoli lectures. Before his maiden speech he had a pint of champagne and two glasses of port. 'I received a first class reception and I was much congratulated,' he wrote her.

Ashmead-Bartlett was an ardent protectionist. His parliamentary speeches advocated higher tariff barriers, and he also urged young people to migrate to the dominions. But it was events outside parliament that dictated his political future. His 1924 Labour opponent, J.P. Gardiner, issued writs against Ashmead-Bartlett, his agents and printers over a pamphlet distributed in the campaign.

During the election a campaign worker had issued a pamphlet with the headline 'Parents! Save your children from the socialist Sunday schools', holding up Gardiner as an infidel who would banish religion, make the Bible a closed book and abolish the Ten

Commandments. It was clearly defamatory, and as the damages case progressed Ashmead-Bartlett worried about the costs.

'The truth is this parliamentary life costs far too much money for me and whereas it might lead to a career it is now a terrible burden on my shoulders and I have more difficulty than ever in making both ends meet,' he wrote to Nina, declaring he would not stand again. 'God knows what will happen if they get heavy damages in this libel case. I would then resign and leave England altogether.'

As it turned out, the court awarded Gardiner only £300, which was to be given to charities. But the toll of housing in London, supporting an electorate, gambling, plus his own lifestyle, proved too much. He went bankrupt again, forcing him to resign his parliamentary seat.

The court case proved great copy in the London press. 'Bolsheviks, money-lenders and gambling were discussed in the Bankruptcy Court when Mr Ellis Ashmead-Bartlett, formerly MP for North Hammersmith, was examined,' said one newspaper report. He estimated his liabilities at £11 118 and his assets at £311.

Ashmead-Bartlett openly told the court how the Hungarian counter-revolutionaries had captured a lot of money from the Bolsheviks, giving him a 'big portion', but its value declined, and his share eventually was only about £10 000. As to his present state, he had been in the hands of money lenders since 1921, and £10 000 of his current liabilities were from borrowing. The usurious interest rates showed he must have been rated a poor risk. One lender gave him only £1500 on a promissory note of £2700, and wanted his money back in instalments.

The papers had a field day. The *Daily Mail*, reporting Ashmead-Bartlett telling about the capture of the Bolshevik money and how the counter-revolutionaries had given him a 'commission' on it, continued:

> Mr Registrar Warmington: 'Prize money' (laughter).
> Mr Ashmead-Bartlett agreed and added that he had received a big sum but 'it suddenly collapsed and was worth nothing' (laughter).

> Asked whether the proceeds from the sale of certain land on the Riviera went in gambling, Mr Ashmead-Bartlett said, 'It might have been for politics or gambling. The whole thing is mixed up' (laughter).

It might have had its humorous side but bankruptcy ruined his parliamentary career. He also forfeited £1300 in annual interest from Uncle Willie's estate. Yet Ashmead-Bartlett was prepared to do this, and not save his name by using some of the money he had in Biarritz real estate development. He had estimated to Nina that the project could eventually be worth about 1.5 million francs, yet it does not seem to have figured in the bankruptcy case. Either he felt Biarritz was security for Nina and the children, or it was owned by Nina.

Nina, meanwhile, was having her own money problems. A cousin had defrauded her family of some of their funds in Argentina. Nina's family money, however, largely supported the Paris home, the upbringing of the children and family holidays back in Argentina. Minus Ellis of course, who never visited his wife's native country.

As he had done after previous bankruptcies Ashmead-Bartlett escaped back into journalism, spending the last six years of his life roaming the globe in search of headlines and books, and maybe that elusive business deal as well. The children saw only glimpses of him when he occasionally returned home for a few days. Once he returned with an Indian servant and a revolver, leaving both behind when he departed. His letters home to Nina reveal a man scratching for a living, trying desperately to maintain his standard of living, and sending back money when he could.

By 1926–27 he was in the international settlement of Shanghai, writing articles for the *Daily Telegraph* and apparently also involved in a cotton mill. How he came to manage and apparently own a Shanghai cotton mill is not known. Perhaps it was a last vestige of his Hungarian investments, or the consequence of one of his share deals with Uncle Willie. It was tough work. The mill had to be kept running 24 hours a day, otherwise the losses would be enormous.

Then Chiang Kai-shek's Nationalists assessed the mill for a US$60 000 'contribution' to fight the communists. If it was not paid the cotton would fail to leave the port, and that meant ruin.

Apart from the business distraction, China was in the throes of civil war, with an international force in Shanghai trying to ward off attackers. 'This is an armed camp full of murderers and assassins,' he wrote Nina. 'I never go out day or night without two pistols and I always have my hand on the one in my right hand pocket.' Quite often he stayed up until 3 am cabling reports to meet London's deadlines.

In his papers there is a mysterious letter from Ashmead-Bartlett, dated May 1927, to a Dr Lew Yuk-lin in Peking saying that his 'wife' had died in November 1926 after an acute illness of three days. 'Her death has been a terrible blow to me and at present I feel as though I can never really be happy,' he wrote. Nina, of course, was in France with the children at the time. Did Ashmead-Bartlett have a Shanghai housekeeper whom Chinese acquaintances might have thought was his wife?

Events in China saw Ashmead-Bartlett drifting further to the right politically. The country needed a dictator or foreign cooperation, he said. 'In my opinion other countries besides China will require the establishment of similar dictatorships before very long in view of the fact that so-called democracy has proved an utter failure everywhere.' This was not an uncommon view in that inter-war era.

This right-wing tendency was evident in two interviews he had with Mussolini, the Italian dictator, in 1927 and 1928. Apart from fairly soft questioning, he ingratiatingly told Mussolini that in the 1927 British coal strike 'the thoughts of thousands of Englishmen turned to your excellency and on every side one heard people saying, "If we only had a Mussolini"'.

In a typewritten speech, probably after the 1929 depression started to grip, Ashmead-Bartlett pondered what he would do if he were a dictator. The answer: abolish parliament, where MPs 'loll about smoking and drinking to all hours of the night', and have

Myth Maker

expert commissions quickly decide on new schemes. And just for a spot of fun, he proposed casinos at all seaside resorts as well as banning all politicians from making speeches for at least five years until the country recovered.

In 1928 the *Daily Telegraph* sent him to Russia to research a series of articles on the 11-year-old communist regime. Stalin was just ending the New Economic Policy, which allowed limited peasant agricultural trading, and beginning the forced collective farm program. Ashmead-Bartlett, no friend of the 'Bolos' as he called them, was astounded they even let him in.

Wanting to go, but anxious not to obtain a permit by false pretences, he devised a formula of words to give to the Soviet embassy in Paris. Sure, he disliked communism, but every country had a right to choose its own form of government. If communism suited Russia, it was not his affair. But he would oppose it vigorously in England. Therefore, he argued, he could go to Russia with an 'open mind'. The embassy was satisfied, and he secured a visitor's permit.

Stalin's gang regretted it. Ashmead-Bartlett found life was hell for ordinary Russians. 'The whole nation has sunk down into an abyss of misery,' he wrote Nina. 'It has fallen in the social scale to a primitive state of civilisation.' But there was no chance, he believed, of Stalin's regime being toppled. His articles, written after he returned, openly spoke of communist murders and warned foreign investors against setting up businesses. A Moscow friend wrote to him: 'Your stuff excellent. They are behaving as if you had raped their grandmother after a weekend in Mahomet's paradise at their expense. Can't understand it. Poor dears. Such ingratitude. We suppose you aren't coming back.'

In November 1929 the *Daily Telegraph* sent him to India to cover the campaign by the Nationalist leader Mahatma Gandhi for independence from Britain. He did not want to go, but needed the money. 'I need so many things and I have no money to spend on them,' he wrote to Nina. 'This will be my last journey I hope. I have never seen India and the situation there is very grave. It will complete my education on World Affairs.'

Debt problems pursued him in India. In one letter to Nina he promised to send her 'some of the debt I owe' shortly, and had already cabled some to a 'Cocando', reducing the debt to him to 5000. Details of the Cocando debt, and the currency involved, are not known.

Ashmead-Bartlett had not lost his nose for news, however. Hearing that Gandhi was to be arrested, he left Bombay at 4 am and drove to a spot where he found police waiting with three cars to capture Gandhi from a train. He upbraided the police.

'You will occupy the same place in history as the Roman soldiers who arrested Christ,' he told them. 'You will be accursed for all time.'

The police sergeant responded: 'I'll take my chance on that. I want my breakfast.'

Gandhi, dressed only in a cloth tied around his waist, was arrested when the train stopped. He gave Ashmead-Bartlett, the sole journalist present, a 'farewell message' before being taken away. Ashmead-Bartlett cabled the 'dramatic account' to London. Later, he told his son Francis in a letter that he would appear in the 'Indian's bible' when it was written as one of the few persons present at the arrest of India's god.

At one point in his wanderings in February 1931 he was in London, and in a letter Nina accused him of only being with people who thought of enjoying themselves. Ashmead-Bartlett was stung, as in Britain his bankruptcy actually debarred him from making any money. In a somewhat sad letter he replied:

> I can assure you the past two months have been the worst I have ever spent in my life without one single iota of enjoyment. Your ideas of life are really too absurd for comment. You can imagine how one enjoys oneself without money but what is worse being cut off from all one's friends because one has no clubs and nowhere to meet them. It is also very agreeable living in third rate public houses year in and year out. The conditions under which you live are a paradise compared to mine.

This was marriage by mail. The two corresponded irregularly, with only occasional meetings. Nina would sometimes express her anger either by not writing for long periods, or by sending him letters with no return address. Ellis reacted in his usual ironic style, saying he had not received letters she had obviously left lying about the house.

In early 1931 the *Daily Telegraph* wanted to send him back to Russia, but dramatic events in Spain drew him to the action there instead. The seven-year dictatorship of Primo de Rivera had ended, with elections producing a swing to the republican left. King Alphonso resigned after calls from the newly elected revolutionary leader Alcala Zamora.

'You have probably realised I am in Madrid,' he wrote Nina from the Ritz Hotel. The monarchy had collapsed 'like a pack of cards', while the nobility had behaved 'like the useless pack of privileged cowards they are'. Spain, he told her, was just at the beginnings of her troubles — another of his unnervingly accurate forecasts. The country later descended into civil war.

'I have no time to write more. I enclose 2000 francs. I could not send it because the Banks have been shut. I hope all are well at home. I expect I shall stop here for some little time ... Love to all ... Ellis.'

It was a poignant prediction for his last letter home as stay a while he did. He died in Lisbon a little more than a fortnight later, after going there to cover the arrival of the Prince of Wales. He had been unwell, and his illness developed into 'congestion of the lungs'. Ashmead-Bartlett died in a local Portuguese nursing home on 4 May 1931, aged 50. Nina arrived to be by his side, and two days before his death he converted to Catholicism.

Probably no other journalist had seen so many wars and campaigns, said the *Daily Telegraph*'s Campbell Dixon in their obituary the following day. It carried four decks of headlines — 'The Man on the Spot', 'Brilliant career of E. Ashmead-Bartlett', '30 Years of War', 'His letter that made History' — and reported many of his great scoops, his Dardanelles coverage and the letter to Asquith revealing the failure of the Gallipoli expedition.

'On the smallest as on the biggest assignment he wrote with unsurpassed vigour, lucidity and colour, and his rivals will be the first to admit that his death has taken one of Fleet Street's most brilliant and spectacular figures,' Dixon concluded.

Charles Bean, his Gallipoli rival, was even more generous. Ashmead-Bartlett's initial Gallipoli dispatch, he said, was probably the finest of its kind ever penned by a war correspondent. The dispatch launched Australia's Anzac legacy, a legacy that over the years would grow into the nation's most powerful image of itself.

15

Journalism and the Making of the Gallipoli Myth

AN accident of fate cast Ellis Ashmead-Bartlett across Australia's path. When he arrived at Gallipoli in early April 1915 with Lester Lawrence from Reuters news agency, the Navy quickly divided the pair to cover the big landings of 25 April. Ashmead-Bartlett was assigned to the battleship HMS *London*, while Lawrence went to HMS *Triumph*. As it turned out, the *London* was a lead ship for the Anzac landing, while the *Triumph* covered British troops landing south at Cape Helles. So it was from the bridge of the *London* that Ashmead-Bartlett peered through the grey dawn of 25 April 1915 to see if the untried Australian and New Zealand troops could prove themselves in battle, opening the blocked Dardanelles Strait for the capture of Constantinople.

His report of that landing electrified the world, according to his colleague Charles Bean. It wrote Ellis into the Australian story. Indeed, it became the most important page of that story. Had Ashmead-Bartlett been assigned to the *Triumph*, Australia might have a very different Anzac legend, if one at all.

Not that the English journalist knew much about Australia. While he admired the Australian troops he had watched training for the landing, he confessed later to Charles Smith, a Melbourne *Argus* correspondent at Gallipoli, that he and most of his countrymen knew almost nothing about Australia itself. Ashmead-Bartlett said that Kitchener's New Army that went to the peninsula in July fully expected Australians to look like Indians. Smith was astonished that a journalist who had so quickly captured Australia's imagination knew nothing of the country's trans-continental railway, its federal capital, or even of Melbourne's famous cable trams.

Ashmead-Bartlett, said Smith, did have one piece of intelligence about Australia, however. A returned traveller at his London club had remarked that the girls were pretty. Such attraction Ashmead-Bartlett would later verify for himself. Indeed, the local women, the prowess of Australia's soldiers and the beauty of Sydney's harbour were among the few aspects of Australia that the nation's myth maker actually liked when he visited for the only time in 1916. Then, he found the food terrible, service non-existent, the hotels unbearable, the press lazy, the politicians second rate, and censorship worse than in England. Worst of all for him was the trade union dominance.

Ashmead-Bartlett's main focus was not on Australia as a country. Outside his diary, he never published a word about the country or his speaking tour. Even when visiting he still thought Tasmania was a separate country. For Ashmead-Bartlett, Gallipoli and the fighting ability of the Anzacs — or 'colonials' as he continued to call them — was his sole focus. For him, Gallipoli was what is known in the newspaper trade as a 'good story' — an article that qualifies for page one or splash treatment. And in 1915 he needed a good story. Having just survived his second brush with bankruptcy, Gallipoli's flow of books, lectures and even film provided much-needed income.

Gallipoli may have been just another 'good story' for Ashmead-Bartlett, like his Moroccan, North African, Hungarian and Balkans yarns, but unlike the others it was one he could not shake. From the moment of his expulsion in September 1915, he and Sir Ian Hamilton settled into a personal and at times vicious war over the Dardanelles expedition that was to last well beyond Ashmead-Bartlett's death in 1931. Hamilton, desperate to apportion blame for Gallipoli's failure, at one point even sought to paint the press as traitors who delivered the expedition to the enemy.

After his campaign to relieve Hamilton and have the troops withdrawn, Ashmead-Bartlett took up the baton again at the Dardanelles Royal Commission in September 1917. He criticised the useless waste of life in frontal attacks, the poor medical facilities, Hamilton's failed strategy and his 'amazing proclamations' to the troops.

Hamilton replied in kind, informing the commission that as commander he had received intelligence reports that Ashmead-Bartlett's reports in the *Daily Telegraph* were translated and read out to Turkish troops. 'They had a great effect in giving them hope and courage,' he said.

The commission brushed aside such sniping, letting Hamilton off with some mild criticisms. A commander, its report said, should be judged by the results he achieves. In Hamilton's case, of course, the results were disastrous, although the commissioners said the Gallipoli failure was due to causes 'for which he is only partially responsible'.

Hamilton, however, was prepared neither to forgive nor to forget. In 1920 Ashmead-Bartlett received a 'bolt out of the blue' — an offer of a CBE in the Order of the British Empire for his 'work connected with the war'. At first he was offended, writing to Lord Burnham that all the shepherded correspondents on the Western Front had received the KBE, which gave them the much sought-after prefix of 'Sir', while he was being offered only the lower CBE. Rather than place himself in a lower category he would prefer no award at all. Burnham advised him against it, and in the end Ellis accepted the CBE.

In fact, he was lucky to receive the offer of any award at all. Behind the scenes, Hamilton had done his best to block it. When the War Office asked Hamilton for a 'special report' on Ashmead-Bartlett, who they said was in line for an honour, the Gallipoli commander let fly. He repeated to the War Office the intelligence report on how Turkish troops were cheered by Ashmead-Bartlett's report, throwing in for good measure other reports on the noted pessimism of the journalist. Hamilton saved his most damning remarks for the smuggled letter to Asquith incident. Whether or not Ashmead-Bartlett had the right to make such a communication (he had, the Royal Commission was told), he had broken the censorship rules in smuggling it out. 'Further, [he] had broken his word of honour,' he wrote, a phrase no doubt aimed at eliminating his adversary from any royal honours list.

Having failed, Hamilton shot a public broadside in his 1920 two-volume *Gallipoli Diary*, mocking both Ashmead-Bartlett's Bulair landing strategy and his idea of encouraging Turkish defections by offering every deserter ten shillings. His sharpest barbs, however, were aimed at both Keith Murdoch and Ashmead-Bartlett for their letters to politicians on Gallipoli. 'Reckless scraps of hearsay' and an 'irresponsible statement by an ignorant man', he thundered of the letter Murdoch had given to Asquith after Ashmead-Bartlett's had been seized in Marseilles. Hamilton detected the hand of an unnamed 'unscrupulous person' in the Murdoch letter. Dealing with Murdoch's accusation that officers at Gallipoli had been ordered to shoot their men should they waver, Hamilton wrote:

> Murdoch must be mad, or is there method in this madness? Mr Murdoch was not a war correspondent; he is purely a civilian and could hardly have invented this order on his own. No soldier could have told him this. Someone not a soldier — someone so interested in discrediting the Dardanelles Campaign that he does not scruple to do so, even by discrediting our own troops — must have put the invention about per Murdoch.

It was a thinly veiled attack on Ashmead-Bartlett, and the journalist quickly outed himself. First, he wrote to Murdoch setting the record straight between them that he was not the source of the order to shoot reluctant soldiers. The two had only met the evening before Murdoch left for London. The next morning Murdoch had asked him to write a letter to the prime minister. 'Thus I had nothing to do with any statements made by you, and you had absolutely nothing to do with any statements made by me,' he said. Their denunciations of the campaign had come from independent sources.

Next, Ashmead-Bartlett went public, ratcheting up the anti-Hamilton rhetoric. 'Hamilton was totally unfitted either by temperament or by training to be entrusted with the handling of great military operations of an extremely difficult character,' he commented on Hamilton's book. Hamilton's published diary was an attempt to throw the blame for the failure of the expedition on everyone from the government, to his generals, the poor quality of the troops, the French and the Royal Navy.

> The main responsibility [for the failure] rests with Hamilton for his own faulty dispositions in every fight in which the army was engaged, and his utter failure to appreciate the true strategical position with which he was faced … he frittered away his army time and time again in a series of badly conceived abortive attacks in which there was never room to deploy a decisive force at any one point, even if he could have found the key to the enemy's position.

Ashmead-Bartlett echoed these remarks in his 1928 book, *The Uncensored Dardanelles*, where he also developed the theme that Gallipoli suffered because of a lack of a British General Staff. Instead Lord Kitchener's one-man reign created internecine warfare between the Western Front, Gallipoli, Egypt and Mesopotamia.

Hamilton pursued the vendetta beyond the grave. In 1933, two years after Ashmead-Bartlett's death, he gave an after-dinner speech to the Buckinghamshire Yeomanry, also known as the Royal Bucks Hussars, Lord Burnham's old regiment, which had been pitched into the last great battle at Suvla Bay. Obviously still piqued by the journalist's criticisms, he sought to justify why he had tried to get Burnham to sack his correspondent.

'I could no longer stand the British public being told that our men were "panic stricken when the Turks began firing", and that there was a feeling of fear afoot on the peninsula, whereas the true spirit that did animate the Bucks Hussars was one of remarkable indifference to every attempt made by the Turks to frighten them,' he told the audience.

Not content with lashing Ashmead-Bartlett, Hamilton, 18 years after the war, turned on the entire Gallipoli press coverage. 'The press at Gallipoli, and especially in bringing about the evacuation, played the same part as the Presbyterian ministers played with Leslie's army of the Scots at Dunbar, when they made them evacuate their positions and delivered them to Cromwell and his Ironsides,' he railed.

Hamilton's vengeance is perhaps understandable. After Gallipoli friends cut him in the street. He was offered no further wartime position, and spent much of the postwar years unveiling war memorials, speaking at veterans' meetings and writing books to tell his side of the story. He later angled, surprisingly, for a diplomatic posting to Turkey, but was never offered any such position.

The press became just another of the groups he blamed for Gallipoli. While some of the London newspapers did campaign for evacuation, the final decision only came after it was recommended by the military itself. Hamilton's direct hit at the 'press at Gallipoli' — the correspondents — overlooked the fact that, apart from Ashmead-Bartlett, none of them actually criticised the campaign. One had even betrayed Ashmead-Bartlett and Murdoch over the letter to Asquith. Apart from Ashmead-Bartlett, Hamilton himself had been treated tenderly by the Gallipoli correspondents. Bean described him as a weak character under the command of Braithwaite, who 'gilded the pill' with his beautiful literary style. But this was only said in Bean's diaries, not made available to the public until 1979. In his later official war history, Bean described Hamilton as a man of vision and courage, but lacking 'a certain element of solidity which is essential for true greatness in a commander'. Hamilton's character, said Bean, was 'no firm base for an expedition such as that at Gallipoli'. Nevinson, also in a later book, laid the blame for failure of the August offensive on the poor quality of the new English troops, mischance and misjudgement of the tough terrain involved — in short, everything except Hamilton's leadership.

Hamilton's 1933 outburst against the Gallipoli media failed to acknowledge a very curious episode in his divide-and-rule tactics to control the correspondents — a postwar, manipulative friendship with Sydney Moseley, the other journalist he had sent home. Moseley, who was at Gallipoli for about a month for the Central News Agency, seems to have drawn the ire of most of his colleagues, as we have noted. Nevinson thought him 'unfitted to associate on terms of social equality with officers or his fellow correspondents'. The correspondents all complained to Hamilton, who had the hapless Moseley invalided home.

Moseley was not without guile, however. After the war he sent an ingratiating series of letters to Hamilton, who readily recognised a soulmate in hatred of their 'mutual friend' — Ashmead-Bartlett. After Hamilton arranged a job as a clerk for him, Moseley told Hamilton that Ashmead-Bartlett's campaign against the general was inspired by personal spite. He also offered Hamilton the chance to use his (Moseley's) proposed book 'to say through me any new points you might desire to make public'.

Hamilton later helped Moseley get jobs (he was invalided out of one suffering a mental illness termed psychasthenia), and also closely advised him on the manuscript. The book certainly revealed Moseley's loyalties in the general–journalist slanging match. Hamilton, he said, 'is a born commander, of independent judgement, a great breadth of vision — a charming personality'. Ashmead-Bartlett, on the other hand, was a 'culprit' in regarding himself as a mentor to the commander-in-chief. The duty of correspondents, said Moseley, was to only record facts and impressions of what they actually saw.

Hamilton pursued his link to the ill Moseley, ostensibly showing concern for his multitude of ailments, but his actions also showing a high level of desperate manipulation of an unfortunate ally.

After the *Sunday Times* reviewed Moseley's inconsequential book, Ashmead-Bartlett wrote to the editor, saying this was an example of a sensational title being foisted on the public by authors with no real

Ashmead-Bartlett energetically took both still and movie photographs of the tragic drama of Gallipoli. Beach chaos at Anzac: dugouts, supplies, mules, donkeys.

A group of Turkish prisoners of war

Anzacs having a dip: this was more than pleasure — it was an issue of hygiene, and at any time enemy artillery could strike.

Anzac diggers — continually creating foxholes, walkways, dugouts, steps and ramps

One of the genuine chaps — for a senior officer. Lieutenant General Sir William Birdwood (Birdie) clearly enjoying his Anzac dip. (AWM G00401)

An historic group of Anzacs rests during battle. The man in the unusual forage cap on the right is almost certainly Simpson of Simpson and his donkey fame. There are very few verified pictures of Simpson, an iconic Anzac.

'Firing a trench mortar at Quinn's Post': Ashmead-Bartlett's own caption from his 1916 lecture tour

It was hard to keep the Anzac spirit down: troops playing cricket despite enemy fire. (AWM G01289)

The terrible reverse side of Gallipoli: the dead and wounded. Filming of this reality brought the censors crashing down on Ashmead-Bartlett, and much of his film was consequently confiscated and lost.

Australian wounded waiting for treatment

Nurses at Lemnos await the next boatload of casualties from the Gallipoli lines.

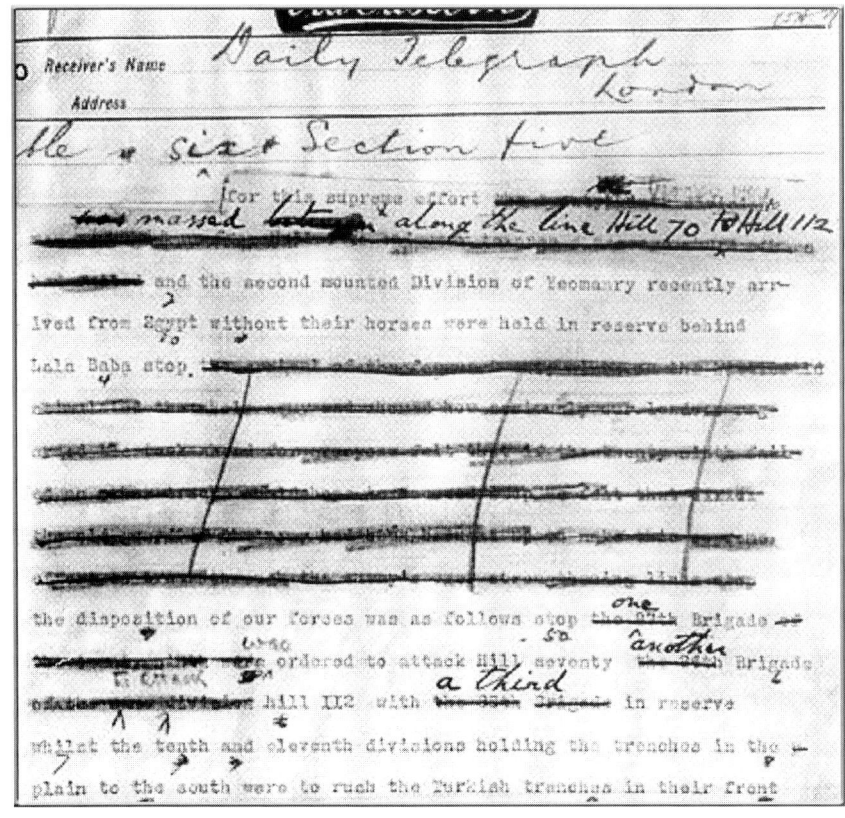

One short example of the crushing censorship faced by Ashmead-Bartlett during the Gallipoli fiasco (Mitchell Library)

By 1916 Ashmead-Bartlett had become a lecture-circuit celebrity in England, America, Australia and New Zealand. The brilliant public speaker illustrated his talks with his own photographs, maps and diagrams.
(State Library of New South Wales)

A 1916 Australian poster describing Ashmead-Bartlett's film. The final appeal reads: 'You couldn't be there, boy, but you can see what your pals had to do'.

(ABOVE) Another widely distributed Australian poster advertising the famous film *A Hero of the Dardanelles*, which featured Ashmead-Bartlett's dispatches, photos and footage
(NFSA 360590-1001-1)

(RIGHT) A New Zealand advertisement to promote Ashmead-Bartlett's 1916 lecture tour. As happened in Australia, officials attended the lectures in case he did not toe the government line and encourage recruitment.
(State Library of New South Wales)

knowledge of the subject. Moseley, he said, had spent most of his month at the Imbros correspondents' camp in an easy chair reading books. He had spent one hour in a trawler off Anzac, a few hours at Cape Helles, and was never within six miles of Suvla Bay. Lester Lawrence backed him up, saying that when the unwell Moseley accompanied him to the Cape Helles beaches he had spent all his time resting in a cabin aboard the beached *River Clyde*, going to the beach only once.

Hamilton's 1933 claim that Ashmead-Bartlett had written a story that allied troops were 'panic stricken' sparked the *Daily Telegraph* into action. The newspaper said it had checked his published stories but no such words as 'panic stricken' were ever published. When the paper asked, Hamilton replied that he had censored the reference. Whether other parts of the cable ever got to London he did not know. 'I do not think any of it was ever published,' he said. 'Your late war correspondent, Mr Ashmead-Bartlett, was no admirer of my methods — far from it — but he was no perverter of facts. Though in himself a brave man, who took big risks, he was subject to fits of depression about the expedition, and when he said our troops were panic-stricken he probably thought so for a moment.'

The exchange sparked a renewed debate about the famous letter from Ashmead-Bartlett to Asquith via Keith Murdoch, which the War Office 'lost' in transit across Whitehall to No. 10 Downing Street. Hamilton came up with a new theory about it. Ashmead-Bartlett had believed that if he were commander-in-chief for a day the peninsula could be taken by an attack on Bulair. So his famous dispatch disappointed those arguing that Gallipoli should be evacuated. Therefore, it 'vanished'. The lost dispatch, he said, 'is a story predestined to shine like the diamond necklace of Marie Antoinette out of the pages of history'. For a military man, Hamilton certainly had a colourful turn of phrase.

The family of Ashmead-Bartlett was not so colourful, but they made some telling points when they weighed into the debate. Sister Audrey took objection to Hamilton's comments. Her brother, she said, was a truthful war correspondent who could not praise too highly 'the troops he saw fighting a forlorn hope against forlorn odds'.

'It is true that he cared not a jot for any man's opinion,' she said. 'He was always sure of himself. He did not stoop with flatteries to get any position. He despised a man who thus wormed his way to high places.' Just to ensure Hamilton got the message, she added that had anyone back in England been so foolish as to supply Hamilton with the extra troops he demanded, 'their bodies would have joined that wonderful band of heroes that now sleep under the Turkish soil'.

Brother Seabury, now adorned with the Burdett-Coutts name, joined in, saying that Ellis's actions back in England after being expelled from the peninsula contributed largely to the eventual evacuation. Hamilton, he said, failed to foresee the result of his actions in sending Ellis home. 'I think that after his first feelings of resentment faded away my brother was grateful to Sir Ian Hamilton for having given him the opportunity, however unwittingly, of saving the lives of the men whom he is now so unjustly accused of having maligned.' It was a telling point.

Hamilton might have regarded his press corps, and particularly Ashmead-Bartlett, as traitors for delivering Gallipoli to the enemy, but in fact he was fortunate to have such a compliant group of journalists — with that one exception. It was Hamilton himself who created the climate of confrontation with his attempted manipulation and lies.

Ashmead-Bartlett was the only Gallipoli journalist who wanted to take a wider view of the military tactics used at Gallipoli. Charles Bean from Australia and Malcolm Ross from New Zealand were mainly interested in their national troops, and Bean also had an eye to his history project. Henry Nevinson of the British provincial press and Lester Lawrence of Reuters, given their editorial outlets, were more interested in the day-to-day flow of battles. Here was a largely docile, if somewhat fractious press corps, that Hamilton could have easily brought on side for his battles with the War Office for more serious attention to be paid to the Gallipoli expedition, which all along was something of a sideshow. Even Ashmead-Bartlett initially believed the expedition could succeed and take Constantinople. And he was always prepared to put a favourable spin on events.

One of the unwritten laws of journalism is that reporters will usually side with their best contacts. The Gallipoli journalists offered Hamilton an outstanding platform to lobby the War Office and Cabinet, just as the egotistical General Douglas MacArthur did in the World War II Pacific campaign. It is an interesting analogy. MacArthur briefed his accompanying press, supplying them with great copy that boosted his island-hopping campaign as it competed for military resources against the war in Europe. But woe betide any reporter who stepped out of line.

Historian Nicholas Hiley, after studying the early censorship of World War I, concluded that war correspondents would always reproduce the views of the armies to which they were attached, only falling back on claims to represent the public if deprived of news or the means to send it. 'If Hamilton had grasped this he could at any time have won over the NPA [Newspaper Proprietors Association], and through them, have controlled Ashmead-Bartlett,' said Hiley. Instead, Hamilton made his own intransigence the story, inadvertently handing Ashmead-Bartlett a future role as the man who told the truth about Gallipoli.

The willingness of the Gallipoli press corps to 'toe the official line' and not expose the disastrous reality of Gallipoli was remarkable. Admittedly it was wartime, and journalists are nationalists. Yet Ashmead-Bartlett, it seems, was the only one who took an increasingly dark view of the mounting losses and poor tactics, eventually becoming sufficiently depressed to write to his prime minister.

The numbing effect of the censorship affected Ashmead-Bartlett deeply. 'It is heartrending work having to write what I know to be untrue, and in the end having to confine myself to giving a descriptive account of the useless slaughter of thousands of my fellow countrymen for the benefit of the public at home, when what I wish to do is to tell the world the blunders that are being daily committed on this blood-stained Peninsula,' he confided in his diary. He also wrote of trying to minimise the Suvla defeat, 'an almost impossible task', adding that 'we have landed again and dug another graveyard'.

Yet his colleagues stayed quiet. The visiting Keith Murdoch could see the scale of the disaster within four or five days, and to his credit joined Ashmead-Bartlett. Phillip Knightley, in his best-selling book *The First Casualty*, a history of war correspondents, argues that if the correspondents in France had been as enterprising as Ashmead-Bartlett and Murdoch, the whole war might not have continued on its ghastly course.

Hamilton's treatment of his small, largely compliant press corps is a case study in how to mismanage the media. Rather than wrapping the journalists into his cause, Hamilton played mind games with them. Welcoming and apparently generous, he promised them they could go where they liked and enjoy relative freedom. Yet he applied several levels of censorship, used spies in their camp and set out to play 'divide and rule'. Not only that, he had literary pretensions of his own and wanted to compete with them. The journalists sometimes found their copy was delayed until Hamilton's own official, and usually optimistic, accounts went through for publication.

In Ashmead-Bartlett's case, Hamilton was guilty of provocation. Hamilton used his connection to Lord Burnham, the *Daily Telegraph* proprietor, to have the troublesome journalist recalled. This crude attempt to pull strings around the old boys club failed.

For all the emphasis he placed on a gentleman's word of honour, when it came to expelling Ashmead-Bartlett for breaking censorship, Hamilton himself indulged in lies. When Nevinson asked Hamilton about the expulsion some few days later he was told it was a result of orders from the War Office, and that Hamilton himself regretted it. Bald-faced cheek. Hamilton ordered the expulsion against direct orders from the War Office to hold his hand until London advised him.

Clearly Hamilton stooped to some low tactics to get rid of Ashmead-Bartlett. Writing to your prime minister is not a hanging offence, despite Hamilton's claim that it breached the censorship rules. Censorship is all about stopping military information falling into the hands of an enemy, not those of the prime minister.

Breaching censorship is something many journalists wear on their sleeves these days, but in wartime 1915 it was seen as a serious offence. Defending Murdoch, and by implication himself, from the charge, Ashmead-Bartlett said his colleague may have been guilty. 'But is any patriotic man going to allow a technicality to stand in the way of endeavouring to save thousands of his fellow countrymen from a miserable end and the Empire from grave disaster?' he asked. If placed in the same position 'I would not hesitate to act in the same manner again'.

Amazingly, none of Ashmead-Bartlett's Gallipoli colleagues supported him. They believed either that he had broken censorship, or that if he felt strongly about the issue he should have returned to London himself. None sought to even make a story out of the expulsion. Yet they all knew about the incident. A report along the lines of 'Gallipoli correspondent expelled for writing to Prime Minister' would have made the headlines. It might not have passed Hamilton's censorship, but it would have presented him with an embarrassing situation. None of Ashmead-Bartlett's colleagues even tried it. Journalists all too often sit on the best stories they know. Ashmead-Bartlett was also guilty of this. He knew of the bid by officers to pull the Australians off the beach on the first night, but did not mention it in his initial historic dispatch of the 25 April landing.

Gallipoli was the first modern attempt at what is now known as an 'embedded' media — one living with the military. Only a few accredited correspondents were permitted, the rest kept in places like Cairo. The system was not as regulated as that subsequently adopted for the Western Front, where the five correspondents were kept in a tight, shepherded group, briefing each other on what they saw and living in the same house, along with censors. This was a style Ashmead-Bartlett detested. He ached to roam freely and report what he saw. After he was thrown off Gallipoli he lamented the 'death' of old-fashioned war correspondents. 'The rough and ready, quarreling, jealous crowd have gone,' he wrote. 'But they deserve well of history. They have preserved the most vivid stories of great events that have changed the face of the world. They took great risks, and brought off some amazing scoops. They were either the delight or the horror of their editors. The sums of money they spent were fabulous, and several papers owe an early demise to their attempts to beat rivals.'

The highly controlled new 'war writer' was a different breed, part and parcel of the Army, who wrote purely in the interests of the Army. There was no rivalry, and there were no scoops. 'They are looked after, fed, watched and housed by the Army ... The strictest code of morals and deportment has been drawn up by the military authorities for their guidance. They have no worries and no anxieties, for all their news is despatched at the same hour and appears on the same day ... they are invariably shown the same thing so that every paper each morning has the same tale told in a different writer's language ... Every word they write is carefully censored, not a note of criticism is ever allowed to creep in, and only successes gained over the enemy are ever allowed to be commented on.'

Ashmead-Bartlett showed his scorn for this new breed of military-controlled journalists. 'They are, in fact, the "good boys" of the army, and can hold their positions as long as they do as they are told, and write what they are told,' he said.

As the war progressed the old war horse also developed a cutting view of wartime censorship. Truth had been eliminated from the written word, he argued in an article titled 'The Great Conspiracy'. The war, he said, had seen a vast conspiracy to deceive the public and conceal the truth. Responsibility for blunders — the Dardanelles being a classic example — was never attributed to those responsible.

Wartime photography was worse, suffering from 'suggestio falsi' in its selective presentation of pictures and captions, such as 'The Tommy and the French girl', or 'An Australian being kissed by a French General'. It was the photography of perpetual smiles. 'The men going into action are smiling, the men coming out are smiling, the wounded are smiling and the dead would be found smiling if our dead were allowed to appear in the press,' he wrote.

Ashmead-Bartlett's sharp critique of his wartime colleagues raises questions about his own performance. After all, he suppressed the news of the panic bid to evacuate the Anzacs on the night of the 25 April invasion, and as a film cameraman he spent hours trying to get happy footage of naked Anzacs frolicking in the Mediterranean which he hoped would intrigue the ladies of London. The bigger issue, however, is whether the Anzac myth maker exaggerated.

The simple answer is 'yes', but his exaggerations were more to inject colour into his copy, not deliberate falsehoods. As the fact-conscious Charles Bean commented, Ashmead-Bartlett had a real regard for the truth. But Bean also tackled Ashmead-Bartlett on some of his more flamboyant writing. When asked about whether the allies ever made bayonet charges in which no mercy was given, as he had reported, Bean says Ashmead-Bartlett replied: 'No, they always dropped their rifles and held up their hands for mercy'. Sometimes it was given, sometimes not.

Bean couldn't quite make out his colleague. 'Ashmead-Bartlett makes it a little difficult for one by his exaggerations, and yet he's a lover of the truth,' Bean wrote in his diary. 'He gives the spirit of things, but if he were asked: "Did a shout really go up from a thousand throats that the hill was ours?" he'd have to say "No, it didn't". Or if they said "Did the New Zealanders really club their rifles and kill three men at once?" or "Did the first battle of Anzac really end with the flash of bayonets all along the line, a charge, and the rolling back of the Turkish attack", he'd have to say "Well — no, as a matter of fact that didn't occur".'

London headline writers played up Ashmead-Bartlett's colourful account of New Zealand Maori war cries in their attack during the failed August breakout. 'Maoris terrorise Turks' said one. 'The lion's whelps at the Dardanelles' said another. Ashmead-Bartlett in fact had written:

> The Maoris entered into the charge with great dash, making the darkness of the night hideous with their wild war-cries and striking terror into the hearts of the Turks with the awful vigour with which they used their bayonets and the butt-ends of their rifles ... Although few in number, they closed on the Turks with fury, using their rifles as clubs, swinging them round their heads and laying out several with each sweep.

Ashmead-Bartlett had been at Suvla Bay on the day of this battle, and relied on the New Zealand correspondent, Malcolm Ross, for his detail of the attack, an acknowledgement he freely gave in his cable. Believing the clubbing with rifle butts was not true, Bean asked Ross. No, replied the New Zealander, he had not written this. Ashmead-Bartlett, whom Ross greatly admired, had said to him afterwards: 'I say, I hope you didn't mind my inserting one or two things in your account — one or two things I heard from officers'.

Bean gave Ashmead-Bartlett the benefit of the doubt. 'Bartlett wouldn't invent a description like that,' he said. 'But he had heard something of the sort from some NZ officers and he inserted it without hesitation in a report which the article said he had received from Mr Ross, the NZ Official Correspondent. Bartlett has a real regard for the truth — and that is the astonishing part about him, that and his industry.'

The line between envy and concern for journalistic integrity in Bean's equivocation on Ashmead-Bartlett's work was thin. He had admitted to a 'pang of jealousy' when he first heard that another war correspondent was moving about his Anzac patch, and one who beat him to the first accounts of the landing. Yet he praised

Ashmead-Bartlett for writing 'close to the truth'. Then, when he wrote about the eventual evacuation in December 1915 (Ellis was then back in London) he thought it 'the only chance one has had of even attempting to rival Bartlett's work'.

Still, Ashmead-Bartlett's injection of colour disturbed the historian in Bean. 'Well, I can't write that it occurred if I know that it did not, even if by painting it that way I could rouse the blood and make the pulse beat faster — and undoubtedly these men here deserve that people's pulses shall beat for them,' he wrote. 'But war correspondents have so habitually exaggerated the heroism of battles that people don't realise that the real battles are heroic.'

Bean agonised about the role of war correspondents. How could they write about the horror, beastliness, cowardice and treachery of battle? Writers had to throw a cloak over these. Soldiers, even Australians, ran away and occasionally had to be threatened with a revolver to return. Bean says he had witnessed troops advancing at the same time as 'weaker ones' retreated back through them. This was the true side of war, but he doubted if anyone would believe it outside the Army. 'I've never written higher praise of Australians than is on this page [his diary], but the probability is that if I were to put it into print tomorrow the tender Australian public, which only tolerates flattery and that in its highest form, would howl me out of existence,' he said.

Yet Bean generously acknowledged that it was Ashmead-Bartlett's first account of 25 April — which concluded with the 'flash of bayonets' — that did so much to influence the tradition of Anzac. Incidentally, the Australian may have been critical of such colourful flourishes, but he used them himself. His own report of the landing had an Australian brigade surmounting a summit 'like a whirlwind, with wild cheers and bayonets flashing'.

In an era of mass communications it is difficult to appreciate the depth of the effect of Ashmead-Bartlett's 25 April report on the Australasian psyche of 1915. Newspapers, the only popular medium then, gave it blanket coverage. The *Sydney Morning Herald* reported men turning up to enlist carrying the newspaper report. Within 10 days the New South Wales Department of Public Institution had published Ashmead-Bartlett's report, along with Bean's, in a pamphlet for schoolchildren titled *Australians in Action: The Story of Gallipoli*.

Other pamphlets of his landing account followed. One, with a ribbon binding and titled *Our Australian Heroes of the Dardanelles* was sold to help raise war loans. Ashmead-Bartlett's 25 April report was even reprinted on a theatre playbill.

Perhaps the most telling account of the impact of the landing story was told by Western Front veteran Fred Farrall in an interview with Alastair Thomson for his 1994 book *Anzac Memories*. Fred Farrall was 15 at the time of Gallipoli, and recounted to Thomson:

> When the landing was made in Gallipoli, of course, we all had to have it read to us from the papers after tea at night. It was sort of ... almost something like a religious service, and we listened to it, and we believed it.

Ashmead-Bartlett's cable, colourful and perhaps exaggerated, was held up as gospel by the Australian public. When the first feature film, *The Hero of the Dardanelles*, was released just three months after the landing, the producers knew how to give it the ring of authenticity. 'Most graphically and faithfully portrayed in accordance with Ashmead-Bartlett's historic despatch,' they proclaimed in billboards.

Australia's embrace of Ashmead-Bartlett's stirring account in 1915 was understandable. The new nation's army was untested, and many in Britain thought it an undisciplined colonial rabble. Hell raisers amongst the troops in Egypt had already been sent home in disgrace. Ashmead-Bartlett touched this nerve, when reporting the cheering wounded on 25 April: 'They were happy because they knew they had been tried for the first time, and had not been found wanting'.

It was almost as if Ashmead-Bartlett had relieved a national anxiety, replacing it with a nascent sense of national pride. Ashmead-Bartlett's account of 25 April — stirring, colourful and even exaggerated though it may have been — gave Australia its first presence on the world stage. The convict past was not wiped away, just supplanted by a tale of courage. The nation had a new identity, one that showed its people had real character. Gallipoli, said Bean, was the dawn of an Australian consciousness. The very fact that it was a dawn first lit by an Englishman made it more acceptable to Australians, still craving praise from the 'mother country'.

It was not just a sense of pride that these dispatches imbued. Gallipoli showed Australians they were different from the English, physically better built and with different national traits. Gallipoli blended pride with the stirrings of independence.

Unconsciously, Ashmead-Bartlett helped mould the view of Gallipoli as the birth of Australia's own story. It may have been just another 'good story' for him, but his telling of it, and his injection of vivid and colourful phrases, meant that for Australians it became their story. And it was an Australian story that pushed the new nation into the headlines of the world's press. As Bean noted in his official war diaries, Ashmead-Bartlett's 'brilliant despatch' put the efforts of the Anzac soldiers before the world as if the landings were the affairs of Australasian troops alone. The British effort was virtually forgotten. Such was the effect of Ashmead-Bartlett's fortuitous presence at Anzac Cove on 25 April.

Nationalism was not strong in Australia at the outbreak of war. Federation of the colonies had not produced anything like the national identity that gripped Americans after their war of independence. Australians were still coming to grips with their large, mysterious country with its convict inheritance. Bush balladeers like A.B. 'Banjo' Paterson had romanticised the bush, while C. J. Dennis was carving out a larrikin city culture with his *Sentimental Bloke*. But there was no national story that reflected what Australians thought of themselves.

If nationalism is the need for communal identity, Ashmead-Bartlett's 25 April cable gave it to Australians, as also did Bean's later dispatch. Australians saw a reflection of their nation that gave them great pride, reinforcing their individual identity. Gallipoli was an enormously powerful force in 1915, and remains so today.

The *Bulletin* even drew a direct line from the Eureka Stockade to Gallipoli in terms of drawing the landing into Australia's emerging nationalism. Eureka was the true beginning of Australia's history, said the magazine, and it was fitting there should be a member of the Lalor family at Gallipoli, as there had been at Eureka. 'Old Peter gave an arm; the grandson, his life,' it said.

For others, Ashmead-Bartlett and the Gallipoli story was not so much a continuation as the filling of a void. Australia was almost a blank sheet. Geoffrey Serle in his *From Deserts the Prophets Come*, a history of the creative spirit in Australia, quotes the young playwright Louis Esson, fleeing Australia for Europe in 1911, disgusted with his native country for being too young, with no culture, folk-songs or bohemian life, and too crude.

This was the blank page that greeted the reports of the heroic Gallipoli landing. Both Ashmead-Bartlett's and Bean's accounts of the landing had overtones of jingoism and a heroic-romantic view of the Australian soldier. But at least it was Australia's own story.

Run a line through Ashmead-Bartlett's original 25 April dispatch, and some of his and Bean's later cables, and it is easy to see the elements of the Gallipoli story that so appealed to Australians. Ashmead-Bartlett had the Australians brushing aside opposition to scale cliffs, clinging on despite a determined enemy, displaying enormous bravery against the odds, and all the time with a cheeky, somewhat carefree anti-authoritarian demeanor. It was as if Gallipoli combined the stoicism of the Australian bush with the 'have a go' culture of the city larrikins.

Another element of the Gallipoli legend can be traced back to Ashmead-Bartlett's 25 April dispatch — the 'victory'. Gallipoli, of course, was a major defeat, yet Australians celebrate it with almost a religious zeal. Ashmead-Bartlett (and Bean) wrote of the bravery of the landing and the scaling of the cliffs, and then the persistence and initiative of holding on despite the odds. That is the 'victory' of Gallipoli.

The Australians at Gallipoli were tailor-made for a writer with Ashmead-Bartlett's flair. Although he and others praised the physiques and courage of the Australians while lamenting their discipline, he turned that indiscipline into an independence of spirit, blending it with a sense of humour that marked out the troops from 'down under'.

Ashmead-Bartlett's portrait of General Birdwood as the 'soul of Anzac' is a classic illustration of this style. 'Birdie', as he was known to the troops, fortunately operated with a no-frills style that suited that of the Australians. Often he walked around the lines with his sleeves rolled up and a stick in his hand, unrecognisable as a general. Accompanying Birdwood on his daily round one day, Ashmead-Bartlett recalled that the general was wearing his ribbons when they passed two Australians in a trench. One of them looked up, saw Birdwood's ribbons, and turned to his companion, remarking, 'Bill, the — — Army ain't going to know me long enough to get a row like that'.

Apocryphal or not, such stories burnished the developing Anzac legend. Ashmead-Bartlett had an uncanny ability to get to the heart of the Gallipoli story — the diggers. Although they were not known by that name then, Ashmead-Bartlett brought out all the strands of the digger legend — the combination of anti-authority nonchalance and bravery that so captured the hearts of Australians. He even found a goldminer soldier who swore the country reminded him of an Australian goldfield.

Although Ashmead-Bartlett had little more to do with Australia after his visit, Charles Bean nurtured the Gallipoli legend to full flower. The legend began to blossom even as early as 1916, when Ashmead-Bartlett visited Australia. Plans were already being made for an annual celebration. In that year the ceremonies at home joined those by troops in Egypt, England and France. Ken Inglis says that by 1918 it became customary to hold services on 25 April. Over the years Anzac Day became the nation's premier celebration, replacing Empire Day, even overshadowing the official Australia Day, 26 January. Every attempt to promote alternatives such as the Eureka Stockade or the exploits on the Kokoda Trail in World War II as more representative of Australia and its ideals has failed.

Myth Maker

Ashmead-Bartlett's legacy to Australia is more than just igniting the Anzac legend with his report of the landings. He took the only cinema footage of the expedition, a priceless piece of the national heritage. Perhaps most importantly, he helped blow the whistle on a failed campaign, ensuring the troops were evacuated without further loss of life.

But it was his 25 April report that made him such a celebrity in Australia in 1915, although his role has not been given the recognition it deserves. When Charles Bean compiled his best-selling *Anzac Book* with contributions from the troops, one of the soldiers wrote the following words on the impact of Ellis Ashmead-Bartlett:

> How private Bill made his Kangaroo-like leap up the ridges of Gallipoli has been told by a war correspondent to a public which had, up till then, been vaguely aware of his existence as a poor relation from a South Sea island. It is fairly certain that future historians will teach that Australia was discovered not by Captain Cook, explorer, but by Mr Ashmead-Bartlett, war correspondent.

As Ashmead-Bartlett found, soldiers usually say it better than historians.

Appendix 1

Report of the Gallipoli Landing

Ellis Ashmead-Bartlett's cabled report of the Gallipoli landing on 25 April 1915, which appeared in major Australian newspapers on 8 May.

It required splendid skill, organisation and leadership to get the huge armada under weigh from Mudros Bay without accidents. The warships and transports were divided into five divisions. Never before has an attempt been made to land so large a force in the face of a well-prepared enemy.

At 2 o'clock on April 24 the flagship of the division conveying the Australasians passed down the long line of slowly-moving transports, amid tumultuous cheering, the flagship being played out of the bay by the French warships. At 4 o'clock the ship's company and the troops assembled to hear the Admiral's proclamation to the combined forces. This was followed by the last Service Before Battle, during which the chaplain uttered a prayer for victory, and called for a Divine blessing on the expedition, all standing with uncovered and bowed heads.

At dusk all lights were put out, and the troops rested, to be ready for the ordeal at dawn. It was a beautiful, calm night, with a bright half-moon. By 1 o'clock in the morning the ships had reached the rendezvous five miles from the landing-place. The soldiers were aroused and served with their last hot meal.

The Australians, who were about to go into action for the first time under trying circumstances, were cheerful, quiet, and confident, showing no sign of nerves or excitement. As the moon waned the boats were swung out, and the Australians received their last instructions. Men who six months ago were living peaceful civilian lives began to disembark on a strange, unknown shore, in a strange land, to attack an enemy of different race.

Each boat was in charge of a midshipman, and was loaded with great rapidity, in absolute silence, and without a hitch. The covering force was towed ashore by ships' pinnacles. More of the Australians' brigade was carried aboard the destroyers, which were to go close inshore as soon as the covering force landed.

At 3 o'clock it was quite dark, and a start was made shore-wards, amid suppressed excitement. Would the enemy be surprised or on the alert?

At 4 o'clock three battleships, line abreast and four cables apart, arrived 2,500 yards from the shore, with their guns manned and searchlights made ready. Very slowly the boats in tow, like giant snakes, moved inshore. Each edged towards the other in order to reach the beach four cables apart. The battleships moved slowly in after them, until the water shallowed.

Every eye was fixed on the grim line of hills in front, menacing in the gloom, the mysteries of which those in the boats were about to solve. Not a sound was heard not a light seen, and it appeared as if the enemy would be surprised. In the men's nervy states the stars were mistaken for lights ashore.

The progress of the boats was slow, and dawn rapidly was breaking. At 4.50 the enemy showed an alarm light, which flashed for ten minutes and disappeared. The boats appeared to be almost on the beach, and seven destroyers glided noiselessly inshore.

At 4.53 am a sharp burst of rifle fire from the beach. The sound relieved the prolonged suspense, which had become almost intolerable. The fire lasted a few minutes, and then a faint British cheer came over the waters, telling that the first position had been won. At 5.30 the fire was intensified, and by the sound we could tell our men were firing. The firing lasted twenty-five minutes and then died down somewhat.

The boats returned, and a pinnace came alongside with two recumbent figures on deck and a small midshipman cheerfully waving his hand, although he had been shot through the stomach. The three had been wounded in the first bout of musketry.

The boats had almost reached the beach when a party of Turks entrenched ashore opened a terrible fusillade with rifles and a Maxim. Fortunately most of the bullets went high.

The Australians rose to the occasion. They did not wait for orders or for the boats to reach the beach, but sprang into the sea and formed a sort of rough line. They rushed the enemy's trenches, although their magazines were uncharged. They just went in with cold steel.

It was over in a minute. The Turks in the first trench either were bayoneted or ran away, and the Maxim was captured.

Then the Australians found themselves facing an almost perpendicular cliff of loose sandstones, covered with thick shrubbery. Somewhat about half way up the enemy had a second trench, strongly held, from which a terrible fire poured both on the troops below and the boats pulling back to the destroyers for a second landing-party.

Here was a tough proposition to tackle in the darkness, but those colonials were practical above all else, and went about it in a practical way. They stopped for a few minutes to pull themselves together, get rid of their packs, and charge their rifle magazines. Then this race of athletes proceeded to scale the cliff without responding to the enemy's fire. They lost some men, but did not worry, and in less than a quarter of an hour the Turks had been pushed out of their second position, and were either bayoneted or fleeing.

Appendix 1

As daylight came it was seen that the landing had been effected rather further north of Gaba Tepe than originally was intended, at a point where the cliffs rise very sheer. The error proved a blessing in disguise, because there was no glacis down which the enemy could fire. The broken ground afforded good cover for troops once they had passed the forty yards of flat beach.

The country near the landing-place is formidable and forbidding. To the sea it presents a steep front, broken into innumerable ridges, bluffs, valleys, and sandpits, rising to a height of several hundred feet. The surface is bare, crumbly sandstone, covered with thick shrubbery about six feet in height, which is ideal for snipers, as the Australasians soon found to their cost. On the other hand, the Australasians proved themselves adept at this kind of warfare.

In the early part of the day heavy casualties were suffered in the boats conveying troops from the destroyers, tugs, and transports. The enemy's sharpshooters, hidden everywhere, concentrated their fire on the boats. When close, at least three boats broke away from their tow and drifted down the coast without losing control, being sniped at the whole way, and steadily losing men.

The work of disembarking proceeded mechanically under a point-blank fire. The moment the boats touched the beach the troops jumped ashore and doubled for cover; but the gallant boat crews had to pull in and out under a galling fire from hundreds of points.

All through 25th April this went on, the boats landing troops, ammunition, and stores. When daylight came, the warships endeavoured to support them by heavy fire from secondary armaments; but not knowing the enemy's position this support was more moral than real.

When the sun had fully risen, we could see that the Australasians had actually established themselves on the ridge, and were trying to work their way northward along it. The fighting was so confused and occurred on such broken ground, that it was difficult to follow exactly what happened on the 25th; but the covering forces' task was so splendidly carried out that it allowed the disembarkation of the remainder to proceed uninterruptedly, except for the never-ceasing sniping. But then the Australians, whose blood was up, instead of entrenching, rushed northwards and eastwards, searching for fresh enemies to bayonet. It was difficult country in which to entrench. They therefore preferred to advance.

The Turks had only had a weak force actually holding the beach, and relied on the difficult ground and their snipers to delay the advance until reinforcements came. Some of the Australasians who pushed inland were counter-attacked and almost outflanked by oncoming Turkish reserves. They had to fall back after suffering heavy losses.

Myth Maker

The Turks continued to counter-attack throughout the whole afternoon; but the Australians did not yield a foot of the main ridge. Reinforcements poured up from the beach, but the Turks enfiladed the beach with two field guns from Gaba Tepe. This shrapnel fire was incessant and deadly.

The warships vainly for some hours tried to silence them.

The majority of the heavy casualties during the day were caused by shrapnel, which swept the beach and ridge where the Australasians were established. Later in the day the guns were silenced or forced to withdraw, and a cruiser moving close inshore plastered the village with a hail of shell.

Towards dusk the attacks became more vigorous, the enemy being supported by powerful artillery inland, which the ships' guns were powerless to deal with. The pressure on the Autralasians became heavier and their line had to be contracted.

General Birdwood and his staff landed during the afternoon, and devoted their energies to securing the position so as to hold firm until next morning, when they hoped to get field guns into position.

Some idea of the difficulty can be gathered when it is remembered that every round of ammunition had to be carried over the water, landed on a narrow beach, and carried up pathless hills through a valley several hundred feet high, to the firing line. The whole mass of troops was concentrated in a very small area, and was unable to reply, though exposed to relentless and incessant shrapnel fire, which swept every yard of the ground. Fortunately most of it was badly aimed, and burst too high.

A serious problem was the getting of the wounded from the shore. All those unable to hobble had to be carried from the hills on stretchers, and then hastily dressed and carried to the boats. Boat parties worked incessantly throughout the entire day and night.

The courage displayed by those wounded Australians will never be forgotten. Hastily placed in trawlers, lighters or boats, they were towed to the ships. In spite of their suffering they cheered the ship from which they had set out in the morning. In fact, I have never seen anything like these wounded Australians in war before.

Though many were shot almost to bits, without hope of recovery, their cheers resounded. Throughout the night, you could see in the midst of the mass of suffering humanity, arms waving in greetings to the crews of the warships. They were happy because they knew they had been tried for the first time, and had not been found wanting.

For fifteen mortal hours they occupied the heights under incessant shell fire, without the moral or material support of a single gun ashore, and subjected

Appendix 1

the whole time to a violent counter-attack, by a brave enemy, skilfully led, with snipers deliberately picking off every officer who endeavoured to give a command or lead his men.

There has been no finer feat in this war than this sudden landing in the dark and the storming of the heights, and above all, the holding on whilst reinforcements were landed. These raw colonial troops in these desperate hours proved worthy to fight side by side with the heroes of Mons, the Aisne, Ypres, and Neuve Chapelle.

Early on in the morning of the 26th, the Turks repeatedly tried to drive the Colonials from their position. The latter made local counter-attacks, and drove off the enemy with the bayonet, which the Turks never face.

The Turks, who were largely reinforced overnight, prepared a big assault from the north-east. The movement began at 9.30. From the ships we could see the enemy creeping along the hilltops, endeavouring to approach under cover. They also brought up more guns, and plastered the position with shrapnel, while the rifle and machine-gun fire became unceasing.

Seven warships crept close in, with the Queen Elizabeth further out as a kind of chaperone. Each covered one section of the front and opened a terrific bombardment on the heights and valleys beyond.

As the Turkish infantry advanced, they met every kind of shell our warships carry, from "Lizzie's" 15-inch shrapnel to 12-pounders. Our shooting was excellent, while their artillery not only shelled our positions, but tried to drive off the ships.

The scene at the height of the engagement was sombre and magnificent. It was a unique day, perfectly clear, and one could see down the coast as far away as Seddul Bahr. Three warships were blazing away, and on shore the rifle and machine gun rattle was incessant. The hills were ablaze with shells, while masses of troops stood on the beaches waiting to take their places in the trenches.

The great attack lasted two hours. We received messages that the ships' fire was inflicting awful losses on the enemy.

Then, amidst the flash of the bayonet and a sudden charge by the Colonials, before which the Turks broke and fled amidst a perfect tornado of shells from the ships, they fell back, sullen and checked.

They kept up an incessant fire throughout the day, but the Colonials had now dug themselves in.

Some prisoners were captured, including officers, who said that the Turks were becoming demoralised by our gunfire, and that the Germans had difficulty in getting them to attack.

Appendix 2

Letter to the British Prime Minister

This is the text of the letter Ellis Ashmead-Bartlett wrote to the British prime minister, Herbert Asquith, in September 1915, and which the Australian journalist, Keith Murdoch, tried to smuggle back to London. It was seized from Murdoch in Marseilles. Later the War Office claimed it had been 'lost' in Whitehall while being sent to Downing Street.

September 8, 1915

Dear Mr Asquith

I hope you will excuse the liberty I am taking in writing to you, but I have the chance of sending this letter through by hand, and I consider it absolutely necessary that you should know the true state of affairs our here.

Our last great effort to achieve some definite success against the Turks was the most ghastly and costly fiasco in our history since the Battle of Bannockburn.

Personally, I never thought the schemes decided on by Headquarters ever had the slightest chance of succeeding, and all efforts now to make out that it only just failed, owing the failure of the 9th Corps to seize the Anafarta Hills, bear no relation to the real truth.

The operations did, for a time, make headway, in an absolutely impossible country, more than any general had a right to expect, owing to the superlative gallantry of the Colonial troops, and the self-sacrificing manner in which they threw away their lives against positions which should never have been attacked.

The main idea was to cut off the southern portion of the Turkish arm by getting astride the peninsula from Suvla Bay. Therefore, the whole weight of the attack should have been concentrated on this objective; instead of which the main attack, with the best troops, was delivered against the side of the Turkish positions which are a series of impossible mountains and valleys covered with dense scrub.

The Staff seemed to have carefully searched for the most difficult points, and then threw away thousands of lives in trying to take them by frontal attacks. A few Ghurkas obtained a lodgment on Chunuk Bair, but were immediately driven off by the Turkish counter-attacks, and the main objective, Koja Chemen Tepe, was never approached.

The 9th Corps, miserably mishandled, having failed to take the Anafarta Hills, is now accused of being alone responsible for the ultimate failure of the operations. The failure of the 9th Corps was not due so much to the employment of new and untried troops, as to bad staff work. The generals had but a vague idea of the nature of the ground in their front, and no adequate steps were taken to keep the troops supplied with water.

In consequence, many of the unfortunate volunteers went three days in very hot weather on one bottle of water, and were yet expected to advance, carrying heavy loads, and to storm strong positions.

The Turks, having been given ample time to bring up their reinforcements to Anafarta, where they entrenched themselves in up to their necks, were again assaulted in a direct frontal attack on August 21st. The movement never had the slightest chance of succeeding and led to another bloody fiasco in which the unfortunate 29th Division, who were brought up especially from Helles, and the 2nd Mounted Division (Yeomanry) were the chief sufferers. As a result of all this fighting our casualties, since August 6th, now total nearly fifty thousand killed, wounded and missing.

The Army is in fact in a deplorable condition. Its morale as a fighting force has suffered greatly, and the officers and men are thoroughly dispirited. The muddle and mismanagement beat anything that has ever occurred in our military history.

The fundamental evil at the present moment is the absolute lack of confidence amongst all ranks in the Headquarters Staff. The confidence of the Army will never be restored until a really strong man is placed at its head. It would amaze you to hear the talk that goes on amongst the junior commanders of divisions and brigades. Except for the fact that the traditions of discipline still hold the force together, you would imagine that the units were in an open state of mutiny against headquarters. The commander-in-chief and his Staff are openly spoken of, and in fact only mentioned at all, with derision. One hates to write of such matters, but in the interests of the country at the present crisis I feel they ought to be made known to you. The lack of a real Chief at the head of the Army destroys its discipline and efficiency all through, and gives full rein to the jealousies and recriminations which ever prevail amongst the divisional leaders.

At present the Army is incapable of a further offensive. The splendid Colonial Corps has been almost wiped out. Once again the 29th Division has suffered enormous losses, and the new formations have lost their bravest and best officers and men. Neither do I think, even with enormous reinforcements, that any fresh offensive, from our present positions, has the smallest chance of success.

Myth Maker

Our only real justification for throwing away fresh lives and fresh treasure in this unfortunate enterprise is the prospect of the certain co-operation of Bulgaria. With her assistance we would certainly pull through. But as I know nothing of the attitude of Bulgaria or Greece or Italy, I am only writing to give you a true picture of the state of the Army and the problems with which we are faced in the future, if we are left to fight the Turks alone.

Already the weather shows signs of breaking, and by the end of this month we cannot rely on any continuous spell of calm for the landing of large bodies of troops at some other point on the coast. In fact the season will soon be too late for a fresh offensive, if another is contemplated. We have therefore to prepare against the coming of the winter or to withdraw the Army altogether.

I am assuming it is considered desirable to avoid the latter contingency at all costs for political reasons, owning to the confession of final failure it would entail, and the moral effect it might have in India and Egypt. I am convinced the troops could be withdrawn under cover of the warships without much loss, far less in fact than we suffer in any ordinary attack. I assume also that the future of the campaign out here must be largely dependent on the offensive in conjunction with the French in the West.

It is no use pretending that our prospects for the winter are bright. The Navy seems to think it will be able to keep the Army supplied in spells of calm weather provided a sufficient reserve of food, munitions, and ammunition is concentrated on the various beaches while the weather holds.

The outlook for the unfortunate troops is deplorable. We do not hold a single commanding position on the Peninsula, and at all three points, Helles, Anzac, and Suvla Bay, we are everywhere commanded by the enemy's guns. This means that throughout the winter all the beaches and the lines of communications to the front trenches will be under constant shell-fire. Suvla Bay is especially exposed. The Turks are firing a fair amount of ammunition, but it is obvious they are feeling the shortage, or else are carefully husbanding their supply, otherwise they could shell us off the Peninsula at some points altogether. But it must be remembered that as soon as they are absolutely certain our offensive has shot its bolt, and that we are settling down in our positions for the winter. They will be free to concentrate their artillery at certain points, and also to bring up big guns from the forts, and therefore we must expect a far more severe artillery fire on the beaches during the winter months than we are exposed to at present.

A great many of the trenches which we hold at present will have to be abandoned altogether during the winter as they will be under water. This will mean concentrating the Army at certain points on dry ground, and preparing a series of defensive works which will ensure us against sudden surprise

Appendix 2

attacks. We could thus hold our positions with fewer men and rest some of the divisions from time to time in the neighbouring islands.

We ought to be able to hold Helles without much trouble, but even if we commence our preparations in time, we shall face enormous difficulties at Anzac and Suvla Bay. Our troops will have to face the greatest hardships from cold, wet trenches, and concentrated artillery fire. I believe that at the present time the sick rate for the Army is roughly 1,000 per day. During the winter it is bound to rise to an even higher figure. I know one general, whose judgement is generally sound, who considers we shall lose during the winter in sickness alone the equivalent of the present strength of the Army. This may be an exaggeration, but in any case our loss is bound to be very heavy. The whole army dreads, beyond all else, the prospect of wintering on this dreary and inhospitable coast. Amongst other troubles, the autumn rains will once more bring to view hundreds of our dead who lie under a light covering of soil.

But I suppose we must stay here as long as there is the prospect of the Balkan Alliance being revived, and throwing in its lot with us, even if they do not make a move until next spring. I have laid before you some of the difficulties with which we are faced in order that they may be boldly met before it is too late.

No one seems to know out here what we are going to do in the future, and I am so afraid we shall drag on in a state of uncertainty until the coming season is far too advanced for us to make proper preparations to face the coming winter in a certain measure of comfort and security. At the present time some of our positions, gained by the Colonial Corps high up on the spurs of the hills on which the Turks are perched cannot be considered secure. A sudden counter-attack, vigorously delivered, would jeopardise the safety of our line, and might lead to a serious disaster. There will have to be a general re-shuffling of the whole line, and some of our advanced posts will have to be abandoned during the winter months.

I have only dealt with our own difficulties and troubles. The enemy of course has his. But to maintain, as I have seen stated in an official report, that his losses in this recent fighting were far heavier than ours, is a childish falsehood which deceives no one out here. He was acting almost the whole time on the defensive, and probably lost about one-third of our grand total.

You may think I am too pessimistic but my views are shared by the large majority of the Army. The confidence of the troops can only be restored by an immediate change in the supreme command. Even if sufficient drafts are sent out to make good our losses, we shall never succeed, operating from our present positions. A fresh landing on a grand scale north of Bulair would probably ensure success, but the season is too late, and I suppose the troops are not available. If we are to stay here this winter let orders be given for the Army to start its preparations without delay. If possible have the Colonial troops taken off the Peninsula altogether because they are miserably depressed since the last failure, and, with their active minds, and the positions they occupy in civil life, a dreary winter in the trenches will have a deplorable effect on what is left of this once magnificent body of men, the finest any Empire has ever produced.

If we are obliged to keep this Army locked up in Gallipoli this winter large reserves will be necessary to make good its losses in sickness. The cost of this campaign in the East must now be out of all proportion to the results we are likely to obtain now, in time to have a decisive effect on the general theatre of war. Our greatest asset against the Germans was always considered to be our superior financial strength. In Gallipoli we are dissipating a large portion of our fortune, and have not yet gained a single acre of ground of any strategical value. Unless we can pull through with the aid of the Balkan League in the near future, this futile expedition may ruin our prospects of bringing the war to a successful conclusion by gradually wearing down Germany's colossal military power.

I have taken the liberty of writing very fully because I have no means of knowing how far the real truth of the situation is known in England, and how much the military authorities disclose. I thought, therefore, that perhaps the opinion of an independent observer might be of value to you at the present juncture. I am, of course, breaking the censorship regulations by sending this letter through, but I have not the slightest hesitation in doing so, as I feel it is absolutely essential for you to know the truth. I have been requested over and over again by officers of all ranks to go home and personally disclose the truth, but it is difficult for me to leave until the beginning of October.

Hoping you will, therefore, excuse the liberty I have taken.

Ellis Ashmead-Bartlett

The Rt Hon H.H. Asquith
10 Downing Street

Bibliography

Books

Alomes, S. 1988, *A Nation at Last? The Changing Character of Australian Nationalism, 1880–1988*, Angus & Robertson, Sydney.

Ambrosy, A. 2001, *A Brave Nation: A Short Political and Social History of Twentieth Century Hungary*, Hungarian Life Publishing, Melbourne.

Anderson, M. & Ashton, P. 2000, *Australian History and Citizenship*, Macmillan, Melbourne.

Andrews, E.M. 1994, *The Anzac Illusion: Anglo-Australian Relations During World War I*, Cambridge University Press, Cambridge.

Ashmead-Bartlett, E. 1910, *The Passing of the Shereefian Empire*, William Blackwood and Sons, London.

— 1913, *With the Turks in Thrace*, in collaboration with Seabury Ashmead-Bartlett, William Heinemann, London.

— 1915, *Despatches from the Dardanelles*, George Newnes Ltd., London.

— 1915, *Our Australian Heroes of the Dardanelles*, London.

— 1918, *Some of My Experiences in the Great War*, George Newnes, London.

— 1923, *The Tragedy of Central Europe*, Thornton Butterworth Ltd, London.

— 1928, *The Uncensored Dardanelles*, Hutchinson & Co, London.

— 1929, *The Riddle of Russia*, Cassell & Company Ltd, London.

Ashmead-Bartlett, E. & Bean, C.E.W. 1915, *Australians in Action — the Story of Gallipoli*, New South Wales Department of Public Instruction, Sydney.

Bean, C.E.W. 1940, *The Story of Anzac*, 2 vols, Angus & Robertson, Sydney.

Bennett, C.N. 1911, *The Handbook of Kinematography*, published by the *Kinematograph Weekly*, London.

Berend, I.T. & Ranki, G. 1974, *Hungary, a Century of Economic Development*, Barnes & Noble Books, New York.

Bertrand, I. 1978, *Film Censorship in Australia*, University of Queensland Press, Brisbane.

Bowers, P. 1999, *Anzacs: The Pain and Glory of Gallipoli*, Australia Post, Melbourne.

Boyd, W. 1987, *The New Confessions*, Penguin, London.

Brenchley, F. & Brenchley, E. 2001, *Stoker's Submarine*, HarperCollins, Sydney.

Carlyon, L. 2001, *Gallipoli*, Macmillan, Sydney.

Carver, Field Marshall Lord 2003, *The National Army Museum Book of the Turkish Front, 1914–1918*, Pan Macmillan, London.

Coe, B. 1981, *The History of Movie Photography*, Ash and Grant, London.

Decil, H. & Liddle, P.H. 1998, *At The Eleventh Hour: Reflections, Hopes and Anxieties at the Closing of the Great War 1918*, Leo Cooper, London.

Dennis, P., Grey, G., Morris, E. & Prior, R. 1995, *The Oxford Companion to Australian Military History*, Oxford University Press, Oxford.

Denton, K. 1986, *Gallipoli: One Long Grave*, Time-Life Books, Sydney.

Fewster, K. (ed) 1983, *Gallipoli Correspondent: The Frontline Diary of C.E.W. Bean*, Allen & Unwin, Sydney.

Gibbs, P. 1929, *Realities of War*, Hutchinson & Co., London.

Gilbert, Sir Martin et al. 2000, *The Straits of War: Gallipoli Remembered*, Sutton, Stroud, Gloucestershire.

Gordon, H. 1976, *An Eyewitness History of Australia*, Rigby, Adelaide.

Grenville, J.A.S. 1976, *Europe Reshaped 1848–1878*, Fontana, London.

Hamilton, I.B. 1920, *Gallipoli Diary*, 2 vols, Edward Arnold, London.

Hickey, M. 2000, *Gallipoli*, John Murray, London.

Higgins, T. 1963, *Winston Churchill and the Dardanelles: A Dialogue in Ends and Means*, Collier-Macmillan, London.

Inglis, K.S. 1998, in John Lack (ed), *Anzac Remembered*, University of Melbourne Press, Melbourne.

Jones, B.E. (ed) 1915, *The Cinematograph Book*, Cassell & Company Ltd, London.

Keegan, J. & Knightley, P. 2003, *The Eye of War*, Weidenfeld and Nicholson, London.

King, J. & Bowers, M. 2005, *Gallipoli*, Fairfax Publications/Doubleday, Sydney.

Knightley, P. 1976, *The First Casualty*, Harvest, London.

Laffin, J. 1985, *Damn the Dardanelles: The Agony of Gallipoli*, Sun Papermac, Melbourne.

Lee, C. 2001, *Jean, Lady Hamilton: A Soldier's Wife, 1861–1941*, Celia Lee, London.

Lee, J. 2000, *A Soldier's Life: General Sir Ian Hamilton 1853–1947*, Macmillan, London.

McCarthy, D. 1983, *Gallipoli to the Somme: The Story of C.E.W. Bean*, John Ferguson, Sydney.

McGregor, A. 2004, *Frank Hurley: A Photographer's Life*, Viking Penguin, Melbourne.

Mackenzie, E.M.C. (Compton) 1929, *Gallipoli Memories*, Cassell & Company, London.

— 1963, *My Life and Times, 1915–1923*, Octave 5, London.

McLachlan, N. 1989, *Waiting for the Revolution: A History of Australian Nationalism*, Penguin, Melbourne.

Macleod, J. 2004, *Reconsidering Gallipoli*, Manchester University Press, Manchester.

Malins, G.H. 1993, *How I Filmed The Great War*, facsimile edition, Imperial War Museum, London and Battery Press, Nashville (first published 1923).

Mayer, H. 1968, *The Press in Australia*, Lansdowne Press, Melbourne.

Molnar, M. 2001, *A Concise History of Hungary*, Cambridge University Press, Cambridge.
Moorehead, A. 1998, *Gallipoli*, Wordsworth, Ware, Hertfordshire.
Moseley, S.A. n.d., *The Truth About the Dardanelles*, Cassell & Company, London.
Nevinson, H.W. 1928, *Last Changes, Last Chances*, James Nisbet & Co. Ltd., London.
— 1935, *Fire of Life*, James Nisbet & Co. Ltd., in association with Victor Gollancz Ltd., London.
Perry, R. 2005, *Monash*, Random House Australia, Sydney.
Piggott, M. 1983, *A Guide to the Personal, Family and Official Papers of CEW Bean*, Australian War Memorial, Canberra.
Pike, A. & Cooper, R. 1980, *Australian Film, 1900–1977*, Oxford University Press, Melbourne.
Reade, E. 1975, *The Australian Screen: A Pictorial History of Australian Film Making*, Lansdowne Press, Melbourne.
— 1979, *History and Heartburn: The Saga of Australian Film, 1896–1978*, Harper and Row, Sydney.
Reynaud, D. 2005, *The Hero of the Dardanelles and Other World War I Silent Dramas*, National Film and Sound Archive, Canberra.
Rhodes, J.R. 1999, *Gallipoli*, Random House, London.
Ross, J. 1985, *The Myth of the Digger: The Australian Soldier in Two World Wars*, Hale & Iremonger, Sydney.
Salt, B. 1983, *Film Style and Technology: History and Analysis*, Starwood, London.
Schuler, P. 1916, *Australia In Arms*, T Fisher Unwin, London.
Seal, G. 2004, *Inventing Anzac: The Digger and National Mythology*, University of Queensland Press, Brisbane.
Serle, G. 1973, *From Deserts the Prophets Come: The Creative Spirit in Australia 1788–1972*, Heinemann, Melbourne.
Shirley, G. & Adams, B. *Australian Cinema: The First Eighty Years*, Currency Press, Sydney.
Souter, G. 1981, *A Company of Heralds*, Melbourne University Press, Melbourne.
Stanley, P. 2005, *Quinn's Post, Anzac, Gallipoli*, Allen & Unwin, Sydney.
Steel, N. & Hart, P. 1995, *Defeat at Gallipoli*, Papermac Macmillan, London.
Sulzberger, G.L. 1977, *The Fall of Eagles — the Death of the Great European Dynasties*, Crown, New York.
Talbot, F.A. 1912, *Moving Pictures: How They Are Made and Worked*, William Heinemann, London.
Thomson, A. 1995, *Anzac Memories: Living with the Legend*, Oxford University Press, Oxford.

Walker, R.B. 1976, *The Newspaper Press in New South Wales, 1803–1920*, Sydney University Press, Sydney.
Williams, J.F. 1999, *Anzacs, the Media, and the Great War*, University of New South Wales Press, Sydney.
Williams, V. 1938, *The World of Action*, Hamish Hamilton, London.
Younger, R.M. 2003, *Keith Murdoch, Founder of a Media Empire*, HarperCollins, Sydney.
Zwar, D. 1980, *In Search of Keith Murdoch*, Macmillan, Melbourne.

Newspaper and journal articles; library and museum papers; and privately held unpublished papers

Ashmead-Bartlett, E. Memento and Souvenir of Gaba Tepe, Ashmead-Bartlett's Thrilling Story of the Australian Heroes at the Dardanelles
— Du Maurier's great patriotic play, *An Englishman's Home*, National Library of Australia.
— 1915, *Sunday Times*, 17 October.
— 1915, *Times*, 24 November.
Bean, C.E.W. 1931, Ashmead-Bartlett obituary, *Sydney Morning Herald*, 9 May and 16 May.
Burness, P. 2005, 'The Anzac yarn', *Wartime* (the official magazine of the Australian War Memorial), no. 29.
Carlyon, L. 2001, Charles Bean and the Gallipoli journalists, address to C.E.W. Bean Foundation, August.
— 2004, Gallipoli in a nation's remembrance, Australian War Memorial Anniversary Oration, 11 November.
Daily Telegraph 1931, 'The man on the spot: brilliant career of E. Ashmead Bartlett', 5 May.
Dardanelles Commission 1917, 5 February (43rd day), evidence 16335–16545 of Keith Arthur Murdoch; and 3 May (75th day), evidence 26756–27018 of Ellis Ashmead-Bartlett.
Dutton, P. 2004, '"More vivid than the written word": Ellis Ashmead-Bartlett's film, *With the Dardanelles Expedition, 1915*', *Historical Journal of Film, Radio and Television*, vol. 24, no. 2, June, pp. 205–22.
Fewster, K. 1982, 'Ellis Ashmead-Bartlett and the making of the Anzac legend', *Journal of Australian Studies*, no. 10.
Grimshaw, C. 1958, 'Australian nationalism and the imperial connection 1900–1914', *Australian Journal of Politics and History*, vol. 3, pp. 140–62.
Hamilton, General Sir Ian 1915, memorandum on a letter from Mr K.A. Murdoch, Committee of Imperial Defence, 26 November.
Hiley, N. 1993, '"Enough Glory for All": Ellis Ashmead-Bartlett and Sir Ian Hamilton at the Dardanelles', *Journal of Strategic Studies*, vol. 16, no 2.
Huxley, J. 2004, 'Birth of a nation', *Sydney Morning Herald*, November 27–8.

Imashev, G. 2000, Gallipoli: the film *With the Dardanelles Expedition: Heroes of Gallipoli*, the Joint Imperial War Memorial Study Tour to Gallipoli, September.
— 2002, 'Gallipoli on film', *Wartime*, issue 18, no. 54, April.
Inglis, K.S. 1965, 'The Anzac tradition', *Meanjin Quarterly*, vol. 24, no. 1, March.
— 1970, 'The Australians at Gallipoli', parts 1 & 2, *Historical Studies*, vol. 14, no. 54, April.
McLachlan, N. 1968, 'Nationalism versus the divisive digger: three comments', *Meanjin Quarterly*, vol. 27, no. 3, pp. 302–8.
Prior, R. 2005, The strategy behind Gallipoli, Australian Strategic Policy Institute, April.
Sekuless, P. 2000, Australian War Memorial address, 3 May.
Sunday Times (London) 1915, 'The Near East situation: Mr Ashmead-Bartlett's views', 17 October, p. 10.
— 1915, 'A year-and-a-half of war, by Ellis Ashmead-Bartlett', 19 December.
Wright, T. 2005, 'Why we remember', *Bulletin*, 26 April.

Other sources

Diaries of C.E.W. Bean, Australian War Memorial, August–September 1915 (3DRL 606 item 16) and June–September 1915 (3DRL 606 item 10)
Diaries of Lady Jean Hamilton, the Liddell Hart Centre for Military Archives, King's College, London
Letters of Ellis Ashmead-Bartlett to his wife, Nina, between 1919 and 1931 (in the possession of Francis Ashmead-Bartlett)
Archives of Sir Ian Hamilton, the Liddell Hart Centre for Military Archives, King's College, London
13: Hamilton: 17/64 Newspaper and journal cuttings
14: Hamilton: 7/1/1 Letters from Hamilton to Rt Hon Winston Leonard Spencer Churchill MP
15: Hamilton: 7/1/11 Letters from Hamilton to Rt Hon Herbert Henry Asquith MP
17: Hamilton: 7/3/1–12 Papers relating to Ellis Ashmead-Bartlett and Keith Arthur Murdoch, war correspondents on Gallipoli, 1915–1969
18: 7/3/1: May 13 1915 to Mar 12 1919 (Ellis Ashmead-Bartlett)
19: Hamilton: 7/3/10 'War Memories of the Dardanelles'
20: Hamilton: 7//3/11 Newspaper cuttings of reviews of *The Uncensored Dardanelles* by Ellis Ashmead-Bartlett
21: Hamilton: 7/3/2 Correspondence between Hamilton and the Hon Harry Lawson Webster Levy-Lawson MP
22: Hamilton: 7/3/3 Correspondence between Hamilton and Maj Gen Sir Charles Edward Callwell

24: Hamilton: 8/1/48 Correspondence between Hamilton and Sydney Alexander Moseley
29: Hamilton: 8/2/41 Typed copy of evidence of Keith Arthur Murdoch
30: Hamilton: 8/2/6 Typed copy of evidence of Ellis Ashmead-Bartlett
31: Hamilton: 9/2 Correspondence between Hamilton and the War Office
32: Stern: 1/20/3 File of papers entitled 'Anecdotes'

British Library Document Supply Centre — British Thesis Service
Hiley, N.P. 1984, Making war: the British news media and government control, 1914–1916, unpublished Open University PhD thesis, 3 vols

British National Archives (Public Records Office) Kew, London
1. PRO CO 616/33/440-1 F.G.A. Butler to D. Davies, 28 December 1915
2. PRO CO 616/53/207-211 Lord Burnham (Harry Lawson) to Bonar Law, 10 February 1916
3. PRO CO 616/53/205, 216, Sir Cecil Spring-Rice, 18 and 19 January 1916
4. PRO CO 616/59/294, 295 Sir Cecil Spring-Rice, 7 and 9 February 1916
5. PRO CAB. 19/30 88-93+ War Office reports on correspondents at the Dardanelles
6. PRO HO 139/23 and 2/97 Press correspondents at the Dardanelles
7. PRO ADM 1/8427/205 Adm to Riddell, Brade to Greene, Greene to Brade, Robbins to Greene, Greene to Balfour
8. ADM 1/8427/205 8 May 1915 – 11 July 1915 letters from Bernard Alfieri of Alfieri Picture Service to Sir W. Graham Greene; general correspondence to and from Admiralty to GOC MEDEX, and War Office

Institute of Commonwealth Studies, University of London, Ashmead-Bartlett Papers
ICS 84/A: diaries 1897–1925
ICS 84/A/1: diary of a tour in Turkey, 1897
ICS 84/A/2: diary South Africa 1900
ICS 84/A/3: diary France, Monte Carlo and England 1901
ICS 84/A/4: diary London 1901–1902
ICS 84/A/5: diary London, Martinique, West Indies 1902
ICS 84/A/6 and 7: diary England 1906 and 1907
ICS 84/A/8: diary London and Morocco 1908
ICS 84/A/9: diary England 1909
ICS 84/A/10: diary America, England, France, Italy 1911
ICS 84/A/11: Dardanelles campaign diary 1915
ICS 84/A/12, 12/1 and 12/2: diaries kept during the aftermath of the Dardanelles campaign 1915–1916
ICS 84/A/12/3: diary America, Australia and New Zealand lecturing on the Dardanelles campaign
ICS 84/A/13, 13/1–7: diaries of the Hungarian Bolshevist Revolution 1919–1920

ICS 84/B 1892–1930: personal correspondence files

ICS 84/C 1899–1930: press articles

ICS 84/D: photographs 1880–1930, including family photographs, and photographs taken by Ashmead-Bartlett during the Russo-Japanese, North African, French and Dardanelles conflicts

ICS 84/E: press cuttings 1891–1933, ranging from the life and death of Sir Ellis, to Ashmead-Bartlett's own cuttings, reviews of articles and book reviews

ICS 84/F: publications 1899–1929; printer's proofs and unpublished manuscripts

ICS 84/G 1915–1919: additional papers on the Dardanelles campaign

ICS 84/H Maps 1905–1920: miscellaneous maps from war zones covered by Ashmead-Bartlett

ICS 84/1: personal papers 1892–1931, relating to political career, passports, curriculum vitae. Awards, publicity and obituary, 1931

National Archives of Australia, Canberra

Papers relating to the visit of Ellis Ashmead-Bartlett to Australia in 1916: Series A11803 — 14/89/209, 89/209/5; 14/89/209, 89/209/3a;14/89/209, 89/209/ Ashmead-Bartlett's lecture of 12/2/1916; 14/39/209, 89;209/ newspaper articles from the *Sunday Times* re. Ashmead-Bartlett's Anzac Story; 14/89/209, 89/209/9; 14/89/209, 89/209/6; and 89/209/7, matters relating to censorship

National Archives of Australia, Melbourne

Matters relating to censorship of Mr Ashmead-Bartlett's lecture tour of Australia: Series no. MP 390/8, items 1915/6 B/C 3578435, Australian commercial diaries 1915/16

Australian War Memorial

Ashmead-Bartlett, E., *With the Dardanelles Expedition: Heroes of Gallipoli*, film, F00069.

Documents relating to films taken at Gallipoli by Ellis Ashmead-Bartlett (AWM 264/003/105)

Bean, C.E.W. August–September 1915, 3DRL 606 item 16

— June–September 1915, 3DRL 606 item 10

National Library of Australia

Ellis Ashmead-Bartlett papers on Gallipoli, Mfm M2581—M2586 (also held at the State Library of New South Wales)

Papers of Keith Arthur Murdoch, MS 2823

In the Newspaper Reading Room, major Australian newspapers, including the *Sydney Morning Herald*, *Daily Telegraph*, the *Age*, the *Argus*, Melbourne *Herald*, Adelaide *Advertiser* and Brisbane *Courier* for 8 May 1915; *Sydney Morning Herald* and the *Age*, selected issues March–September 1915, February–March 1916.

National Film and Sound Archive, Australia (formerly ScreenSound)

With the Dardanelles Expedition: Heroes of Gallipoli (Australian War Memorial F00069). This film in a re-digitised form is controlled by the Australian War Memorial.

The Spirit of Gallipoli, 1928 (incorporates *Hero of the Dardanelles* footage at 32–40 min).

Australasian Gazette No. 278, ID 0040451-0000, second segment at 2 min 24 s. Arrival of British war correspondent in Australia in 1916 at start of his Australia-wide lecture tour.

Gallipoli and Other WWI Scenes, ID AVC 0 22226.0544745-0003: possible original Gallipoli footage, most re-enactment. Scenes of battleship sinking, possible Ashmead-Bartlett voice-over: 'My camera was trained on the battleship ... when she was hit'.

Australasian Gazette, ID 10135-01, at 12 min 16 s. Turkish guns demolished during Gallipoli landings; scenes of trenches, troops, guns, plus shots of the sections of the Narrows they commanded.

Pathe Animated Gazette No. 0346, RVCO 14477 0373653-0003. The first NZ VC at Gallipoli, Corporal Bassett, at 3 min 54 s; and camera similar to Ashmead-Bartlett's being unloaded at 5 min 48 s.

The Noade Film, circa 1920s. Cut and paste editing shows some original Ashmead-Bartlett footage in good condition. National Screen and Sound Archive and Madeleine Chaleyer, Australian War Memorial, are investigating this recently discovered film.

Index

Abul Hamid, Sultan, 6
Achi Baba, 93, 95, 97, 98, 127, 156, 161
AE2, 73
Aeroscope, 132–3
  learning to operate, 134–6
  in use, 141, 142–3
'affairs of the heart', 11–12, 13, 22, 31, 199
Agamemnon, 57
Alfieri Picture Services, 35, 134, 138, 139
Anafarta Hills, 160–1
Annesley, Lady, 22
anti-Hamilton rhetoric, 244
Anzac Day, 92, 203, 259
Arcadian, 95, 113
Armstrong, Capt, 65, 82
Armstrong, Maj. L.F., 194, 198
Ashmead-Bartlett, Ellis
  according to a soldier, 260
  birth, 9
  books, 20, 27, 44 (with Seabury), 60, 65, 95, 111, 140, 226
  buried alive, 141, 160
  CBE, 242
  characteristics, 1–2, 4–5, 13, 16
  death, 238
  ill/injured, 7, 10, 30–1, 34, 35, 168, 183–4, 185, 190, 193
  marriage, 230
  siblings, 2
  thrown off Gallipoli, 174–5
Ashmead-Bartlett, Francis Ellis, 231, 237

Ashmead-Bartlett, John, 231
Ashmead-Bartlett, Madeleine, 231
Ashmead-Bartlett, Nina, 223, 224, 228, 229, 231, 234, 237
Ashmead-Bartlett, Seabury, 17, 37–8, 40, 105, 248
  accepts Burdett-Coutts inheritance, 231
Ashmead-Bartlett, Sir Ellis, 2, 6
  England (newspaper), 3
Ashmead-Bartlett, William (Uncle Willie), 2, 3, 22, 24, 184–5, 211, 225, 231
Asquith, Prime Minister H.H., 49, 105, 107, 108–9, 171
  makes Murdoch's letter a State Paper, 171
Atatürk, Kemal, 68, 81, 172
Australian 11th Infantry, 64
Australian Imperial Force, 61
  impressive physiques, 61–2
Australian, according to Ashmead-Bartlett, 194, 199–201
  women 198–9
Aziz, Abdul, 26, 27, 28

Bachelors Club, 24, 25
Balfour, Arthur, 116
Baltic, 206
bankruptcy, 25, 54, 197, 233–4, 237
Baron Ardrossan, 103
Barton, Prime Minister Edmund, 13
Bean, C.E.W., 55, 75, 76, 77–8, 82, 89, 117–18, 150, 168, 176, 183, 260

Index

Bean, C.E.W. (*continued*)
  on Ashmead-Bartlett, 2, 5, 17, 90, 120–1, 122, 175–6, 177, 186, 239, 254, 255
  at Imbros camp, 120–1
  on national awareness, 91
Bedford Regiment joined, 8
  resigned, 18
Berry brothers, 180
Bertie, Lady Gwendoline, 22, 25, 29, 58
Birdwood, Gen (Birdie), 72, 76, 101, 110, 161–2, 185, 259
  proposed invasion plan, 152–3
Birkenhead, Lord *see* Smith, F.E.
Boer War, 8–10
booklet for schoolchildren, Gallipoli, 89, 90, 256
Brade, Sir Reginald, 46, 137, 207, 212
Braithwaite, Maj. Gen., 58, 97, 99, 114, 124, 126, 159, 174, 182, 207
  'drip feed only', 125
breakout from Anzac, attempted, 130, 140–1, 156, 157
bribe Turkish soldiers, scheme to, 153
British 29th Division, 58, 63, 93, 98, 160
Brookes, Ernest, 135, 141, 142
Bulair landing, 99
Bulair landing, Ashmead-Bartlett's scheme, 99, 108, 110, 123, 153
Burdett-Coutts, Baroness, 3, 22
Burnham, Lord *see* Lawson, Harry
Butt, Alfred, 133, 134, 138, 143

Caledonian, 104
Canopus, 57

Cape Helles, landings, 63, 74, 90, 93, 97
Carlyon, Les, 171
Carson, Sir Edward, 105
censorship, 42, 58, 63, 69, 125, 126–7, 129, 148, 149, 156–7, 162, 173–4, 176, 188, 249
  by the Bolsheviks, 217
Chaleyer, Madeleine, 146
Chocolate Hill, 141, 142, 153, 160
Chunuk Bair, 156, 158, 159
Churchill, Clementine, 2
Churchill, Jack, 25, 58
Churchill, Winston 105, 110
  failed plan to capture Constantinople, 54, 106–7, 108, 181–2
'club-wielding Maoris', 156
consular duties, 10
Cornwallis, 57, 100, 179
counter-revolutionary, Ashmead-Bartlett as, 214, 216, 217, 218–20
Courtenay's Post, 101
Cunard, Lady, 109
Cunningham, Sir Thomas, 216, 221

Daily Telegraph special correspondent
  Austrian invasion of Serbia, 46
  Balkan wars, 37–44
  France, 49–52
  India, 236–7
  Russia, 236
  Spain, 238
dangerous enemy, a, 177–8
Dardanelles Committee of Inquiry (Royal Commission), 17, 164, 165, 242

Dardanelles Strait (the Narrows), 54, 73
  failed attack on, 76, 77
Davis, Jack, 35, 36
Dawney, Maj. Guy, 161, 180
Dawson, Geoffrey, 170
de Crespigny, Capt. Philip, 151–2, 162
de Lisle, Maj. Gen., 162
de Robek, Vice-Admiral Sir John, 57, 65, 103, 113
Delane, John, 16
Dennis, C.J., 88–9, 257
'dig, dig, dig' 73, 74
Dix, Commander Charles, 63
Dixon, Campbell, 238
Dixmunde, battle, 53
Dobson, Jeanie, 87
Donohoe, Martin, 38, 39, 41, 42, 48
Dutton, Phillip, 145

Empire Press Union, 55
Elizalde, Mme Marie Alejandrina *see* Ashmead-Bartlett, Nina
Euryalis, 84
eye witness (official), 47, 49

Farrall, Fred, 256
feature films (about Gallipoli), 90–1, 144–5, 256
Fenton, West de Wend, 179, 180, 184, 189, 210
Fewster, Kevin, 197
film footage of Australian troops, Ashmead-Bartlett's, 112, 141–2, 143, 145, 146, 179, 204
  captioned and edited by Bean, 143–4, 145
First Brigade (NSW), 197
Fisher, Prime Minister Andrew, 61, 80, 163

Fitchett, Rev. W.H., 90
'flying ambulance', 52–3
Fortescue, Capt Granville, 30, 49, 52
Fox, John, 17
Fraser Film Company, 204
French, Field Marshall Sir John, 49, 170
Fyfe, Hamilton, 48, 49

Gaba Tepe, 110
  landing, 88
Gallipoli, Ashmead-Bartlett's report of landing, 65–71, 85, 261–5, 258
  his later description, 70–2, 83
Gallipoli, invasion plan, 56–9
  withdrawal from, 185
gambling, 9, 10, 13, 24, 34, 183, 202, 205, 224, 230
Gibbs, Philip, 52, 207
Gina, 104–5, 179
Godley, Gen., 73, 161
Goliath, 57
'greatest burglar the world has ever known', 218–20
Grenard, Lt Col. Lord, 162
Griffith, Arthur, 89
grizzly bear cub, 205, 206
Gurkhas, 158, 159

Hamilton, Lady Jean, 22, 109
Hamilton, Sir Ian, 55, 57, 59, 77–8, 95, 97, 99, 106, 110, 113, 114, 116, 125, 126, 128, 129, 137, 147, 148, 153, 155, 159–60, 169, 177, 180, 243
  character, 94–5, 182, 245
  controlling correspondents, 58, 117, 118, 121–2, 127, 149
  dispatches, 83, 94, 100, 128

Hamilton, Sir Ian (*continued*)
   friendship with Moseley, 246
   on Ashmead-Bartlett, 149
   on Lawrence, 150
   on Moseley, 149
   on Murdoch, 149–50
   on Nevinson, 150
Harding Davis, Richard, 16, 17, 18, 29–50, 52
Hawk Battalion, 130
Hearst, William Randolph, 14, 192, 193
Herbert, Aubrey, 130
Hiley, Nicholas, 169, 186, 249
Hozier, Blanche, 2
Hughtes, William Morris, 188–9, 193, 224
Hunter-Weston, Maj Gen, 95, 123, 126
Huszar, Count Karoly, 218

Imbros Island camp, 114, 118, 119–20, 148, 151
Implacable, 84
Inglis, Ken, 85, 92

James, Lionel, 35, 38, 39, 41, 42
James, Robert Rhodes, 82
Joffre, Gen., 208

K Beach, 114, 117
Kann, Reginald, 35
Karolyi, Count Mihaly, 215
Keikwansan Fort, 20
Keyes, Commodore Roger, 57, 60, 64, 82–3, 103, 113
Kilid Bahr, 161
Kings Messengers, 104
Kitchener, Lord, 55, 95, 110, 114, 116, 169
   on reporters, 48
   on the public, 49
   recalling Hamilton, 182
Kitchener's 'New Army', 153, 240
Knightley, Phillip, 14, 16, 18, 250
Krithia, attacks, 91, 95, 97, 98, 159
Kum Kale invasion, 95
Kun, Bela, 215, 216–7, 218

Laffin, John, 124
Lancashire landing, 115
law studies, 12–13
Law, Andrew Bonar, 187, 189, 190, 191, 192, 202
Lawrence, Lester, 55, 56, 60, 64, 74, 82, 100, 116, 119, 153, 159, 224
Lawson, Harry (later Lord Burnham), 33, 37, 43, 55, 106, 120, 126, 151, 162, 178, 181, 192, 207, 209–10, 212, 214, 220, 242
lecture tours, 180–1, 183–5
   American, 191–3
   Australian, 193–7, 189, 203–4
   British, 188
   censorship, 191, 193, 194–5, 197–8, 202, 204
   New Zealand, 191, 204–5
Lemnos Island, 56, 113
Lena, 13
Lewis, Col, 30
Limpus, Admiral, 55, 56, 104
Lines of Communication, 118
Lister, Charles, 128
London season, 21–2
London, 57, 60, 61, 63, 64, 66, 68, 70, 71, 74, 84
Lone Pine, 158
Lord Nelson, 57
Lule Burge, battle of, 40–1

Index

Macdonald, Sir Claude, 18
Mackenzie, Compton, 115, 122–4, 137, 186
Macura, 205
'magic passes', 50, 51
Mahon, Gen., 162
Maidos, 81
Majestic, 57, 66, 101 sunk, 102–3
Malins, Lt Geoffrey, 132, 133, 134
Malone, Col. William, 136
maps, the need for accurate, 9, 17, 59
Marlborough College, 1, 5, 6, 20
Massie, Hughes, 111, 112, 133, 139
Maxwell, William, 57, 99, 114, 115, 117, 126
  found War Office memo, 207
McKay, Brig. Gen. W., 96
Methuen, Lord, 104
military strategy, Ashmead-Bartlett's ready grasp of, 8–9
Minneapolis, 153
Mitilini, 168
Monash Gully, 100
money lenders, borrowing from, 12, 17, 24, 54
moneymaking schemes, 26, 29–30, 134, 210, 225–6, 227–8, 230, 234–5
Montagu Street house, 12
Montgomery, Mr, 8
Moolton, 168, 170
Moore, Arthur, 48
Morgan, Gerald, 49
Morocco
  with the French, 23–4
  interviewing Moulai el Hafid, 27–8
Moseley, Sydney, 120, 122, 148, 149, 153

moving news pictures, 131, 132
Mudros Bay, 56, 63, 64, 113
Munro, Gen., 185
Munro-Ferguson, Sir Ronald, 79–80, 190, 201, 203
Murdoch, Keith, 75, 120, 147, 191, 224, 243, 250
  at Gallipoli, 163–4
  carrying Ashmead-Bartlett's letter, 169–70
  in demand, 170–1, 172, 180
  writes his own letter, 170, 171–2

'naked bathers', 136–7
  or nearly, 150–1
National Press Association, 139
'Near East Situation' interview, 183
Nek, the, 158
Nevinson, Henry, 48, 116, 120, 148, 153, 157, 159, 173, 175
  describing Imbros camp, 5–6
  on Ashmead-Bartlett, 121, 177, 186
Newcastle, Duke of, 16
Newspaper Proprietors Association, 55, 111, 115, 138, 140, 211
Niagara, 193
No 9 Japanese Tea House, 18
Nogi, Gen. Baron, 19, 20
Northcliffe, Lord, 181, 190, 191, 212

oasis massacre, the, 36–7
Ostler, Allan, 38

'panic striken' troops, claims of, 247
Parnell, Miss, 199, 204
Pasha, Abdullah, 40

Peace Conference, Versailles, 217, 222, 224
Pearce, Senator George, 80–1, 201, 202, 203
Penfold, Hyland, 203–4
Phlipch, Elza, 11–12
photography, wartime, 253
political career, 31–2, 231–3
  sued, 233, 234
Port Arthur, attack on, 17, 19–20
Press Association, 55
Press Bureau (Sub-press Bureau), 47–8, 139
press control, British wartime, 46–7
Prevost, Colonel, 23
Prevost-Battersby, H., 48
Price, Ward, 38
Prince of Wales, 57, 66

Q Hill, 158
Queen Elizabeth, 56, 64, 66, 73, 74, 82, 101
Quinn's Post, 100, 136

Radcliffe, Maj. Delme, 138, 148, 153, 173, 164, 176
Raglan, Lord, 16
Reid, George, 191
Reims, fighting at, 50–1
Reuters special correspondent
  in Morocco, 30
  in Tripoli, 34–6
Riddell, Sir George, 139, 211
Riverina, 204
Ross, Malcolm, 117, 150, 156, 169, 183
Russell, Herbert, 120
Russell, William Howard, 16, 16
Russo-Japanese War, 17–20

Sari Bair, 88–9, 162
Schuler, Phillip, 120, 150
Scimitar Hill, 155, 160
Serle, Geoffrey, 258
Shanghai wife, 235
siege of Sidney Street, 32–3
Smith, Charles, 120, 240–1
Smith, F.E. (later Lord Birkenhead), 49, 211
smuggled letter (to Asquith), vii, 164, 165–7, 266–70
Smuts, Gen., 217
Spring-Rice, Sir Cecil, 191
Stopford, Lt Gen. Sir Frederick, 154, 155, 157
  9th Corps, 162
Sunik, 56
Suvla Bay landings, 95, 141, 142, 153–4
Swettenham, Sir Frank, 139
Swiftsure, 57, 101
Swinton, Ernest, 49

Tait, Frank, 193
Tait, J&N, 189, 203, 204
Triumph, 57, 60 listing, 101
Tyrrell, Col. G.E., 173, 174, 175, 176, 207

Valestino, Battle of, 7

Walsh, Frances Christina, 2
war correspondents
  character, 15
  cocooned, 207, 209–10
  controlled, 47, 252
  creating new reporting genre, 15–16
  duty, 187
  spending money, 14–15, 35, 38, 120

War Office
  confiscated letter, 170, 172, 247
  gains control of war
    correspondents, 116
  kept Ashmead-Bartlett's Gallipoli
    footage, 137, 139, 141
  organised visits, 53
  questioned right to film, 137, 139
  siezed papers, 206, 210
Ward, Col., 125, 126

Western Front
  accreditation from French, 208
  denied 'official' position, 209, 211
  plan to cover American troops,
    211, 212–3
  resigned, 209
White, Jack, 180
Williams, Valentine, 1, 43
Wilson, Col. Leslie, 130
word of honour broken, 178, 244–5

Also by the author

White's Flight
*An Australian Pilot's Epic Escape From Turkish Prison Camp
To Russia's Revolution*
ISBN 1 74031 1000
Fred and Elizabeth Brenchley

Allan Fels
A Portrait of Power
ISBN 1 74031 0705
Fred Brenchley
Winner of the Blake Dawson Waldron Prize for business literature

AVAILABLE FROM ALL GOOD BOOKSTORES